# In Praise of *Be the*

"All too often, women have a hard tin[...] are so busy giving and doing for others [...] time for ourselves. In *Be the One You Need*, Sophia lays out a road-map for prioritizing ourselves and shows us that meaningful self-care, regardless of your age, is about being able to help yourself so you can truly love and help others."

—**Mika Brzezinski,** bestselling author, founder of
Know Your Value, co-host of *Morning Joe*

"As women, we often put ourselves last. As Black women, we always put ourselves last. Sophia challenges all of us to change that—and put a deeper, more meaningful self-care and soul care regimen into practice so that only then can we fill the cup of others we love to the fullest."

—**Rev. Dr. Bernice A. King,** CEO, the Martin Luther King, Jr.
Center for Nonviolent Social Change

"*Be the One You Need* is about looking after yourself first. If we run ourselves ragged, we're no use to anyone. It's not something anyone should feel guilty about—Sophia Nelson gets that."

—**Katty Kay,** former BBC news anchor, journalist NBC News,
and bestselling author of *The Confidence Code*

"We all need self-care, men and women alike. *Be the One You Need* offers a wonderful blueprint to face the challenge of these difficult days and to be deliberate in seeking your joy."

—**Eddie S. Glaude, Jr.,** Princeton University professor
and author of *Begin Again: James Baldwin's America
and Its Urgent Lessons for Our Own*

"As a leader, I cannot recommend *Be the One You Need* more highly. Sophia has used a combination of her personal experiences to give us 21 powerful life lessons. Every corporate and industry leader, educator, and organization looking to create healthier work environments needs to read this book. She gives us a pathway to deeper self-care habits that last a lifetime and inspires us to take our own personal power back."

—**Col. Nicole Malachowski** (USAF, Ret.), speaker and
first female pilot to fly with the Thunderbirds

"*Be the One You Need* is not a call to be selfish, it's about practicing self-love as you ask yourself what you want, what you need, and how you feel—it's about putting your own self-care first."

—**Elizabeth Hamilton-Guarino,** author of *The Change Guidebook* and CEO of The Best Ever You Network

"*Be the One You Need* is the much-needed self-care guide needed to survive the COVID era. In this book, Nelson gives us a roadmap to create healthier lifestyle choices that will take us through the current pandemic and shows us how to do the hard work that heals our hurts—and allows us to soar."

—**Anushay Hossain,** author, *The Pain Gap: How Sexism and Racism in Healthcare Kill Women*

"What do I want? What do I need? How do I feel? These are three questions author Sophia Nelson forces us to reckon with time and time again in this powerful, poignant, and punch-packing book on radical self-care for the soul as well as for the mind and body."

—**The Hon. Kay Coles James,** former president of The Heritage Foundation, former director, US Office of Personnel Management, and member Women's Suffrage Centennial Commission

"Whether it is in politics or spirituality, Sophia Nelson tells the truth. In *Be the One You Need,* the truth is that we can't love others until we love ourselves. But loving ourselves is surprisingly hard—so she gives us an honest pep talk, a trustworthy map, and a shoulder to cry on. We all need her vulnerable wisdom right now."

—**Dr. Diana Butler Bass,** award-winning author of *Freeing Jesus* and *Grateful,* and one of America's most trusted commentators on religion and contemporary spirituality

"I commend Sophia Nelson on her transparency. It takes real courage to admit we don't care for ourselves with the same love as we care for others. I found *Be the One You Need* to be a powerful and soul-stirring book that carefully and thoughtfully helps us learn how to service ourselves so we can be of even better service to others. This is a must-read for everyone, especially those looking to live a life of true freedom and greater peace."

—**DeVon Franklin,** *New York Times* bestselling author and Hollywood producer

# SOPHIA A. NELSON

# BE THE ONE YOU NEED

## 21

### Life Lessons I Learned While Taking Care of Everyone but Me

Health Communications, Inc.
Boca Raton, Florida
*www.hcibooks.com*

## Author's Note

Actual names, dates, and locations have been changed to protect people's identities and privacy where needed.

Library of Congress Cataloging-in-Publication Data
is available through the Library of Congress

© 2022 Sophia A. Nelson

ISBN-13: 978-07573-2407-9 (Paperback)
ISBN 10: 07573-2407-x (Paperback)
ISBN-13: 978-07573-2399-7 (ePub)
ISBN 10: 07573-2399-5 (ePub)

Publisher: Health Communications, Inc.
        1700 NW 2nd Avenue
        Boca Raton, FL 33432-1653

*"Sonnet 52" used with permission of Abhijit Naskar from his book Giants in Jeans: 100 Sonnets of United Earth, ©Abhijit Naskar 2021.*
*Author cover photo and headshot ©Andrew Sample Photography, Asamplephotography.com*
*Cover, interior design and formatting by Larissa Hise Henoch*

## *To my Front Row Love Council*

Although it has changed some over the past three decades, I would be nowhere and nothing without your constant love, counsel, and support.

*Dani*

*Soror TJ*

*Soror Nicole*

*Soror Kim Reed*

*Soror Rev. Wise*

*Soror Lesleigh*

*Dr. Sabrina*

*Soror Markey*

*Soror Chelle*

*Soror Katina*

*Andy Morris*

*Andrea Agnew*

*Soror Trish*

*PJ & Lauren Riner*

*Vanessa*

*Shonny*

*Soror Pastor Renee*

*Dishan*

*Dee*

*Talaya*

*Tamyko*

*Mrs. C. & Angie*

*Kay C. James*

*My aunts (Belinda, Debbie, Sharon, Brenda, and Evelyn)*

*Crystal Smith*

*Last, but not least, my mother*

*Sandria A. Nelson*

# self · care
*[noun] . [self - kair]*

---

The practice of taking action to pre-serve or improve one's own health;

the practice of taking an active role in protecting one's own well-being and happiness, in particular during periods of stress.

# CONTENTS

## SECTION II: Manage Your Emotions Before They Manage You......................113

*We are by nature emotional beings. To deny that is to deny our most basic humanity. Yet, if we do not responsibly manage our emotions in life, love, business, and relationships we find ourselves isolated and alone. These lessons will help us to recognize and better manage our emotions and use them as powerful tools for self-care and success.*

## SECTION III: Protect Your Peace, It's the Passport to Your Soul..................199

*Every human has a spiritual soul. One that must be nourished, watered, and replenished daily. These lessons help us to take care of the inner self. The part we most often neglect.*

# SECTION IV: Relationships Are Not Transactional— They are Reciprocal ...............................265

*We were made for relationship. We are not meant to do this thing called life alone. We all need the tools to help us win at our relationships and bless others in the process. But our most important relationship is the one we have with ourselves.*

# SECTION V: Fill Your Cup First: Be Intentional About Your Choices, Your Living, Your Life ...........................291

*Successful people are intentional. They live a life that integrates common sense with respect for others, with grace, and collaboration. They are not afraid to compete with anyone, anywhere, but they do so with a firm code that allows them to climb while still lifting others along the way.*

# ACKNOWLEDGMENTS

**F**irst and foremost, to my literary agents, Leticia Gomez and Claudia Menza, I am so blessed to have you representing me and working with me on every book. Onward we go to the next one!

To my publisher, HCI Books, thank you for working so hard on this book. I adore Christine Belleris, Christian Blonshine, and Lindsey Mach; and Larissa Henoch is the best designer and graphics person on earth. You all made a challenging production schedule (my fault) a joy to work through. Thank you!

To Gilda Squire and team, thank you for being the best publicists in the business.

To Denise and Todd Chavers, for allowing me to write this book in your beautiful and quiet farmhouse in Virginia when I needed to get away—I only wish I could have stayed out there for four months. Next time. Next book!

To my younger, wiser sisters of Millennials, Gen Y, and Gen Z: Roxy, Impana, Kerri, Stephanie, Jana, Anushay, and so many others whom I mentor and by whom I enjoy being "reversed mentored." I am proud of you. I am blessed to have you in my life, too! Keep shining. I am here if you need me. To some of the newer women in my ROW—professionally and otherwise—welcome! I look forward to our shared journey.

To Mika and the *Morning Joe* team and *The Sunday Show* team, for always supporting me on air and off. I appreciate you! Thank you to the CNN *New Day* team and entire CNN team for giving me an on-air platform.

To Dean Lori Underwood of Christopher Newport University, for giving me my first opportunity to teach as a professor and as a scholar at a public liberal arts college. I will never forget your faith in me, and I look forward to the work we will do together off campus for years to come.

To my WC "Wine for the Woman's Soul" partner Jennifer Breaux, thanks for supporting me. To Jackie Stone and BK Fulton for being great friends and mentors. Patrice, Dr. Sue Nixon, Lorianna, France, Cheryl Carr, and Carmen, thanks for your special friendship.

Thank you to all my book jacket and *In Praise of* contributors. I know it was a tough turnaround. Thank you. I owe you BIG!

To all the ladies and nurses from INOVA Fair Oaks in Virginia who helped me with mom during her two years of disability—I am forever in your debt. You are true friends, and I would not have made it without you! *Where oh where would the world be without nurses?*

To my neighbors: John (aka "Wiley Coyote") and Marsha, Cliff, Abby, and my sweet little girls, Paul and Barbie Gerardi—love you guys—we all got through the worst of COVID-19 together. *La familigia!*

To my Alpha Kappa Alpha sorority sisters, I'm honored to serve all mankind with you. We help each other.

To the amazing men in my life—whom I value more than words can say—you keep me strong, you keep me clear, you make me smile. Thank you for protecting me and looking out for me, brothers!

To my co-pastors, Jill and Charlie Whitlow, thank you for always being there for me, and for the light Community Church shines in our Northern Virginia community. I am forever in all your debt. Love you much. *Me.*

Lastly, there are too many other names, friends, and supporters to list—but you know who you are, and **I love me some YOU!**

# A NOTE
# FROM THE AUTHOR:
# HOW TO USE THIS BOOK

**M**y goal in this book is to give you the elements that make for a more fulfilling life. No life is perfect. No life offers us all we ever dreamed of when we were young, but you can have a good life, even if your start was not so good. Each of our life journeys is a story that is the sum of all our parts. The good, the bad, and the downright ugly.

This is my fourth nonfiction book in ten years. But this book is deeply personal. It is my hope that in sharing intimate, oft unspoken, and at times painful parts of my journey with you, in the form of twenty-one "life lessons," that you will recognize some of yourself; that within these pages someone has finally given voice to how you have felt for years but have been unable to put into words; that you will be able to free yourself from guilt, shame, fear, or whatever deep emotional burden you have been carrying around secretly in your soul. And, if you haven't started the process yet of truly getting to know yourself, that this book will inspire you to do so starting today.

Sometimes, we cannot recognize or face our own pain or reveal our secrets until someone else shines a light on them. It's always easier to acknowledge what has happened to us when we see that it has happened to someone else. For decades, I kept a deep, dark secret that I had been sexually assaulted as a young girl by a neighborhood teenage boy. He was regrettably allowed to be near and at times even in our home. It was so soul crushing at such a young age that I pushed it down deep and denied for years that it happened. Even when I penned my first book, *Black Woman Redefined,* in 2011 and we devoted an entire section to the issue of sexual abuse and how commonplace it is in the Black community (as well as all communities), I still held it close. I hid it from my editors, my family, and myself. I was ashamed, even though I had done nothing wrong, until one day, during the 2018 Supreme Court confirmation hearings of Judge Brett Kavanaugh, when a Twitter hashtag #whyIdidn'treport went viral.

Famous women and some men from all walks of life began to share the unthinkable: their deep secrets of sexual abuse. I found myself tweeting and then speaking about it for the first time before millions of viewers on national television. It felt freeing and frightening all at once. My mother, who was watching the broadcast and who I had finally told about what happened some months before in a letter, exclaimed simply: "You are very brave. I wish I was more like you." I wasn't trying to be brave. I wanted to be free. And it took a weight off my shoulders that I can never quite adequately put into words.

As you read this book, and it begins to shake you, awaken you, and free you, I encourage you to keep a journal—even something as simple as a notepad—or perhaps a voice recorder as you read along. As you go through each of the lessons in the book, note your reactions and link your experiences. Some will make you laugh. Others will hit you in places you stopped talking about long ago. And others will make you nod your head and think, *Me, too. I have been there, too, Sophia. Thank you for putting into words what I was forced to be silent about for so long.*

It is my profound hope that all of us have walked away from the once-in-a-century time of health and emotional challenges that was 2020–2021 with some powerful life lessons that changed us for the better. If you didn't, you truly missed the silver lining in the storm. I decided to write this book almost a year into the pandemic because it was in the middle of our collective loss, death, grief, financial devastation, and time spent alone taking care of my sick parent that I found myself. I became what I needed after giving so much of myself away for most of my life. Maybe you, too, had a revelation about who you were and how you were living. Whether you did or did not, please stick with this book even when it gets hard. You can never be what you need until you dare to face what needs to be fixed. Or stopped. Or released. Or loved. Or forgiven. Or embraced. Or renewed.

Life is an amazing gift. I hope this book helps you to ask the most important question of all: *What do I want?* And once you answer that question, I hope it unlocks the best YOU in all you seek, and that it propels you to be brave enough to go out

**You can never be what you need until you dare to face what needs to be fixed. Or stopped. Or released. Or loved. Or forgiven. Or embraced. Or renewed.**

**Life is an amazing gift. I hope this book helps you to ask the most important question of all: *What do I want?***

and live a life of honesty, authenticity, kindness, peace, exploration, revelation, and redemption, where needed, for whatever time you have left on this precious side of eternity.

# PROLOGUE

## Let's Be Honest, 2020 Changed Everything— or At Least It Should Have

I have three questions that I need you to ask yourself right now as you begin this book:

1. What do I want?
2. What do I need?
3. How do I feel?

I am now fifty-five years old, and I have begun to ask myself these questions often, if not daily. I don't want you to wait until you are my age to ask them. Start asking yourself these questions daily, quietly to yourself. Write down your answers and then go do what you need to act decisively on them.

My new life mantra at this season of my life is this: "Do no harm. Take no shit."

The truth is that sooner or later we all perish; we all fade away into dust. Death is the great equalizer, and in 2020, we all learned a lot about living and dying. The cycle of life and death was all around us. It was ever present in ways we never experienced before. Our mortality was tangible, and we were helpless to do anything to stop the invisible plague that had literally stopped the world in its place for months. The virus forced us to face and reckon with our own mortality much sooner than we ever expected, to rethink our lives, and to desire something deeper from our living. It hit us all. We read article after article of people quitting their jobs in droves, leaving their unhappy marriages, starting new careers, finding deeper love and connections and stepping back from the busy of life. Maybe it took standing on a collective cliff of death to better embrace the purpose of life.

**Here's the takeaway for me:** except for a chosen few in this life who make history, who leave an indelible mark on mankind, or who leave great inventions and discoveries that last centuries or even millennia, we are gone forever. So, what we do with our time on this earth matters—a lot. Some, like my maternal grandmother, are blessed to live well into their nineties or even to make it to one hundred. But in the scheme of things, life is so truly short—and death lasts forever—so we had better live while we are alive.

In short, the pandemic reminded us that life is more than just what we do for a living, or how busy we are, or how many hours we spend on our phones. It made us focus instead on who we spend our time with and the quality of the time spent. The pandemic shut us all down. None of us could hide from it or escape its impact. In the United States alone, by January 2022, we'd lost an unthinkable 900,000-plus souls in eighteen months. And even as many of us eventually got vaccinated, got boosted, and felt more comfortable taking off our masks, new variants appeared; outbreaks of the virus grew and forced us to go inside, mask up, and cancel travel plans, birthday plans, and holiday plans alike.

Although we are now in the spring of 2022 and have some hope that COVID-19 will end, we are still dealing with the effects of the virus. It's very likely that you know someone who had COVID. Or maybe you, like me, had it yourself (I had it two times). Or worse, you lost friends or family: parents, grandparents, aunts, uncles, spouses, partners, in-laws, or—God forbid—children. None of us escaped the huge mirror that was being held up to our image, letting us know that time is not a friend and that whatever it is that God put us on this earth to do, we should do it—now. I think it finally hit millions of us that you cannot cuddle up under a blanket with your career or laugh at a movie with an iPad—we are made for relationship, love, and human connection.

**None of us escaped the huge mirror that was being held up to our image, letting us know that time is not a friend and that whatever it is that God put us on this earth to do, we should do it—now.**

As we lost millions of fellow human souls around the globe to this invisible virus that shut down our businesses, forced us to shelter in place, and stopped our busy routines cold nearly overnight, many of us went quietly inward. We found ourselves suffering from depression, isolation, emotional fatigue, family overload, Zoom burnout, and loneliness because of a longing for the very human connection and interaction that we so often took for granted.

For me personally, life got tough fast. I had a parent at home living with me as a result of a sudden and unexpected long-term disability. She could not work, drive, or even barely walk without assistance, and I was her only caregiver. My business, like so many, was losing revenue due to the shutdown of business from in-person to virtual, and I had to pivot to make money and make it all work. I had to do this while also figuring out how to manage my own health and wellness as well as that of a now unwell parent. I could not have made it through without the generosity of my friends, Mom's friends, and sorority sisters. They stepped up. They picked up Mom and took her to appointments. They checked on me, and they gave me a safe space to share my feelings when I needed to vent or cry. The upside of all this is that I rediscovered myself in 2020, as I suspect many of you did. At least I hope you did. As the old saying goes *it's not until you get healed that you know how broken you truly were.*

Many have asked me, "What does *be the one you need* mean?" Simply put, it means that there comes a time in your life when you must be there for you, when you must allow yourself to feel, to say what you think, to ask for what you need, and to stop pouring all your time and energy into others, deserving or not. It means you begin to see yourself as a person worthy of your own attention and time, as a person deserving of love, comfort, support, emotional nourishment—and you begin to give that support to yourself.

**Many have asked me, "What does *be the one you need* mean?" Simply put, it means that there comes a time in your life when you must be there for you.**

I learned a lot in the past two years. Getting COVID and being so sick was a blessing in disguise—a jolt of lifesaving lightning to my being. It woke me up in some extremely uncomfortable places. It made me face myself. It made me set boundaries. It made me angry. It made me sad. It made me willing to cut off anyone and anything that no longer made me feel loved, appreciated, or cared for. It also made me want to reach out to people I had not seen in decades who once meant something to me, and for whatever reason we had parted ways. The virus made me weak physically and yet, at the same time, ever so powerful. And it made me willing to speak my mind in ways I had never done with my family and longtime connections that, frankly, needed to hear what I had to say or be cut loose. I was no longer asking the people around me to change. I was changing. And it felt good. It was liberating, and it helped me to break the devastating generational curses that had been looming so large in our family.

Before realizing that I had needs, too, I felt like I was drowning, dying a quiet, slow death. While it might have appeared otherwise from the outside, I had long ago stopped truly living. And I didn't even realize that it had happened. I stopped dating. I didn't talk very much. I stopped feeling. I had been hit and hurt too many times by too many things, but I just kept on pressing through them. Grief hollows us out. It leaves a mark. But once channeled into self-awareness, it can be a powerful motivating force that moves us to meaningful change.

> **Grief hollows us out. It leaves a mark. But once channeled into self-awareness, it can be a powerful motivating force that moves us to meaningful change.**

Like so many of you, what had happened to me in my life was catching up, and I was suffering immensely. I wanted out of my self-imposed cage. I wanted out of the family drama, the family dysfunction, and the boxes they had created for me. I wanted out, and I was ready to do whatever it took to take my power back—power that I long ago gave away. No matter the price for speaking up, I was willing to pay it—anything to have the life I dreamed of when I was younger. The life I had looked nothing like the one I had envisioned for myself. While I was proud of my career successes, missing was the love I so desperately wanted to give and to receive. I was the tiny sliver of glue that was holding what was left of my immediate family together and it was coming apart at the seams. And for the first time, I accepted that it wasn't mine to save or to fix. They would have to go on without me, one way or the other, because whether you realize it or not, people always go on. They figure it out. We owe it to ourselves to put ourselves first and to be what we need, so that we, too, can go on. And one of the most important things about self-care is simply learning not just to go on but to go in a new direction.

## Self-Care Matters

A real spiritual awakening moment for me, about me, was when one of my best friends who is a licensed therapist and renowned corporate trainer was at my home and was doing Essential Colors for my guests at a small, vaccinated-only Mother's Day gathering in 2021. Essential Colors is a personality assessment tool, like the Myers-Briggs Type Indicator test, and it helps you to understand how you see and operate in the world and how you connect with others.

The psychology-based test breaks people down into four types: Blue (all about people); Orange (all about action); Gold (all about order); and Green (all about ideas). When my test results were revealed, I felt sad that I was not a Blue but instead a glaring Gold. Blues are social, compassionate, insightful, and inspiring—all that good mushy stuff. Blues are all about helping, teaching, and building meaningful relationships, and they work well with others. Golds are dependable, honest, loyal, and organized. They are all about planning, supervising, budgeting, and order, and they work well with proce-dure. It is all the stuff I do so well, but deep down I understood that somebody had killed my Blue—because those who know me (like my therapist friend) know that I am Blue through and through, but

I rarely let that side come out. I push that side of me down. Yes, I am kind. Yes, I am a helper to others, always. But I am rarely vulnerable, I am rarely easygoing, rarely chill. I love to play my guitar, dance, and sing, but I rarely do those things. And it's sad because I like being that person. I like her a lot. And I really want to see more of her for whatever days I have left on this earth.

Once you awaken from your emotional slumber, you will feel a lot of emotions. The most challenging to grasp will be understanding who you are and what you truly want from your life. Inevitably, when we try to understand all that we have suppressed, we ask, "What's wrong with me?" That's the wrong question. In my quest to better understand *what was wrong with me*, I happened upon a life-changing book written by Oprah Winfrey and Dr. Bruce D. Perry, *What Happened to You? Conversations on Trauma, Resilience, and Healing*. The simple change of the question altered my understanding of all I had been through, why I act the way I do, and why I have found it so hard all these years to be my truest self, in the open, for all to see and know.

The focus of their book starts with a question asking *what happened* to you instead of pointing the finger in judgment, or worse, and asking, *what's wrong with you?* Dr. Perry's work is all about the human brain, human memory, and how our brains adapt to trauma; how we are shaped in the first seven years of our lives by our families, our surroundings, and our life events. As we age, we react to what we remember of our early life—both the good and not so good. Our personal history affects our development into the life we create for ourselves and ultimately leave as our legacy. This instantly resonated with me and stopped me cold in my tracks.

In *Be the One You Need*, I use what happened to me as a means of teaching others the critical importance of focusing first on self-care. I share the sometimes painful yet liberating lessons I've learned while neglecting myself emotionally and otherwise pretty much since childhood. I want to help men and women alike to stop feeling guilty about self-care and to start the healing process by making wise choices and being their authentic selves. The fact of the matter is, we have our first relationship with our parents (family) and then we go out into the world with their values, their faith, their prejudices, their dysfunction, and on and on. It's not until we understand SELF, however, that we are absolutely freed to LIVE. We meet our needs, we follow our desires, our dreams, and in doing so we feed ourselves. Very few people live that way. We spend much, if not all, our lives looking outside of ourselves for what we want, what we need, what makes us feel whole. In truth, the answer is right there in the mirror—the answer is us.

In the final analysis, we all live and we all die. That is our human condition. My challenge for all of you and, indeed, myself is to truly live life on your own terms. In doing so, you will travel less stressed, less worried, less harried, and less hurried. When you live primarily for you and take care of your needs first (which, by the way, is not how we are conditioned as human beings, particularly as female human beings), you are a much better parent, child, spouse, friend, employer, sibling, and caretaker. If you are always feeling exhausted, drained, upset, unfocused, uncared for, and unnurtured, not only do you suffer most of all, but all of those who love you and who are connected to you suffer.

It's time to pivot, time to live your life on purpose. It's time to decide that you are ready to dig deeper and get to know yourself. It's time to live out your values or maybe rediscover what they are.

The funny thing about us as people is that, when you boil it down, we all value and want the same things: community, connection, family, friendship, love, respect, faith in something greater than us, adventure, respite, wealth, career success, and on and on. We aren't really that different at all when it comes to what we want from life. But if there is one big differentiator, it is our beginnings, and how they set the tone for everything in our lives. This book is going to help you to learn how to shift into what I like to call *the best day of your life*—and that is the day that you decide to live your own life for you, not for others. Grab a chair and let's go!

**It's time to pivot, time to live your life on purpose. It's time to decide that you are ready to dig deeper and get to know yourself. It's time to live out your values or maybe rediscover what they are.**

*"Love yourself first and everything else falls into line. You really must love yourself to get anything done in this world."*

—Lucille Ball

# SECTION I

## Notes to My Younger Self:
## You Are Who You Need

*This section deals with the significance of how our lives begin and the role family plays in who we become. The first scenes of our lives happen with the people who raise us and who are tasked with loving, nurturing, and meeting our basic needs during our early years. The goal of Section I is to help us to better understand the real connection between how we start and where we end up in life. This section encourages you to spot your pain points as an adult and to understand how your decisions early in life inevitably affect other areas down the road. The goal is to help you learn from positive and negative experiences alike and to use them as a ladder to gain exceptional decision-making skills. It is important early in life, when we are in a period of self-freedom and discovery, for people to redefine themselves, not based on the definitions, lessons, and limitations imposed on them by family and friends, but instead based on their own purpose, gifts, talents, and dreams.*

# LESSON 1

## Get Out of *Their* Box:
## You Are Not Your Family

*"You are born into your family and your family is born into you. No returns. No exchanges."*

—Elizabeth Berg, *The Art of Mending*

## *Your Family Is Your History, Not Your Destiny*

**F**amily. What a small but powerful word. It is the one decision that was made for us long before we ever took our first breath or saw the light of day. We all have a family, whether big or small; whether we were born to them or taken in by them. We all have roots. We all have a family tree, a family memory, a family blessing, or a family curse. I grew up in what we now call in twenty-first century lexicon a *toxic* family or, at best, a *dysfunctional* one. Like most of you, I did not know it at the time. It was simply my family, my normal. This is not an easy thing to admit to out loud and it is even more difficult to write about it because sometimes telling our truth and sharing our story means we will have to expose others we truly care about as reckless villains or bad actors in our lives. That's not the point, though. It's not about assigning blame for what other people did or didn't do; it's about how we face it and get beyond it so we can do better. But it all starts with admitting something happened to you that needs to be healed.

To those who have not yet admitted that your "normal" was not normal at all, or that trauma growing up was a big part of your family story, know that I was where you are. It took me a long time to get here. To say such words out loud may seem unkind. A betrayal of those who raised us, fed us, clothed us, and thought they did the best they could (no matter how bad that good was) to take care of us. *I feel you.* However, you should know that it is never weak, or unkind to speak the truth about your life, your feelings, your wounds, and your most challenging experiences. In fact, it is strength to speak the truth as you know it. Never shrink from speaking truth. When you learn to live shut down for years, you unwittingly adjust to the dysfunction. I am telling you to stop doing that now. It is okay to speak your truth, spread your wings, and fly.

My hope is that by sharing my story, you may recognize yourself and feel inspired and empowered to pivot in some small or large way—to change, to break free from the past before it swallows you whole. If it helps you to connect to what I am sharing, you should know that I, too, stayed trapped in what I call the "family box" or "their box" for decades of my life. I felt worthless, disliked and unloved by the very people whose sole purpose it should have been to both like and love me. Looking back now, I recognize that I put up with the unthinkable, the unbearable, and the unkind out of some mistaken sense of duty to people who kept going out of their way to be thoughtless, cruel, hurtful, neglectful, envious, and downright mean whenever it suited them. The truth is, I let people get comfortable disrespecting me, silencing me, labeling me, and boxing me. And it only began to stop when I decided it was time for me to change, when I began to deal in healthy boundaries and not boxes, and to stop being the family punching bag and the family scapegoat. I decided it was time for me to *be the one I needed* for me. And that has made all the difference.

You might be nodding your head in agreement. If so, you are there. And I am telling you that you can only escape *their boxes* if you want to, and only when you are ready to do so. To use an analogy, I am the black sheep in my family, and as the old saying goes, "the black sheep blazes the trail for other family members to follow when they finally see the wolf."

**The number one thing I want you to take away from this life lesson is:** we are

**The number one thing I want you to take away from this life lesson is: we are all shaped by our families of origin, but we are not forever defined by them.**

all shaped by our families of origin, but we are not forever defined by them. The decision to put you first and be what you need for you is not an easy one to make. Even when your family has hurt you, neglected you, or mistreated you, somewhere deep inside you still love them and you want them to change—to do better, to apologize, to "get it." You want their love and approval. But you will never regret putting yourself first and healing. Because when you do, you get to design the life you want, not the one they told you that you could never escape.

**The second most important takeaway from this life lesson is:** Dysfunction continues in every family unless and until someone in that family says, "ENOUGH—not me!" That someone was me, later than I liked, perhaps, but I have broken free nonetheless. I am a work in progress for sure, as we all are, but I hope that by reading this opening salvo into the life lessons I have learned, I will help you to likewise break away, build the firewall, and protect yourself from family hurt.

I also think it is important to note that not everyone reading this book has experienced damage at the hands of their families. And yet, all of us suffer on some level from and must recover from our family's ideas about us and the small boxes they can put us in. My literary agent once shared what a therapist told her: "I spend 90 percent of my time helping patients heal from their family drama and wounds." *Amen. Ain't that the truth!*

I challenge you to do something counterintuitive: you must tend to yourself and to your healing first and let others find their own way. When you learn how to feel safe and be vulnerable you can heal. When you slow down, you can hear your own voice speaking quietly to your soul. That's when you learn that you no longer need to beg to be loved or seen; that you no longer need to prove yourself or defend your desire to be different. No more hiding. You simply need to accept right here and now that you are enough. That you have always been enough. And more importantly than how you feel, is what you do. You must do what makes you feel safe and respected as a human being, not as a loyal member of a family clan that has no interest or desire in growing or changing. You must realize, as I did, that I could not change anyone but me. From a place of empathy, let me say that I know firsthand what it is like to be unkindly labeled by your family to others outside of the family. And, ironically, to also hear that your family has bragged about you as the great family success story at the same time.

> **You must do what makes you feel safe and respected as a human being, not as a loyal member of a family clan that has no interest or desire in growing or changing. You must realize, as I did, that I could not change anyone but me.**

*Crazy, right?* Not really.

I have heard similar stories countless times during over thirty years attending Al-Anon meetings and group-sharing therapy for children of alcoholics or drug abusers. Instead of being praised for being a bright light, or for being the emotionally stable one in the family who wants healing, they punish you. And they ostracize you or even cut you off while they tell anyone who listens that it is you who rejects your roots, your family, and that you think you are "too good" for them. And you're left dumbfounded, not understanding what you did wrong. It haunts you as deeply as it hurts you. Know this: it's time for you to stop carrying that pain and let it go. It starts by understanding that **you did nothing wrong**. Let me be clear: it is them; it is not you.

Here's the thing to remember about your family: they do not like it when you break the code of silence and liberate yourself from the limiting and damaging boxes that they have carefully constructed for you. We all get labels in our families. She is the "smart one." He is the "handsome one." He's just like his "no-good father." She is not "as pretty as her sister." We all have been labeled before we even knew who we were. And it's hard to shake those labels as they tend to follow you—in your family circles, at least—all your life. But we are people, we are unique individuals, and we are not labels. We are ever changing, ever growing, and always learning, if we are lucky. You do not have to answer to someone else's name for you. You do not have to stay in a box that someone who knew you at age ten created for you and wants you in that same box at age twenty-five. One of the hallmarks of unhealthy families is that they do not like it when you refuse to play by longstanding generational rules of dysfunction.

Family members who want to remain in their dysfunction expect you to do the same. And when you don't, there will be hell to pay. Let's face it, people do not like to be called out on their wrongs. When you do so, they will either admit their shortcomings and seek to change so that you can heal the rifts and truly reconcile, or they will deny, lie, attack, blame, demean, and come after you with a vengeance.

I know that many of you reading this can relate. I have talked to you over the past decade since I wrote my first book in 2011. I have heard from you on social media, I have had therapists and life coaches on my podcasts, we've met in small groups at conferences and book-signing events, in corporate ERG groups, and discussed it live on national radio or television. You, like me, felt (and may still feel) utterly ruined by these people who were supposed to love you, support you, lift you, and celebrate your successes. Worse, you felt helpless to do anything about it. So, instead of taking care of yourself and being what you needed, you continued to remain in the shadows and grudgingly go to family gatherings even though you dreaded them. You often silenced your own voice so you could fit in. And you shrank back from being your true, evolved, non-childhood self so that the bullies in your life could continue to speak loudly at your emotional expense. And each time you did this, you lost parts of yourself.

I lived that way until I was well into my late forties. As one former beau, who is a pastor and counselor, said to me once, "Sophia, watching you with your family is fascinating. You become a different person. You shrink, you get quiet, and you take care of everyone, which is admirable. But I hope that one day you pick up a coffee cup and throw it against a wall and tell everyone they need to shut up and give you a break." I was shocked because he is such a peaceful, level-headed man. He was telling me to start standing up for myself instead of taking it on the chin for others. His words stuck with me, and I did exactly what he suggested a time or two—minus throwing the coffee cup. But it wasn't until I was about to turn fifty that I truly began to realize how much I had personally lost and sacrificed. The lightbulb went off and I started boldly, and at times angrily, speaking up for myself. Pushing back. Yelling at the top of my lungs. And it did not go unnoticed by my family and friends. I was finding my inner voice and using it all at once. I was setting boundaries. And I was fully grasping how the trauma in my life had shaped me, and how finally asking the right question freed me to walk a different path.

**The third takeaway I want you to get is this:** You must love yourself more than you love them. I know that seems like a radical statement—and it is. It is a statement of self-love, self-care, self-worth, and

> **You must love yourself more than you love them. I know that seems like a radical statement—and it is. It is a statement of self-love, self-care, self-worth, and it is also a statement of release.**

it is also a statement of release. It is a stunning thing to consider how often we allow our family to use us as a personal bank, priest, counselor, and fixer. And when we finally proclaim that we have had enough, they recoil and act astonished. They'll ask, "What's wrong with you?" versus, as Oprah has taught me to ask, "What happened to you?" They tell you that "you need help"—they sneak behind corners and tell each other that you have "lost it." In reality, what you have done is take your power back, speak your peace, and finally found your way out of their drama.

## History vs. Destiny: Breaking Out of the Mold Isn't Easy

When you make the decision to stand up for yourself and lay down the new rules of your engagement with unhealthy or "toxic" family members, prepare yourself for the fallout. You will likely not be greeted with warm fuzzies and hugs. The upside, however, is what you gain. You gain YOU. You gain self-respect. You gain peace of mind. And you take your power back. American author Flannery O'Connor once wrote, "Anybody who has survived his childhood has enough information about life to last him the rest of his days." She was right. My goal in this first life lesson is to have you consider your beginnings. Truly. Because understanding how you began and the tribe you came from will answer a lot of questions you never knew you had. It will also free you from feeling obligated to family members who constantly abuse, traumatize, and disrespect you. You do not have to endure your childhood sufferings and humiliations repeatedly well into adulthood. There is a better way forward. And it all starts with you finding the courage to say two simple words: no more. Your freedom does not have to result in family fights, estrangement, or bitterness from generational family rifts. Your freedom is for you. How others choose to react to the new, healthier, more emotionally balanced you is their issue. It is not yours. So, stop worrying about what others will think. It's time for you to take care of you.

Dr. Maya Angelou said, "When you learn, teach." So, I am teaching you what I have learned. I had to learn to embrace the truth of where I came from so that I could forge a better path to where I wanted to be. I wish that I had learned this first lesson when I was a younger woman, in my twenties, instead of a middle-aged woman now in my

**There is a better way forward. And it doesn't have to result in family fights, estrangement, or bitterness from generational family rifts.**

fifties. I know for a fact that my life would be different—very different— and that I would have had a lot more joy, peace, and happiness. I would likely have made better relationship choices, gotten married, maybe had children, traveled more, ventured out more, loved more deeply and richly. Simply put, I'd have been a much more emotionally healthy human being instead of one who has worn suffocating masks for most of her life, disguising the person I truly was with the façade of one everyone else expected me to be.

I know firsthand what it is like to feel guilt, shame, and blame for things that had nothing to do with me. I just happened to land in a family where unhealthy interactions in our daily life were the norm. In the generation in which I came of age, we still did not know about the power of "self-help" or "healing your inner child." That all changed for me, when Oprah came on the scene during my high-school teenage and college years and enlightened me to a new body of ideas called "healing your inner child." There was a real awakening to mental health and wellness in the 1980s through the 1990s. As Baby Boomers and Gen Xers, we all grew up in a world of secrets. You kept your family's dirty laundry in the house; you did not air it, discuss it, or even dare to understand it. I grew up somewhat aware that both my parents had deeply traumatic childhoods. They were both poor. They both had absent fathers. My father and his two siblings were raised by his maternal grandfather, his uncle, and his single mother in a 700-square-foot house in the country. He was estranged from his biological father, who was married to another woman across town and father to eight other children. My beloved nana, his mother, was a beautiful biracial woman who worked cleaning houses to make sure he and his two siblings never went without. They always had a roof overhead and clothes on their backs, and they had a community that shared food and resources if anyone was hungry. But my father's family drank—a lot. And they would become angry, mean, and violent; a legacy that would unfortunately become part of my childhood reality, too. His trauma became my trauma and also my brother's trauma. And we learned anger as a first response to life's relationship challenges.

While my father was fortunate to have a mother who loved and did her best to protect him, my mom was not as fortunate. She and her two younger brothers (the first three of eleven children) were not with their biological mother or their biological father, who mom says they saw maybe three times in their lives. They were shuffled off to their maternal grandparents, who loved them but could not afford to keep them. They were then sent to live with other extended relatives who did not want them and where they were often left unfed, without clothes, eating out of garbage, emotionally neglected, physically unwell, and sexually abused. Their life was hell. Over the years, I have watched, brokenhearted, as each of them ended up divorced, passing on their trauma to their own children and grandchildren. We've discussed it openly. My mom and her two brothers, now in their seventies, see it clearly. But they carry a lot of guilt that they didn't know how to do better for their own families. They regrettably followed suit of what they experienced.

The point is this, understanding where your parents came from and what they endured is key to understanding your own life's journey. It gives context to the things we simply could not understand as chil-

**I want to encourage you to first understand your history, and then work from there on your destiny.**

dren. There is a great body of work on this generational trauma that I had no idea existed, and I want to make sure you know it exists because much of what we know today was simply not available twenty or thirty years ago. I want to encourage you to first understand your history, and then work from there on your destiny. I love my parents, with all their flaws, weaknesses, and issues. But I would be lying if I said I understood them. I do not. And, likewise, they do not understand me. The world they grew up in was vastly different from mine. I had to learn to factor that in when I was trying to comprehend some of their bad choices that eventually became my burdens to bear.

Another important factor to consider in your family dynamics is how your birth order plays a large role in how you are treated in your family and what's expected of you. Your gender also plays an even larger role. Are you the son they always wanted? Or the surprise third or fourth daughter who was unwanted? Were you adopted by loving parents who could not have children of their own? Or were you an "oops" first baby like me, who forced two young, immature, emotionally traumatized people to marry and try to parent before they were ready? Or, perhaps, you were the later-in-life baby who was desperately wanted by two parents who wed later in life. It matters not if you were born to a single professional mom who decided to go it alone or were fostered by unkind people whose only aim was to collect a check. No matter how you got here, or why your parents had you, understanding who they are will help you understand who you are.

As I will talk about in the next part of this chapter, generational attitudes have shifted dramatically since the 1980s regarding family and emotional wellness. And we can now talk about, analyze, and consider what makes people do what they do in our families, and how it impacts the people we become. According to modern psychologists and leading experts in post-traumatic stress, including Mount Sinai School of Medicine neuroscientist Rachel Yehuda, and psychiatrist Bessel van der Kolk, author of *The Body Keeps the Score*, even if the person who suffered the original trauma has died, or the story has been forgotten or silenced, the memory and feelings of it for those who remain can live on. For example, your grandmother died, but she passed on the trauma to your mother, and she passed it down to you. These emotional legacies are often hidden, encoded in everything from gene expression to everyday language, and they play a far greater role in our emotional and physical health than has ever before been understood. Stated in a simpler way: a growing body of research called "trauma inheritance" suggests that trauma (from extreme stress, abuse, or starvation, among many other things) *can be passed from one generation to the next.* Here's how: trauma can actually leave a chemical mark on a person's genes, which can then be passed down to future generations.

Consider, for a moment, how many times you have wondered why the people in your family never seem to break free of poverty, trauma, certain illnesses, or addictions; and why we see this play out so many times in communities and families for generations. It's because it can be passed down every bit as much as blue eyes, red hair, height, or other genetic traits. This is a game-changing revelation that pioneering psychologists like Mark Wolynn, in his powerful book *It Didn't Start with You: How Inherited Family Trauma Shapes Who We Are and How to End the Cycle,* are helping a new generation of scientists, psychologists, and physicians to better understand generational curses, bad memories, and how it is all passed down long after our relatives have passed on. Better still, he helps us to reimagine our lives by using the power of direct dialogue to create pathways to reconnection, integration, and reclaiming lost love, life, and health for ourselves and our families.

What I am suggesting is simple: Take a step back from your own trauma and try to understand that of your parents. Ask questions if they are willing to discuss it with you. I did this with my mother, and it has given me a deeper understanding of how she does things and how she raised us. I also talked to people who knew my parents or their parents, and I learned a lot about how deep my family's dysfunction went back into the family tree. It was eye-opening and jaw-dropping all at once. By doing this, my anger and hurt has subsided, and it was replaced with more patience, better understanding, and grace. My mom and I actually entered family therapy over the past two years because of the stress of her being unwell and me trying to manage it largely alone.

**At the end of the day, only you possess the power to undo what has been done to you. Only you possess the courage to be different than what you experienced.**

Still, when all is said and done, no matter how much we learn about our family history, or our parents' history, we still must acknowledge and tend to our own wounds. Ignoring them or pressing them down will only make them louder in our silence. At the end of the day, only you possess the power to undo what has been done to you. Only you possess the courage to be different than what you experienced. And, most importantly, what they experienced. Remember: only you can rewrite the bad chapters of your life, instead create new ones that reflect the man or woman you wish to be, not the one your family tree says you must be. You are not in anybody's box. You are not anyone's scapegoat. It's time you stopped acting like one.

## How a New Generation Views Family, Emotional Health, and Wellness in the Twenty-First Century

I opened this lesson with the two words: *family* and *toxic*. And I want to pause for a moment to give you my thoughts on the current generation's overuse of the word "toxic." Dear young people, everything cannot be and is not toxic. It's just like saying everyone is racist or sexist. When you overuse important words, they lose their true meaning and power. *Trauma* and *toxic* are related because toxic people are born out of traumatic circumstances. And when we diminish another human being who has flaws as "toxic," or who tells untruths, as we all do on occasion, or who has made mistakes as we all will (or have), then we set the bar very high for human failings and weakness for ourselves. This new generational shift can best be summed up by the social media hashtag #okayboomer, which is another way of saying, "Whatever, old people. You think you know everything, but you don't." It's a typical blow-off and it is what this generation does as their norm. And that is likely the fault of an iPhone driven, social media culture. We've trained them to accept gun violence and shooter drills as normal as early as kindergarten. We've allowed phones to take the place of old-fashioned conversation at the dinner table, and we've taught them that their hurt feelings entitle them to say anything, post anything, and hurt anyone they feel has hurt them first.

Although there has been a dramatic and positive shift toward talking about mental health, family dysfunction, childhood abuse, childhood trauma, and how we respond to it, and how to break its very damaging and negative hold on our lives, we have also embraced Gen Y's and Gen Z's cancel culture mentality. It is essentially bullying: peer pressure to engage in group think and group identity. And that includes cancelling our own family if they piss us off, or if we perceive they have wronged us. I will address that in Lesson 16 later in the book. But a new generation of young people is redefining what constitutes family, what they will endure, not endure, and when they will walk away for good. This new generation of twenty-somethings and younger have mastered the art of the "cut-off" . . . the disconnect . . . the block . . . delete . . . cancel. As one Instagram GenYer put it, "our generation thinks it's cool to not care. It's not. Effort is cool. Caring is cool. Staying loyal is cool. Try it out." And their favorite of all: "ghosting."

To be honest, I had no idea this was a thing in families until I read a 2021 *New York Times* article titled, "What's Ripping American

Families Apart?" by famed columnist David Brooks, who opined on the state of the family in the United States and why so many are estranged from their closest relatives. I was stunned to learn that what I was personally dealing with was happening in many families around the world but more and more frequently here in the United States.

In his piece, David Brooks writes, "At least 27 percent of Americans are estranged from a member of their own family, and research suggests about 40 percent of Americans have experienced estrangement at some point. The most common form of estrangement is between adult children and one or both parents—a cut usually initiated by the child. A study published in 2010 found that parents in the US are about twice as likely to be in a contentious relationship with their adult children as parents in Israel, Germany, England, and Spain." He goes on to write, "Part of the misunderstanding derives from the truth that we all construct our own realities, but part of the problem, as Nick Haslam of the University of Melbourne has suggested, is there seems to be a generational shift in what constitutes abuse. Practices that seemed like normal parenting to one generation are conceptualized as abusive, overbearing, and traumatizing to another."

That is where I want to park for a moment. Right here: "generational abuse." What a powerfully disturbing and yet liberating term.

**"Practices that seemed like normal parenting to one generation are conceptualized as abusive, overbearing, and traumatizing to another."**

As I discussed earlier in the lesson, there is a whole new body of study on this phenomenon of family and abuse. How we spot it, how we address it, and how we move beyond it to a healthier place. Let me spotlight a key part of what Brooks shares because it is critical to understanding family, and your relationship to your family, in this new world in which we now all must live, love, and learn. Again, let me emphasize this phrase a bit differently: "Practices that seemed like normal parenting to one generation are conceptualized as abusive, overbearing, and traumatizing to another."

This sentence set me free. I had been struggling to understand for the past seven years since my brother's very public, very bitter divorce, why my biracial nieces, whom we indulged, adored, frankly worshipped, spent quality time with, and spoiled beyond reason when they were growing up, have been largely estranged from our side of the family. My brother married a White woman. Their union was ill fated from the start for many reasons, both cultural and familial, but they struggled most of all with being a mixed-race family in the 1990s through early 2000s. They had a very ugly public split that ripped our families in two and left a lot of hurt feelings, deep family rifts, and even deeper emotional scars on their two children. I have literally wept over this many a night because I did not want the same trauma we endured, that our parents endured, to be passed on to those girls. And yet, regrettably, it has been. All my efforts to help my brother see he needed deep counseling, that he needed to change, or he would one day lose his family—as my father did—failed. It wasn't just him, however, both he and his wife needed to do the work. They didn't, and the marriage inevitably suffered. They were literally counseling other couples in ministry when their own marriage was in shambles. It was hard to watch, even harder to feel helpless to stop the inevitable train wreck that occurred.

I do not have children. So, for all intents and purposes my nieces were my children. If you have followed my career, watched me on TV, followed my social media, and read my books over the past fifteen years or more, you have heard me brag about them, dedicate books to them, and gleefully publicly profess my love for them time and time again. They are the sunshine in my world, and now I barely hear from them. One of them has refused to see me and informed me that I, like her father, am "toxic," among a lot of other not nice things that hurt me to my core. We had an argument on Easter Sunday when she was sixteen over an Instagram post and the attention of a nineteen-year-old boy that had been reported to us by another family member. She was being a typical teenage girl—you know, storming upstairs, yelling, "I hate you" at her father—and I dared to correct her as I would have been swiftly and devastatingly corrected if I'd said anything remotely like that to an elder. Her parents coddled her versus correcting her, and it escalated into me attempting to pop her in the mouth—as any of my aunts would have surely done to me. And after they smacked me, I would have been knocked into the next week by my mom, grandma, and my father. Trust me, I wanted to smack her in the mouth, but my brother intercepted me before I could get to her. It was bad. It was hurtful. I was angry and in shock all at once at the level of disrespect. Sadly, this wasn't the first time we had had a run in like this.

This scene has likely happened in households the world over for decades—smart-mouthed teenager pops off and adult family members correct them. While I got an apology note from her as I had with past infractions, I never saw her again. Ever. That was almost eight years ago. This family squabble was enough for her to justify cutting me out of her life for good. And she has only seen my mother (her grandmother) twice in those eight years with very sporadic texts in between). I have written, called, and texted. I've never missed a birth-day, graduation, or any other occasion to show love, forgiveness, and reconciliation despite what happened that day. I got nothing back but vitriol, judgment, harsh unkind words, and ruthless recriminations. That is a true story. It is painful to share with the world. My youngest niece, who is also now grown, was a part of our lives until she graduated high school in 2020. Now she, too, has stopped communicating, ignored letters and gifts sent, not wished us Merry Christmas or acknowledged birthdays. In hindsight, I guess it was inevitable. Their mother turned them against us long ago with the passive acquiescence of their father (this, too, happens in families everyday), and no matter what we did or how much we loved, I think we were always going to end up here. I pray it changes with time. Because none of us ever has enough time. I have watched it break my mother just as deeply as it has me.

The fact is, we are of a different generation. I was raised to never speak disrespectfully to adults, especially not my family elders. I was seen and not heard. I was taught to be silent. Her generation is taught to call 911 on their parents for raising their voice, to fight their parents back if they think they have crossed parental boundaries, call them liars, and most of all to "find their own voice." Get the difference? We have great conflict in our families right now because we have not learned to deal with the differences of how each generation in that family processes self-care, family obligation, love, loss, pain, conflict, trauma, and forgiveness. And therein lies the key to our total healing.

As for my nieces, it has been hard losing them. It feels like someone ripped my heart out of my chest while it was still beating.

> **We have great conflict in our families right now because we have not learned to deal with the differences of how each generation in that family processes self-care, family obligation, love, loss, pain, conflict, trauma, and forgiveness. And therein lies the key to our total healing.**

It's been harder still to see the impact on my mother, their paternal grandmother. Like those comments of so many bewildered parents and grandparents that I've read on family trauma sites, and in online self-help book reviews, Mom just doesn't understand how they can cut off their family. She's bewildered about how they can be so unkind and downright cruel to those who clearly made some mistakes, but consistently showed how much they cared, and how precious they were to us. I share her bewilderment, but I have accepted it and moved on. I pray for them every day, but I will not allow people whom I have loved unconditionally to treat me disrespectfully with impunity. They will have to work that out for themselves when karma does her work—as she always does. My prayer is they will heal from their hurts and work to make peace with their past before it's too late and we have all transitioned from this life. Once people are gone, it's too late to fix things.

## The Impact of Divorce on Families

My parents got divorced when I was twenty and my brother was thirteen. Based on what I saw growing up, my father was largely at fault for their ultimate split. Still, I didn't stop loving him, or cut out of my life my beloved paternal grandmother, aunts, uncles, or cousins. Oh, I let them know how I felt. And I was shunned for it, unlike my Gen Y and Gen Z nieces who are encouraged to "find their voice" and let the adults in their lives know how they feel. I was not allowed to express my feelings, or protest clearly abusive treatment or emotional trauma. Every time I tried to address my father privately via a letter, he would violate my trust and share it with anyone he could find to make himself a victim. His sister (my once favorite aunt) became his biggest protector, a mean bully. She attacked me, her only niece, on social media and verbally to anyone who would listen. And, as people do, they would tell me because they found her conduct out of order and petty. Everyone knew what went on in the Nelson family. It was legend. Too many public episodes, too many broken relationships, too many bar scenes and fights. It was not secret. My teachers knew. My coaches knew. My boyfriends and my best friends all knew. It was embarrassing and deeply scarring all at once.

The point I want you to get from this is that "toxic" families do strange things. I mentioned this aunt, who ironically had many horrific fights with my father. I witnessed them, my mother witnessed them, my brother witnessed them. They would be drinking (too much) get into verbal fisticuffs and then maybe even physical fights, some right out on the front lawn, until someone called the police. How ironic that the aunt I witnessed with my own eyes physically fight with and be wrestled to the ground by my father in front of the whole neighborhood turned out to be his biggest defender. The same aunt who said she detested his drinking, and his behavior, became his most vociferous champion. Worse, too many times to count, they pretended it never happened and then repeated the entire cycle again and again. That's what unhealthy, unhealed, broken people do. They blame *you* for how *they* have treated you. And when you call them on it, or attempt to discuss it face-to-face, they attack you.

My punishment was being slowly banished from the family after my parents' divorce and up until my grandmother's death in September 2000. They loved my brother because he was the silent, religious child. But I was the rebel. I talked back. And that cannot be tolerated. My brother was welcomed to family gatherings with his wife and children; he could vent his feelings to my father and get into heated arguments with no reprisals. No one badmouthed him outside the family. No one blasted him on social media. No, they reserved all that venom for me. For years, I absorbed it, just as many of you have. Until one day, it literally made me sick. Then I got help, and I got healing, and I started to distance myself and accept that, even though I didn't want to cut myself off completely, the situation had become damaging to my mental and emotional health.

As you have already discerned, I grew up in an emotionally and at times physically abusive hellhole. When my parents got divorced in 1990, I was a senior in college. I remember being shocked when my mother finally left my father (she had done so once before when I was in the eighth grade, moving us briefly to California before coming back home to New Jersey) for good. I never thought she would do it. I was glad when she did. I only wish it had been sooner, because I might have had a much healthier relationship with my father. I know my brother and I would not be the deeply damaged adults we became and who now, at midlife, are trying to figure it all out as we stand amidst the relational rubble of our lives.

Many older generations did not believe in therapy. Or talking. Or even seeking pastoral help. Their way of doing things was you got what you got in life, you sucked it up, and you moved on. Your family was your family. And even if they mistreated you, you were still supposed to "honor" them. I heard that a lot growing up. They often used the Bible as a weapon to keep you silent and obedient even in the face of unthinkable abuse. I will be the first one to say, good for this new generation that they realize they do not have to take abuse, or co-sign it for the rest of their lives. However, I have a deep

> I have a deep concern that in redefining what constitutes abuse, we are losing something important—the power of growth, redemption, and restoration.

concern that in redefining what constitutes abuse, we are losing something important—the power of growth, redemption, and restoration. I think we can all agree that how we treat our own family members says a lot about how we will treat others. You can see it every day in our cut-them-off cancel culture. And it's not working out too well for a lot of people. **The reality is this:** human beings are messy, and we are a mess. This is not likely to change. The goal is not to give up on each other, take abuse from one another, or cut off our loved ones. The goal should be to do the work to heal our wounds first, confront what we want changed within our families, and to go forward wiser, healthier, and happier human beings. And if we make that effort and we fail, at least we know we tried.

Bottom line, we need balance. Our parents and grandparents tolerated the intolerable. They endured. They supported. And they took care of their relatives as they aged, even if they were truly undeserving. They just did the best they could to survive. I could never do what my mother did, but I can admire her strength. She's told me her stories of being hit with ironing cords as a child. That was commonplace. She grew up with two of her younger brothers impoverished, hungry, abused, and moved around between family members and foster care. So, in her worldview, whatever we experienced as children was "not that bad" because, filtering it through her lens, we had two parents, we had a home, we had food on the table and clothes on our backs. It's all a matter of perspective.

For the most part, when I was growing up, our family tried to work through our disagreements or unpleasant fights, or simply overlook them. Yes, of course, there were moments where we may have stopped speaking for a week or two, but there was never a total cut-off. Never, "I'm done with you." Never, "If you get sick, I won't check on you." Never, "I won't send you a birthday card or a Christmas gift." I have a very distant emotional relationship with my father, but I've checked on him during the pandemic regularly. I check on him or ask his girlfriend how he is doing. It's just how we were raised. I keep a healthy distance, but I also do my best to keep in the best touch I can.

Not so with this new generation. They are masters at cutting, blocking, deleting, and unfriending. They can be cold and that worries me. That was David Brooks' point. We are entering uncharted territory. How we define *toxic, abuse,* and *stress* is very different from the new generation. And how we choose to move forward is critical, as I mentioned earlier, because cutting off your toxic loved ones does not fix the problem. You still must face and fix yourself. That is the part people miss most of all. And that is why the conflict and abuse continue generationally. It only ends when you do the work on you.

> *"You own everything that happened to you. Tell your stories. If people wanted you to write warmly about them, they should have behaved better."*
> —*Anne Lamott*

## Not All Families Are Forever

Let me say something clearly and emphatically: not all families are forever. No matter how much you may want things to be better, or to have your relationships healed, if people are unwilling to do the work, you must know when to walk away and take care of you. As I have said many times, you can only change you. If you learn nothing else from this first life lesson, please learn this—you cannot change others or threaten them into changing. All change starts with self: self-love, self-respect, and a desire to be a better human being first for you, and then for those you love. At this stage of my life, I am cordial with my father. After years of trying to win his love, of inviting him to key events in my life, having him in my home, striving for a healthy father-daughter relationship—as so many of my friends have with their dads—I finally accepted it wasn't in the cards for me. It takes two. He is who he is. He is not interested in changing. And I am no longer interested in waiting for him to change. Again, it's generational. He simply expects me to play by his rules, and, in his mind, all will be well. I can't do that anymore. It's not good for me. And if I must choose between him or me, I emphatically choose me. Most of our family is estranged. People not speaking to one another, holding grudges, and spreading untrue gossip. It's awful.

**You can only change you. If you learn nothing else from this first life lesson, please learn this—you cannot change others or threaten them into changing. All change starts with self: self-love, self-respect, and a desire to be a better human being first for you, and then for those you love.**

For my part, I can say with a clear conscience that none of this is because I want it that way or because I cut anyone off. Those are lies they like to tell so they can excuse their own behavior. It's easier to say, "Someone cut me off" or "They don't talk to me," or "I have no idea what is wrong," than to admit to yourself and others that you may have some culpability in why people choose to be around you or not. I have written letters. I have called. I have brought in counselors, trusted family friends with counseling or pastoral backgrounds. I even made a video for my nieces back in 2020 during the pandemic, talking to them as the young women they now are as their only aunt (I ran it first by our family therapist, and she approved of the tone, content, and motivation behind it). I thought I could communicate by video, a way they might better relate to and understand, while trying to help them get to know me better as a member of the other side of their family. One never acknowledged the video and the other one literally went off on me in an email riff that was jaw-dropping, angry, upsetting, and heartbreaking all at once.

> *"Nobody trashes your name better than someone who is afraid you will tell people the truth."*
>
> —*Anonymous*

I had to let it go, folks. And so do you. I am getting too old for the emotional stress and strain that family anger and accusation exacts from our lives. I am content to let people be who they are now, so I can be at peace with who I am. Although my mother's family lives far away in California, we see them when we can, we talk to them, text daily with them, and laugh with them. I have five maternal aunts who do love me, support me, and who are very proud of me. My father's eldest sister (by his estranged father), Aunt Evelyn, who is in her eighties, also keeps in touch, and lets me know how proud she is of me and the things I am doing with my life. So, it's not all my family, just some of my family. The West Coast family has had challenges, too; as in any family, not everyone likes everyone else. But family hurt and family estrangement is real, and unfortunately it is common in our society. Of all the lessons I have learned, this first one matters the most because it is the foundation. Your family is your foundation, just like the foundation on a home. It determines everything about who we become, and how we engage our emotions, our relationships, and our self-care.

If you want to have a happy and functional life, you must face the demons of your past, or the ones still with you in your present, and you must seek to make peace with them as best you can so that you can break the family cycle of pain, anger, and eventually estrangement. Running away or calling people names like "toxic" is not the answer. Do the work on yourself so that you can better understand the work that others either cannot do or refuse to do. It's very liberating. The first key takeaway I want you to get from this lesson is that what is normal to one person, or to one generation, may not be so for another. This is most definitely true in my family.

I had to wrestle with this hard truth because it explains a lot of things. I did not understand about how my parents were raised since I did not live their experience, and, in turn, how they parented us. My grandparents, part of the "greatest generation" (as of the writing of this book, I still have my maternal grandmother, alive at age ninety-two), and my parents, classic Baby Boomers, born right after World War II in 1945 and 1947, respectively, had shared life values and connections with their parents. Their only technology growing up was radio, then, in the 1950s, television. These things and the newspaper were the only means of getting news from around the world or being connected to the rest of the nation.

But the Baby Boomers were seen by their parents as rebellious, out of control, liberal, and going against the order of things. The greatest generation literally saved the world from fascism and tyranny in World War II. They married young and they stayed married. They honored the nuclear family. They took care of their elders, often caring for aunts and uncles and grandparents in the family home. They fueled the industrial boom, they lived in relative peace and prosperity after the war, built new cities and towns, and moved west. And they cherished extended family. Their kids, however, protested Jim Crow. They disrupted the old social order around race and gender. They practiced free love. They went to Woodstock and rolled around in the mud. They went to Vietnam, protested Vietnam, took over student-union buildings, started dating interracially and having friends from different cultures and classes. They turned the prevailing order on its head so that American families and culture began to change quite dramatically. It was the beginning of women's rights, civil rights, and affirmative action. Divorce for women was no longer a stigma. It was a huge shift from what had previously shaped American families.

I am a Gen Xer, born in 1967. My parents were young when they had me, so they were more in touch with my generation's music, politics, and culture. Unlike our parents and grandparents, we had no great causes to fight. We were the latchkey kids. Our moms worked, and we learned quickly how to be self-sufficient. We lived under twelve straight years of the Cold War and Republican presidents during our formative years. We were barely five years old or so when Nixon had to resign the presidency. We don't remember the Vietnam War or Kent State, Jimmy Carter, or Gerald Ford. We were the benefactors of the women's liberation and civil rights movements. We went to fully integrated schools and worked on computers.

Many of us turned out to be conservative and traditional, although many women, like me, did not get married and have children until later in life, and some did neither because we had professional careers that made many of us "firsts" in our field. Trailblazers can rarely have it all. Fast forward to the present day: a woman is vice president of the United States. A woman is Speaker of the House of Representatives. And my nieces' generation (born in 1998 and 2002, Gen Z) can now take for granted that a Black man can be president and a woman can be vice president. Why am I going through the generations and what shapes them? Because the time in which we grow up matters—a lot. The same for our parents, grandparents, and their parents.

We are all shaped by our home environment, our external societal influences, and the time in which we are born and live. More importantly, we must acknowledge that generational "curses" are real. Generational blessings are also real. And families are always a mixture of both. But for this life lesson, I am talking to people, like myself, who did not have healthy, "normal" families. I am talking to people who have struggled their entire lives with toxic parents, siblings, and family ties. I want you to understand that you do not have to put up with narcissistic behavior, abusive behavior, or people who really do not like you, much less love you. At some point, you must decide that you are going to define who you are. You will choose not to be like them without looking down on them. You will do your best to put them in the proper context of their life experiences, traumas, and the like, and let them be. I had to learn, as you will, that I cannot change people as much as I may want to. For my own well-being, I had to accept that I can only change myself. Period.

Part of your being what you need to live a happier life is relieving yourself of the stress and shame that comes from being part of a dysfunctional family. It is stress that makes us unwell. It affects our body, mind, and soul. The more you can step back and begin to see those who hurt you as victims of the same abuse and trauma, the more grace you will find for them. And, ultimately, you can forgive them and free yourself.

## You Must Forgive Your Family for You (Even if They Never Ask)

Oprah's book taught me something important that I want you to understand, too: *Nothing is wrong with you.* It is all *what*

**Family is a huge thing in our lives. It molds us, and either enables us to grow and fly or cages us in a life of emotional chaos.**

*happened to you.* No matter how badly or sadly your life may have begun—or even how unsettled it might look right now, as Walt Whitman said, "You are the master of your fate." You are the captain of your soul. You still get to write the rest of your story if you are willing to do the work of facing the things that hurt you, disappointed you, broke you, wounded you, or scarred you. Your family was just the shepherd that watched over you until you reached adulthood. How well they watched over you, how kind or unkind they were to you, how much love or anger you were exposed to, only you can say. But I promise you, once you begin to process the hurts of your childhood abuse, neglect, loss, grief, or sufferings through a lens of not "what's wrong with me" but instead "what happened to me," everything will shift in your world. It will feel like someone opened your eyes for the very first time.

To paraphrase Buddha, "Praise and blame, gain and loss, pleasure and pain are part of the dance of life."[1] How true. Some of you had great parents. You had wonderful, idyllic childhoods. Or maybe you just had normal, no drama, no trauma, with a family who loved you, wanted you, celebrated you, nurtured and encouraged you. Growing up as the older child of one raging, always angry parent and another submissive, saintly parent was difficult, to say the least. It was filled with lots of confusion and trauma: emotional, spiritual, relational, and even physical. As a female child, the older child, and only daughter, it was rife with life-changing peril. The relationship between father and daughter is an important one because it is a girl's first glimpse at what men are and how she relates to them.

---

[1] Actual quote: "Praise and blame, gain and loss, pleasure and pain, fame and disrepute are the eight worldly winds. They ceaselessly change. As a mountain is unshaken by the wind, so the heart of a person is unmoved by all the changes on this earth." —Buddha

My father was present in our home my entire childhood into my teenage years. He always had a job and provided for us. When I was very young, he was my hero. I adored him. The sun rose and set on him. I saw him as strong, handsome, smart, and my protector. That all started shifting when I was about seven and became more aware of what was going on around me. My mother cried constantly. Most of my childhood memories are filled with horror and heartache. I began to see my father through the lens of who he really was. He drank often and a lot. And when he drank, he changed. He became like the Incredible Hulk, which ironically was one of my favorite childhood TV shows. He turned into a monster. My hero became unrecognizable when he drank. This was my normal. This was my childhood.

I hated family holidays because I knew how they were going to turn out. They always started off nicely. My mom or paternal grandmother started cooking up a feast early. There were gifts, friends, family—and plenty of alcohol. Inevitably, however, my father's family would drink too much and start fighting with one another, sparring verbally at first, which would then sometimes turn physical—literally threatening, menacing, and even audibly growling at one another. It was like something out of a bad movie. Looking back on this with adult eyes, I realize how traumatic it was to see and hear the people I loved fighting, cursing, and being so disrespectful to one another. Boundaries were nonexistent—just lots of anger and rage that manifested from their unresolved childhood wounds and traumas. Alcohol gave them "liquid courage" but also took away all their inhibitions. The next day, oddly, they would act as if it never happened—until it would happen again. Adding to the confusion for me was that my mother was like a saint, the opposite of the rage and venom. She took us to church every Sunday, she did not curse, she was kind and very naïve. She was a stay-at-home mom for most of my early child-hood, even when she worked part-time. But, as my father's drinking became worse, my mom changed. She withdrew. She stayed locked in her home office after she successfully became a registered nurse. Her personality type is passive—she avoids conflict at all costs. It's the ostrich approach: If you don't see it, then it doesn't exist. If you ignore it, it will go away. Obviously, this is also not a good, healthy, or sustainable way to live your life.

As of this writing, I am still in the process of working through things with my mother. We are in family therapy, and we have made progress. It's been slow. It's been difficult. Through this process, I have come to give her credit for being willing to stand in the arena and fight for her family at such a later season of her life. We couldn't have two more different personalities, but we both have a deep and abiding faith. The odds were stacked against my mom when she decided to get an education while in a really bad marriage with two young kids. Yet, she succeeded, got a profession, and one day stood up for herself and left the drama behind, knowing that she could stand on her own two feet. For that, I applaud and admire her immensely.

But no matter how I was neglected, or how many hurtful and callous things have been done to me out of ignorance, I have never abandoned her. She has already lost too much. She is a good woman, and she did the best she could with what she knew at the time. I get that now. I understand that she had zero coping tools coming from a tough childhood then moving straight into marriage at nineteen years old and expecting a baby while living halfway across the world in Germany. She did the best she could, even if her best has left deep scars on me and my brother. I have learned that I can only hold her to what she knew at the time—not what she and I now know. My father is a different story. He has never apologized. He has never tried to build a father-daughter relationship with me. He is great with his niece and his two granddaughters, likely because he no longer drinks. He gives them money and buys them things, and they think he is awesome. They do not know the man their father and I endured. They only know him as "Pop-Pop." Good for them. I had to make peace with the fact that the little girl I once was is not to blame for the father who failed her so deeply. I hoped the father I once adored would come back, but he did not. I do not know this man at all, and he certainly does not know me.

All of this takes a toll. I suppressed my hurt and anger. Even worse, as children often do, I turned that anger inward and blamed myself for my parents' behavior. I had bleeding ulcers as a teenager and college student. The older I got, the more I started to suffer from the effects of my childhood. Depression. Drinking. Even suicidal thoughts.

I don't want that for you. You must accept that, yes, you are a grownup now, but no matter how you try to hide it or suppress it, you are still trying to deal with the scars of your past. And let me be direct—it is not a healthy coping mechanism to live an isolated, lonely life, or to suffer from anxiety every day of your life, or worse, continue to bounce from dysfunctional, abusive relationships time and time again.

I want you to know you are not alone—too many of us grew up with emotionally damaged and ill-prepared parents. They simply didn't have the ability to love us as we deserved. What's done is done. While this might have shaped you, it doesn't define you. The mold is not set. You can't change your past, but you sure as hell can change your present and your future. It's time to stop suffering from the emotional baggage that was never supposed to be yours to carry forever.

I have healed—or at least I am in the process of healing—from my childhood trauma. The Sophia Nelson the world sees on TV, on the big stage, or reads about in my books, is no different than you. Once you understand the root of your problem—your family—you can create the more peace-filled life you deserve.

## Now That You Know Nothing Is Wrong with You— What's Next?

If you cannot repair the things you did not break (and you usually cannot), the pain you feel over what was lost should not be avoided. You must know that once you have grieved, mourned, and wailed, there is more to your life and your living. You must hold on to two truths: You can change. And other people can change only if they want to. I now know that, despite all that has happened to me, nothing is wrong with me. And if you hear nothing else I have said in this lesson, I want you to know that nothing is "wrong" with you that some time, some good people, some patience, some good counsel, some love, some empathy, and some faith cannot fix.

> You must hold on to two truths: You can change. And other people can change only if they want to.

It might sound trite but it's true: *hurt people hurt people.* And our families can be a place full of hurt people. Once you fully accept—acceptance is key—that your parents, and whoever else hurt you in life, are also hurt people, it gives you the power to forgive them, release them, embrace them, re-engage them, help them, have courageous conversations with them, or simply love them from afar. What I will never tell you to do is to reconnect your life with people who have sexually abused you, violated you, been emotionally or physically abusive and unkind to you, or otherwise subjected you to deep trauma. You have every right to cut those people off and protect yourself. If those people have changed, gotten professional help, and try to apologize to you or make amends, only you can decide if that is a path you want to walk with them.

When I have spoken to people who have been cut off from family members, they are devastated. Many times, they are clueless as to why it happened. Reading comments on some of the books that deal with family trauma and pain will surely make you tear up. There are parents left alone in their later years, cut off from their grandchildren, rejected when they reach out to talk. They are labeled as "toxic," "abusive," "narcissistic," and they are utterly lost as to what happened. They did not beat or abuse their kids, but maybe they had strict rules that created resentment and eventually estrangement once the child got free and on their own.

Let me say this from the bottom of my heart: You should not be cutting off a family member or parent because you felt entitled, because you didn't get a car when you were sixteen. Or because your mom didn't make all your football games because she had to work to put food on the table. Being corrected when you act disrespectfully as a child or teen, or even as an adult, is not abuse. We should be careful in this modern world of changing definitions of how we treat the people who loved us and did their best by us. Respecting people is important. You can forgive people if you want to, and if they come to you humbly, sorry, and contrite. What I am telling you to consider doing is to try to give people the same grace you want for yourself. This is where most human beings fail. Empathy—we all need to find some. You can have hope. You can rewrite your family's history. You can be the change. You can be the one. Sometimes, it takes loss to be found. You don't have to fully let go of your parents. But you must

**What I am telling you to consider doing is to try to give people the same grace you want for yourself. This is where most human beings fail.**

*Empathy—we all need to find some.*

learn how to separate the person you love from the actions that hurt you.

## How to Make This Life Lesson Work in Your Own Life

There are two applications of this life lesson. The first, if you have not started to get out of the family box. And the second, if you have already started but are a work in progress. Now is time to develop the skillset to start healing yourself instead of shrinking. I want to challenge you to ask and answer some key questions that you should have gathered from this lesson. The first key takeaway I want you to really grasp is that what is normal to one person, or to one generation, may not be so for another. You simply cannot push your values and your life experiences on others, nor can they do that to you. You need to find a way to successfully integrate and create cross-generational dialogue in your family. It's the only way forward. For those who are just starting the journey of healing, ask yourself a series of questions about your parents and family interactions:

- Do you feel you lost your childhood because you had to grow up and become the parent? Did you have to regularly take care of your younger siblings? Did you need to work to help your family financially?

- Did you have to deal with emotionally unavailable, substance-addicted, or self-centered parents who neglected you and your siblings' needs? Or maybe just your needs?

- Did your parents pit you and your siblings against one another; playing favorites, offering, and withholding love, causing fractures and division?

- Did you feel unloved, unseen, or uncared for no matter how much you achieved or excelled?

- Did you walk on eggshells, making sure none of your actions would upset or irritate your parents or an angry abusive parent?

For those of you, like me, who have been walking this path for a while, you need to ask some different questions—or do some work around these questions:

- What label have I been given—what role have I played in being the family fixer, the empath, the people-pleaser, and scapegoat? How do I stop?

- What can I learn from role models, mentors, and others who are positive in my life on how to let go of negative or harmful relational ties?

- How do I act around my family or what is my identity around my family versus being my true self around them?

If you answered yes to more than two of these questions in the first section, you need to start taking better care of yourself and what you need outside of your family. In the section below, I want to encourage you to take the following steps outlined and challenge yourself to break free and create the life and the family dynamics that you want.

## Actions You Can Take to Heal from Your Family's Crazy

Here are several specific tasks you should consider if you want to move forward as a happier and emotionally healthier human being.

Challenge yourself to start setting the boundaries you know in your heart are necessary to protect you from your family dysfunction.

- Get counseling. It is a game-changer.

- Join support groups where you can find a safe space to share your story with others who have experienced what you have. There is healing power in opening up and finding common ground, from adult children of alcoholics or substance abusers, sexual abuse survivors, or veterans with PTSD, there are many organizations that offer help for free.

- Know that people can change. You can change. Have faith in that truth.

- Lastly, you are not your family. Challenge yourself to get out of that box.

In sum, your beginnings have everything to do with the *deep unhappiness that comes from living your life to please other people versus being what and who you want to be.* And no place is more likely to cause us to feel like we simply aren't measuring up than within our own families. I like to say that adulthood is how we spend our lives trying to overcome or make up for our childhoods. Every story has a beginning. And more often than we know, our beginnings shape everything about who we become, what we do, where we live, how we worship, how we love, what we value, and how we live.

This first life lesson is a hard one. But if you want to live a fulfilled life, it will not come from things, achievements, or even other people. A truly fulfilled life is one based on truth—truth with yourself—and one where you give yourself permission to grow up and out of the boxes that others prepare for you long before you even know what a box is. A box confines you. It is a prison not of your own making, but one that you continue to live in long after you were free to leave it. Adulthood is our release from all the things we could not control, did not like, or caused us great harm as children. So why is it that so many of us, generation after generation, continue to live in these boxes that suffocate us, make us sad, make us feel less than, and break us repeatedly? My job here is to help you to break the cycle—early—but to do so in a way that causes healing not further estrangements, restoration where possible, and ultimately release where restoration is not possible, no matter how much we might wish it so.

*"Anybody who has survived his childhood has enough information about life to last him the rest of his days."*

—**Flannery O'Connor**

All of us, in some small or big way, are dealing with a form of trauma because of the pandemic. For me, it's when I finally had to admit I couldn't take it anymore. That there had to be changes with me, first, and then with my family or I was going to have to literally pack my bags and move away—leave my home, friends, work, and just get out. It became that acute. Because, as I said at the outset, you can never, *ever*, outrun you. And when you get quiet, you will come to understand that you can stop running.

If you do not have a healthy family, this first lesson is for you. My goal is to help you to learn how to work through what happened to you (not dwell on *what's wrong with you*) and learn to set critical boundaries with your family, to better learn how to talk to and with them, and most importantly how to call one another out in love when necessary. Every one of us needs a family. It is the very heartbeat of our soul landscape, and it is the place where, if we are willing to do the constant work of love, forgiveness, encouragement, grace, and hope, we can find our greatest joy.

I intentionally chose the topic of family to begin this book. Because it is the other thing, along with self, that we can never outrun. Family is always with us, even if we are estranged from them. Families are complicated. The truth is that all families have good memories and bad memories, strong members and weak members. All families have secrets. All families have "codes of conduct." And all families are at first created by chance (your dad met your mom), and then ultimately by choice (we stay in, and we do the work of family). If we can make peace with the fact that families are both chance and choice, then we can head in a positive direction when it comes to deciding how we love, engage, and even separate from our families if necessary. If we do not have a family, we will find ways to create one, and in doing so we belong. All of us need to belong. And all of us wrestle with our beginnings. Adulthood is when we spend a lifetime trying to correct or deal with from our childhood.

*"Fear of breaking family loyalty is one of the greatest stumbling blockages to recovery. Yet, until we admit certain things we would rather excuse or deny, we cannot truly begin to put the past in the past, and leave it there once and for all. Unless we do that, we cannot even begin to think of having a future that is fully ours, untethered to the past, and we will be destined to repeat it."*

—Ronald Allen Schulz

# LESSON 2

## Take Care of Your Mental and Emotional Health First

*"It's up to you today to start making healthy choices. Not choices that are just healthy for your body, but healthy for your mind and for your soul."*

—Steve Maraboli

## *Yourself*

I am going to say and share a lot of things in this book. Some will be raw and maybe a bit shocking. Others are soothing and revealing. But nothing I say to you will be more important than what I am going to tell you right now: *Guard your mind, guard your spirit, and guard your energy.* In other words, guard your mental and emotional health. Of all the life lessons I have learned, this one is the greatest.

As you know from reading Lesson 1, I did not learn how to truly embrace and value my own well-being until I was well into my late forties and early fifties. Do not wait that long to get this one right. Life's too short. Time lost can never be reclaimed. Young people, hear me on this one—start out as you mean to continue in your life. Set healthy boundaries around your mental and emotional wellness and be firm with them. No means no. You time is your time. And guarding your peace is essential in our modern, busy, fast-paced world.

After we deal with our family of origin issues, the second greatest obstacle in life is the person looking back at us in the mirror—you. This might sound counterintuitive, but part of getting out of your own way is setting up a system of valuing yourself before you value anyone or anything else. I imagine that this sentence made most of you bristle, or feel uncomfortable, which tells you how deeply conditioned we are as human beings to not put self-first—women even more so. But I am going to keep repeating this until you believe me. As I mentioned in the last lesson, we are conditioned by our families, and by our society, to take care of others first—again, women more so than men. And this is where it all begins and ends for most of us.

Part of learning is being willing not just to hear, or to see, but to put into practice what you now know. What I know for sure is that when you do not put your mental and emotional health first, everything else goes off track. Your life becomes a blur, badly out of focus, and only you can fix it. My nana used to say,

> **What I know for sure is that when you do not put your mental and emotional health first, everything else goes off track.**

"There's a running day and a catching day." She was spot on. You can only run from yourself for so long before you will have to pay a very expensive emotional bill for all the years of self-neglect, self-abuse, and lack of self-care. But here is the good news: it does not have to be this way. You can start out by practicing good emotional health and wellness habits, or you can correct course at midlife like I did. It is not too late to have a peaceful, fulfilling, and happy life. Your life is what you decide it's going to be. Remember: As I said at the outset of this book, you are responsible for you. Not your family. Not your friends. Not your spouse. Not your pastor. Not your church. Not your work colleagues. **Bottom line:** if you don't love you, you cannot expect to be loved back. You have got to decide what's next in your life, at every season of your life. And once you decide, you must have a strategy in place to get there.

We live in a culture where "being productive" is prized. Translated, that means we are always on, always exhausted, always overwhelmed, and stressed the hell out. This is no way to live, no matter your age. A better, healthier way to live is to focus on balance. Meaning, yes, you can work hard. You can also be productive. But you balance these things by setting limits. The workday has changed dramatically since I started my professional career in the mid- to late 1990s. While cell phone ownership was starting to become more widespread, this was before the advent of smart phones that compelled people to be connected 24/7. We were not expected to be available anywhere at any time. I was a young attorney working in government and then in private practice. Our workday usually ended at 6:00 PM and then we all went out for a drink or to dinner, or we would play softball on Capitol Hill. On the weekend, we would go to a club and have fun. Even though we didn't know it at the time, we were taking care of our mental and emotional health. We played as hard as we worked, and we loved both. Not so much now.

With our gadgets and devices always at hand, the workday is now literally never ending. Let me be clear: your workday needs to end. Just as it has a beginning, it must have an end. You must begin work at a certain time each day, and likewise you need to have a time when you put down your phone, close your laptop, and walk away from work. You need to be able to shift between the professional you and the personal you. When you work, work. When you are at home, be present. Be with your kids. Be with your spouse. Be accessible. Be there. If you don't get this life lesson quickly, what inevitably happens is that you become less and less emotionally available, first to yourself and then to your family. You become grouchy, short-tempered, maybe even mean and judgmental, snapping at everyone and everything. The reason is because you are not happy with you, and intellectually you know it—hell, you even whisper it to yourself under your breath every day: "I need some rest." "I need a vacation." "I need to get away or I am going to lose it." Ever say any of those things? I know I have. And it wasn't until I started doing something about it that my life started to change, and I started to change right along with it.

Know this: the best day of your life is the day you decide that your life is yours. Although you can and should love and respect and want to look out for other people, you need to treat your time as a valuable gift. Life is 100 percent about the choices you make. Once you accept this age-old truth, and accept true responsibility for your life, you can literally do, be, or have anything you desire. Just remember that no one is entitled to your life. Or your time. Or your wellness. The key is to operate from a state of emotional wholeness, a healthy place from which you can offer others love, friendship, and care. You are entitled to peace of mind. You deserve and need time to catch your breath . . . time to hear yourself think . . . and time to take care of you. And that is the only way you can love and care for others.

This is not hard stuff, folks. It's easy. The Millennials, Gen Yers and Gen Zers have truly mastered this in that they are very protective of their time and space. They like to explore and travel—especially in packs. And they understand the importance of rest. Once again, as I mentioned in Lesson 1 about family, some of this stuff is generational. So don't be too hard on yourself if you find yourself at forty, fifty, sixty, or older and you feel like you simply cannot get out of your own way. You can. You just must be willing to pivot and change. It always comes back to you and to me.

> **The best day of your life is the day you decide that your life is yours.**

## There Is a Big Difference Between Mental and Emotional Health

We often confuse mental and emotional health when in reality they are very different. So, let's clear this up at the outset: Mental health is the umbrella that covers our emotional, psychological, and social well-being. Emotional health is how we manage our feelings, our relationships, and our challenges in life. It's a combination of our fears, worries, regrets, sorrows, joys, grief, anger, hopes, aspirations, insecurities, and so forth. I've learned in my fifty-some years of living that, although it is wise to plan ahead and to have goals and dreams, even expectations for yourself and others, it is wiser still to go with the flow of life and adjust as you need to in order to get to where you want to be, to be the human being you want to be. In my humble opinion, if you want to have a happy life, you must accept three things as true (by the way, acceptance is the key to a truly peaceful and happy life, but we'll get to that later in the book):

1. **Life is like a roller-coaster.** It has amazing highs and lows, twists and turns, ups and downs, hills and valleys. Sometimes, life moves very fast, and, if you are lucky enough to live a long life, it slows down at the end. So, you must be flexible. You must be resilient. You will have to be kind to and forgiving of yourself. And you must be able to pivot and shift as needed based on life's ever-changing circumstances.

2. **If there is love, just feel it.** Embrace it. Don't question it or analyze it. Don't reject it or abandon it. Most important of all, return it. Part of what breaks so many of us is simple: Lack of love. Lack of protection. Lack of connection.

3. **Communication is key.** Say how you feel and let others do the same. No judgment. Just listen as you, yourself, would like to be heard. Speak your truth. Good, honest, respectful communication is a powerful tool for living well. Resist the temptation to push your true feelings down, or stuff your emotions in a box. That is not a healthy way to live, and I promise it will catch up with you at the most inconvenient of times—I know this from

experience. Have courageous conversations because people are not mind readers. Are you? Of course not. So, a simple rule to follow for smart living and drama-free relationships is to communicate often, communicate well, and communicate clearly what you want and what you need. And allow others to do the same with you.

**Here's the bottom line:** if you can stay 100 percent honest first with yourself, and then with others, and let others do the same with you, you will be investing in your mental health in ways untold. If you can be a space for those you love, and a true friend before you are anything else, you will alleviate a lot of stress from your life and from the lives of those around you. If you can accept these three things mentioned above and make them your constant companions in your day-to-day life, you can get through anything life throws at you. Your mental health is made up of parts; your emotional health is how you manage those parts. See the difference?

The way you keep mentally healthy is the same way you keep physically healthy. You exercise and tone your parts. You eat healthy foods. You drink water. You get adequate sleep. You take vitamins. You get regular medical checkups. You stay in tune with your body, and if you notice something is wrong you do something about it. In the past several years, as God is my witness, I have had friends and extended family members literally just drop dead. And there is nothing worse

> The way you keep mentally healthy is the same way you keep physically healthy. You exercise and tone your parts. You eat healthy foods. You drink water. You get adequate sleep. You take vitamins. You get regular medical checkups. You stay in tune with your body, and if you notice something is wrong you do something about it.

because those who are left behind are in shock. There is no goodbye. There is no "I love you." There is just an empty space for that person you loved. Each one of these individuals I lost were not healthy, and they suffered sudden heart attacks or strokes. These were men and women who were carrying too much stress and distress. They had symptoms and ignored them. And they are no longer with us.

I think of my Uncle Johnny, who died when he was in his sixties. He was a healthy eater, drank water, and kept his body in great shape. His grandson told us after he passed that he had been having chest pains. My grandmother and cousins wanted to call 911, but Uncle Johnny said, "It's just gas." He died the next day at work after having a massive heart attack. This is a mistake many make. Afterward, my aunt found some heart medication, and then we found out about the emotional stressors he was dealing with financially and with his only daughter. He was trying to take care of everyone, including raising his grandkids and looking after his aging mother (my grandmother). Despite having people around he was isolated. He had divorced decades earlier and never remarried. He did not date much. He stayed to himself and didn't have a lot of friends. A good man, he attended church, read his Bible, and prayed a lot. But, as I look back on his life, I can see so clearly now that he was likely very depressed, lonely, and didn't want to be a burden to anyone, so he didn't share his feelings, tell anyone about his health issues, or reach out for help. That bothers me because it is such a common response, for men and for women as well. For communities of color, there is a great deal of pressure to stay strong, always push yourself harder, and never ask for help. That needs to change, folks—and change now.

You might ask, "Well, how do I know the difference between when I am not taking good care of my mental health and when I am?" That's a great question. The answer is to practice good mental health care daily. We wake up every day. We shower. We groom ourselves. We work out. We walk the dog. We grab coffee, tea, or juice and we have tasks that we consider a priority. The way you know if you are practicing good mental and emotional health care is by making both a priority in your life every day, just as you do those other things I listed. There is no magic formula to mental and emotional wellness, but there is a process, a routine, an intention that we can all practice that is

**A simple rule to follow for smart living and drama-free relationships is to communicate often, communicate well, and communicate clearly what you want and what you need. And allow others to do the same with you.**

guaranteed to yield positive results. Here are a few things you should consider incorporating into your day-to-day living:

1. **When you get up in the morning, set aside time to command your day before it takes hold of you.** This is a must-do. You need time to just sit with your thoughts. Meditate. Read. Drink your coffee quietly. Light a candle (I do that every day, and I spray this wonderful lemon spray mist that makes the house smell amazing). It's the little things that calm you and center you for the new day ahead.

2. **Know what makes you happy and *who* makes you happy.** You also need to know what does not. Consider limiting the access of those in or around your life who make you feel less than or bad about yourself. People's energy and how it impacts us is a huge factor in managing our mental wellness. This one can be tough if you have a toxic boss, a toxic marriage, or other

unhealthy attachments. However, the key is to manage them so that your energy stays positive and you stay mentally well. Don't let others' drama become a drain on your life.

3. **Move your body.** This is an absolute must. Your body and your emotions are 100 percent directly tied to one another. Moving, walking, running, stretching, swimming, whatever it is that you like to do—do it! Get moving. Don't work inside at a desk all day then come home and sit on the couch all night. It's physically unhealthy for you. It's a known fact that sitting raises your risk of heart disease, diabetes, stroke, high-blood pressure, and high cholesterol. You might have heard the phrase that "sitting is the new smoking" and this is true. You have to move every day. It is super good for your emotional well-being because it causes your body to release happy and healing hormones.

## Setting Boundaries Will Change Your Life

My most profound wish for you is that you desire only *what* and *who* are good for you, and that you will no longer desire, connect yourself to, or be around anyone and anything that is no longer beneficial. Easier said than done? Not really. You just must decide. All of life is a choice. You decide—or you let others decide for you. Choose one. But, believe me, if you do not choose yourself first, you will not have a happy life. You will not be the great spouse you can be. You will not be a nurturing, present parent to your children, and you will not be able to be there for your parents as they age. Turning down the noise of life and being intentional about self-care is essential. Ironically, the COVID-19 pandemic helped us in one way because it literally made us stop and re-evaluate our lives. People were forced to *re-engage, restructure,* and *re-learn* how to be in close quarters with their families, how to talk to their kids, how to be around their spouses all day in the house 24/7, and how to be considerate of other people's needs, feelings, and health.

I had a lot to deal with during the first wave of the pandemic, because I got COVID in 2020 (pre-vaccine). I run a boutique consulting firm, I teach at the college level, I write books, and speak all over the world, not to mention my duties as a columnist and my TV appearances as a regular on-air political pundit. Couple that with the fact that I had a sick parent out on long-term disability who was unable to drive, work, and sometimes barely walk. My only sibling lives in the Northeast and was not engaged. Mom lives with me, so I had to figure out how we were going to get through this—together—and both keep our sanity. It was not easy.

But I quickly realized we were going to have to have the help of a mental-health professional. Luckily, in my circle of amazing women, we have a few qualified therapists and medical professionals to choose from. Despite many in her generation embracing therapy, my mom resisted this kind of assistance. I pushed and demanded (as respectfully and firmly as I could) that we had to do things differently or we would not make it. I told Mom that we had to occupy the same space differently. We each had to protect our physical health and our mental health. Neighbors whom I trusted, and whom I consider good friends, and I organized Friday nights in the backyard. There were usually about six of us, and we social-distanced, played music, had themed events (luaus, Mexican-food night, Italian feasts, Chinese cuisine, etc.), and we always had some wine and spirits handy. Looking back on that period of fellowship, I see that it kept us all sane. It kept us all connected. It kept us laughing.

And Mom, who is now seventy-five, really started to do better. I got her off her twelve-hours-a-day TV regimen and got her moving, connecting, and laughing. We started family therapy, which we had badly needed for decades, and we started working through long-silenced family issues. It was not easy, but I applaud Mom for being willing to stick with it once we got started. We are still working through things, but we have both learned more about each other, our communication styles, our quirks, and now we have more empathy and healthier emotional boundaries. I am free to speak truth versus being muted, or told not to speak, or told, "Can't we just have a nice day?"—which is Mom-speak for "I do not want to deal with that." And if things go off track, the therapist and our support network are there to step in and make sure the courageous and necessary conversations happen. This was critical to surviving 2020 in my home and family. And it is critical to surviving and thriving throughout the rest of my lifetime.

The reason I decided to engage in therapy is because I have a dear girlfriend whose mother died suddenly a few years back and it almost sent her to an emotional and physical death of her own. She and her mother had serious longstanding issues that had never been addressed. She had lost her father many years earlier and is an only child. She is also one of the kindest people I know—thoughtful and caring—but she takes care of everyone but herself. Sadly, she never got to say the things a daughter should be able to say to her mother, or to ask the questions we all need to ask if our childhood experiences were not healthy. And once her mother passed, it was truly finished. There would be no conversations. There would be no explanations or apologies, or maybe even much-needed forgiveness. There was just a parent who no longer walked this earth, a parent she never really got to know, and, more importantly, never got to be known by. It devastated her, and I have heard of so many other stories just like this from other friends, colleagues, and family.

When I saw the way this experience impacted my friend and her mental health (it also badly impacted her physical health), I decided I did not want to be that way at my own mother's gravesite one day. I have accepted that this is my fate with my father, but at least with him I know I tried. And everyone around me knows I tried for years to please him, make him love me, value me, be proud of me, treat me as a father should his only daughter. I am not his favorite child. I accepted that long ago, too. Sometimes when I see my girlfriends— grown women like me—with their fathers, I envy them in a good way. I never had that. And I never will. But I was willing to fight for the relationship with my mom because we are closer and always have been. With my father, I had to do as one therapist friend, who knows our family history and my father, told me: "This is not emotionally healthy for you. I've watched you try for years to be Daddy's girl, and do the right things, and include him in your life, and it's just not good for you. You've done all you can. He's done nothing to truly even meet you halfway. You need to move on."

**What I am saying is this:** The secret to good mental health is YOU. This life lesson is one that you must get down early in your life because all of us operate either with good habits or bad ones. And bad habits are hard to break as you age. The earlier you can know yourself, establish healthy patterns of relational conduct and self-love, and, most important of all, know when it's time to walk away from someone or something, the better your life will be.

**The secret to good mental health is YOU.**

## How Gender and Culture Can Affect Our Mental Health

As I mentioned in Lesson 1, I did not really start taking care of myself and my emotional health until my late forties and later. I was so conditioned, as the older child, as a woman, and more so as a woman of color (see my first book, *Black Woman Redefined*, where I write about how our race and culture defines much of our lives) to always be strong. Always be tough. Always be taking care of others and, worst of all, to be made to feel guilty when I stood up for myself. I had to unlearn all of that and start tending to my emotional needs. I had to be strong my entire life as a child growing up in a challenging, emotionally disconnected home filled with anger and strife. I learned some very unhealthy ways of coping with—or rather not coping with—my emotions, and I often just walled myself off.

By the time I had hit my thirties, I was suffering with some health challenges and then serious depression once I learned I could not have children. My doctors discovered that the culprit was Addison's disease (President John F. Kennedy also had Addison's). I was constantly in fight-or-flight syndrome as a child, living with nearly unending stress and fear. This emotional response took a serious toll on my body's ability to produce cortisol and aldosterone. I was very tiny most of my life (size zero until I was forty). I was sick a lot with stomach problems, infections, colds, you name it. Yet, to look at me, you would never know it. In high school, I was a varsity track athlete, played in the marching band, was elected class president, and dated the star quarterback of the rival high school football team.

For years, I just kept pushing through all my mess—until it caught up with me. I was at a place in my early forties where I didn't want to go on. I felt empty, unloved, unhappy, and, frankly, a bit suicidal. This is when I finally hit rock bottom and had to ask for help. I was lucky enough to have a few close friends who came to my rescue, because, as you guessed it, the family I had saved, given counsel to, financial support to, been there for, and helped time and time again was not there for me in my darkest hour.

The point I want you to get from all of this is that your birth order, your gender, your race, your religion, where you grew up, what you were exposed to—all of it plays a part in how you view and take care of your mental health. For example, we know that many people of faith will often substitute prayer for mental-health counseling. I know I did for years. That was wrong. I was told to "pray it away," or just "pray harder." No. Prayer is a great and necessary component of how we address our shortcomings, needs, and wounds. But it is not the only way.

We also know that we raise our sons to be tough. To "act like a man." To not show emotion or to cry. To not verbally express or communicate their feelings, and, if they do, we label them as "soft" or as a "sissy." And then when these little boys become hardened, emotionless men, we are confused. Men are not given the same grace socially as women—to cry when hurt, or to seek therapy, or to share their feelings. Men are told to just go shoot some hoops, run, or hit harder on the football field. They are told to stuff their emotions down or they are not acting manly. Although we have made some strides in addressing this toxic masculinity, every day we still see the horrible acts of domestic violence, murder-suicides of wives and children, sexual assault against girls and young women, gun violence, and anger incidents that boys, young men, and grown men take part in daily.

We cannot continue to function as a healthy democracy in America, or anywhere around the globe, if our leaders are not emotionally healthy. The January 6, 2021, insurrection at the US Capitol showed us what happens when people are repeatedly fed disinformation by those with ill intentions who are only interested in their own narcissistic need for total control; when those telling the truth are gaslighted; and when displaced, pent-up anger is fanned and explodes into unfettered rage.

Beyond politics, we are living in a very dangerous time for our collective mental well-being. We have seen some of the world's greatest athletes express the need for more focus on mental health, from superstar gymnast Simone Biles at the Tokyo Olympics, to tennis superstar Naomi Osaka, to iconic swimmer Michael Phelps. I could go on and on, but you get the point.

To whoever out there is reading this lesson with tears in your eyes right now, I want you to know I am bowling down your alley, and I want you to go back and reread Lesson 1. This time, with a highlighter and sticky notes. You have to dare to be the one who puts your mental health and wellness first, starting right now. You do not have to live depressed, afraid, stuck, isolated, alone, lonely, unheard, unloved, and uncared for. You can change your life by creating a mental-health and emotional-wellness plan. You and I are like human automobiles. We must be serviced regularly and replenished with all the things that make us run well. We must be charged. We must be refueled. Or we simply won't run at all.

## How to Make This Life Lesson Work in Your Life

Here is the good news. Whether you are eighteen, twenty-seven, thirty-nine, forty-five, fifty-six, sixty-five, or older, it is never too early or too late to start taking care of yourself. *Right now* is a good time. Good self-care is more than just routines and rituals, though. It's a lifestyle change. It's a pivot. Life happens right now. Not later. It doesn't wait. It doesn't give us many do-overs, either. So, you have got to do two things right now: 1.) Decide. 2.) Be intentional. Realize that the journey of life is not about wearing a mask or pretending to be okay when you are not. It really is about learning and growing every step of the way.

**You have to dare to be the one who puts your mental health and wellness first, starting right now. You do not have to live depressed, afraid, stuck, isolated, alone, lonely, unheard, unloved, and uncared for.**

Challenge yourself to stop being stuck in unhealthy emotional health patterns: dating the wrong people; staying friends with toxic people; letting your family's generational dysfunctions become your own; ignoring wise counsel from trusted family or friends; sitting on the couch instead of exercising; putting your vacation off until next year; staying in alone instead of being out with friends; running from love because you are scared of being hurt; keeping to yourself instead of being connected. Instead of continuing to feel stuck, drained, exhausted, angry, lost, or unloved, you are going to have to embark on a new adventure: your life. And you are going to have to dare to choose yourself first. I promise you with all my heart that it will be the best decision you ever make.

## Actions You Can Take to Protect and Heal Your Mental Health

Now that you know you must make your mental and emotional health a daily priority, just as you do your work, your family, eating, grooming, etc., let's talk about how we do so. Here are several specific tasks that you can take, no matter your age or stage in life, to make your mental health the top priority.

1. Create a "you space" in your home, car, basement, prayer closet, or park; somewhere you can be undisturbed. It's a you-only zone.

2. Have morning rituals where you take command of your day and your thoughts. The power of life and death is not just in our words, as Scripture tells us, but also in our thoughts. Choose your thoughts each day. Don't let them choose you.

3. Seek out free therapy or invest in yourself with some paid therapy. Choose a good and reputable therapist who practices what they preach in their day-to-day life.

4. Use your voice. Speak your truth. Get it up and out. Do not push your feelings down. You need a trusted circle—I call mine the "love counsel" because they give me loving advice, prayer, admonitions, and support—that will have your back.

5. Don't carry the emotional bricks of your past any longer. Do the work to change yourself or you will never be free. Don't expect to change or fix others. You are the one you need. It's time to start being that person.

*Your mental health is a priority.*
*Your happiness is essential.*
*Your self-care is a necessity.*

# LESSON 3

## Take Risks: Learn How to Succeed Even When You Fail

*"Life is either a daring adventure or nothing at all."*

—Helen Keller

## *Your Choices*

Life is so much clearer once we have lived a little bit and made mistakes that help us to grow wiser. There is no better teacher in life than experience. And there is no quicker way to learn about life than to dare greatly, as Dr. Brené Brown says, and also to be willing to fail greatly. Taking personal, professional, and relational risks is a necessary evil in life. Nothing can be accomplished, gained, or even dreamed unless you are willing to take a leap, go it alone, or risk it all. That's the deal you must be willing to make with yourself if you want to make something of yourself. Anyone who tells you anything different isn't telling you the truth.

People ask me all the time how I got to where I am, and I respond by saying two things: First, this is not at all the life I imagined for myself when I was seventeen, or twenty-five, or even thirty-five. Second, the road to success of any kind is fraught with choices, sacrifice, disappointment, failure, betrayals, and oftentimes lots of thankless, hard work. If you want to succeed in this life, it's best to start when you are a young woman or young man and believe me when I say it will absolutely take a village of supporters, encouragers, mentors, sponsors, and loyal friends who stand by you for the rest of your days. None of us, and I do mean none of us, gets anywhere in life alone. If you can learn this life lesson while you are in your twenties, you are going to soar!

**Life is all about having something to look forward to.**

But let me say this: there is no shame in not reaching all your goals in life. People change. Desires change. Life throws us curveballs. We often must reset or shift in another direction that we never envisioned. The only shame in life is in not trying. And worse than not trying is not even having goals to reach, not having a dream to chase, not daring to reach beyond your own imagination and limitations to something bigger. Life is all about having something to look forward to. Never forget that. You must constantly and continuously reinvent yourself, re-evaluate your plans, and press on using the gifts that God has given you, including the great privilege of aging. Like all of you, I have lived. I have loved. I have lost people who were dear to me. I have been knocked down by life's curveballs. But the reason I am successful is not because I am smarter, more able, more educated, or more confident than the next person. It is because I have mastered the art of resilience: the art of getting back up again and again. And the reason I can keep getting back up is that I live by a code of conduct that is rooted in my faith, and in my belief that the only way you truly succeed in life is to first experience setbacks and failure. In failing, we learn, we gain perspective, and we become stronger. In surviving the worst that life can throw at us, we can also learn to thrive.

**If you hear nothing else that I say in this book—hear me on this—successful people trust their own voice.**

My code of conduct is a universal one. It's common sense. It's practical, yet purposeful. It is a code people have practiced for thousands of years. It is timeless, yet time relevant! It is a code of making calculated risks, of knowing my value, and of trusting my own voice most of all. *If you hear nothing else that I say in this book—hear me on this—successful people trust their own voice.* Yes, of course, they take wise counsel. Yes, of course they build consensus. But the truly successful, the truly exceptional leaders, are risk-takers. And they march to the beat of their own drum. If I had listened to every naysayer, every detractor, or every person who told me what a young woman, or a young woman of color, coming of age in the 1980s and 1990s *could not yet do*, I would still be in my small blue-collar hometown, likely married to a local guy from high school, and likely stuck in a generational cycle of abuse, of limited opportunity, limited exposure, and limited access. Instead, I marched to the beat of my own drum. I took the road less traveled by. And as my favorite poet Robert Frost once said: *that has made all the difference.*

First off, let's define the word *risk*. What does it mean anyway, to take a risk? *Merriam-Webster* defines taking a risk as: to do something that may result in failure or loss. I define it differently, as taking a running leap into your soul's landscape and continuing headlong into your destiny. Whether it be professionally, personally, or relationally. We all take risks. Every day we wake up, we risk something once we step outside our door. Here's the thing about being a risk-taker, about being a dreamer. You must know the way when no one else believes it's possible. You must see what others do not see. You must hear what others do not hear. You must think big when others can only see the big obstacles standing in your way. You will have to give yourself permission to aim high in all you do—both professionally and personally. And you will need to make the time to plan your dreams and be willing to keep changing and adapting your plan to make those dreams come true.

You must be committed. You must be willing to do what others will not do and to go where others have not yet gone. You must believe in your story, in your destiny, in your dreams, in your passion for something or someone. You must be willing to falter or even to fail despite what you desire. That's what it truly means to take a risk. People will always look at your outward glory, but they rarely know your backstory. Yes, I am an award-winning, bestselling author, journalist, national television commentator, an attorney, and so. But that does not define my life. The moments that have and continue to define my life—don't miss this—were the hard ones. The lonely ones. The broken ones. Those moments forced me to find my voice; to step up when I wanted to sit down; to honor my dreams, and to keep moving forward no matter what. I want you to know that wherever you are and whatever you have been through, I promise you that you CAN and WILL get back up again but you must SHIFT. YOU are the one that you have been waiting for. You are the hero on the white horse that will come to rescue you. You are the author of your story.

For those of you who now find yourself at midlife or older, and who feel stuck, that will be your truth only if you want it to be true. I am speaking from firsthand experience. At age forty, I made a huge career change from big-firm lawyer to aspiring author and journalist. I wrote my first bestselling book at forty-three. I first

**Here's the thing about being a risk-taker, about being a dreamer. You must know the way when no one else believes it's possible. You must see what others do not see. You must hear what others do not hear. You must think big when others can only see the big obstacles standing in your way.**

tried to sell a book to big New York agents and publishers at age thirty. They all told me that I had great potential, and that someday I might be a published author, but they turned me down, gently. I never gave up on my dreams of being an author. I would sit in the Barnes and Noble, B. Dalton, and Borders bookstores and imagine myself being an author and signing my books. It took me thirteen years to get there—but I got there. My first book signing was in May 2011, in the beautiful flagship Barnes and Noble store at 555 12th Street, NW, in Washington, DC, before a packed crowd of over three hundred people who turned out to hear me speak, read from the book, and get my autograph. It was surreal.

**Here's my point:** If you think you are too old now to take a risk, you are wrong. If you think it's too late for you, that your moment has passed, you are wrong. Throughout history, some of the greatest men and women who have accomplished amazing things were well past their youth and their prime. For instance:

- Rosa Parks was a forty-two-year-old seamstress in Montgomery, Alabama, in 1955 when refused to give up her seat in the White section at the front of the bus and move to the Colored section in the back. Her defiant stance prompted a year-long boycott of the Montgomery bus system and lit a spark for the civil rights movement.

- Sir Winston Churchill became Prime Minister of Great Britain at sixty-six, overseeing Britain's involvement in World War II, and then, after a short time out of office when his party was defeated after the war, winning another term in office at the age of seventy-seven.

- Julia Child began her career as a researcher with the government, but then pivoted to cooking, graduating from the famous Cordon Bleu school in Paris when she was nearly forty, and then publishing her classic *Mastering the Art of French Cooking* when she was forty-nine and starting her groundbreaking television show a few years later.

- Colonel Harland Sanders had a number of jobs early in life, from insurance salesman to gas station operator, and developed his "secret recipe" for cooking chicken when he ran a roadside restaurant in a filling station he owned in Kentucky. He was sixty-two when he franchised his first Kentucky Fried Chicken.

**If you think you are too old now to take a risk, you are wrong. If you think it's too late for you, that your moment has passed, you are wrong.**

- Vera Wang resigned from her job and started her bridal wear design line when she was forty. Interestingly, she was a highly ranked competitive figure skater when she was younger and turned to fashion design when she failed to make the US Olympic Team.

- Tom Brady won two Super Bowls after the age of forty after most players are long retired. After a storied career with the New England Patriots, at forty-three, he was the oldest player to be named Super Bowl Most Valuable Player (MVP) and win a Super Bowl as the starting quarterback for his new team, the Tampa Bay Buccaneers. He was also voted as the oldest NFL MVP at age forty in 2017.

- Sam Walton, the founder of Walmart and Sam's Club, regarded as one of the greatest project entrepreneurs in the retail chain industry and who was included in *Time* magazine's list of 100 most influential people of the twentieth century, was forty-four when he launched his first Walmart store.

- Ray Kroc was a milkshake-mixer salesman in the mid-1950s when he sold some of the equipment to the McDonald brothers, who owned a small restaurant in Southern California. Kroc saw the potential in the company and became their franchise agent. He bought the company in 1961 at age fifty-nine and the rest is history. He is credited with the global expansion of McDonald's, turning it into the most successful fast-food corporation in the world.

- Dyana Nyad is regarded as the world's greatest long-distance swimmer because of her open-water achievements, including a record-breaking swim around Manhattan. After this achievement in the 1970s, she spent the next thirty years as a sports broadcaster and journalist. In 2013, after several other failed attempts, she became the first person to swim from Cuba to Florida without the aid of a shark cage, swimming 111 miles in fifty-three hours from Havana to Key West. She accomplished this remarkable feat, a longstanding dream, at sixty-four years old.

- John Glenn—in my favorite story—was the first American to orbit the earth. After he retired from NASA, he began a second career at age fifty-three when he was elected as a US Senator, serving the people of Ohio for over two decades. Remarkably, he went back to space at age seventy-seven in the space shuttle Discovery, making him the oldest person ever to do so.

These are just a few examples of people who made a shift, accomplishing something remarkable later in their lives. They made a pivot. And they took a leap of faith. They took a risk. They dug deep to find that wellspring of youth and they dared to follow their dreams. In doing so, in the middle or at the end of their lives, they found great success and new beginnings where most people at the same stage of life would have simply settled in and accepted their fate for whatever it was at the time.

My goal in this lesson is to encourage young people to run hard after your dreams. Your twenties and thirties, the productive decades of your youth, is a time of great growth and change. Use this magical time wisely. It's the perfect time to blaze new trails, create new technologies, explore new places, to travel, to build, to run, to wonder as well as to wander. Most people in this life don't aim high. They are afraid. They stay in those boxes that I talked about in Lesson 1. They stay stuck in generational expectations, and they never venture out. They aim lower, safer, and they take the road most traveled by, the path of least resistance. For the record, there is nothing wrong with that. But you wouldn't be reading this book if that was enough for you. Right?

For those like me who are older, midlife is the busiest time of your life. It is also the most productive, according to studies on brain activity, which peaks in our fifties but continues pretty high even throughout our early eighties. So, stop pining away for your lost or misspent youth. It's in the rearview mirror. Accept it and move on to this present moment where you can finally slow down and enjoy life. This is the stage where you have the acquired wisdom to separate what is truly important to you and what is just window dressing. Nothing is stopping you from finally getting to know yourself, what you value, and for what you want from the precious remaining years of your life. This is not a time for regret or melancholy. Aging is a gift that frees you to make better, more fulfilling choices.

My advice to those over forty is to get up and shout out loud: "*This situation, this pain, this loss, this setback, this regret, this guilt that I have right here and right now is NOT how my story will end.*" And then start making sure, from that point forward, that whatever is left of your life is the best of your life.

Not all risks are alike. There are three types of risks that I think are important to understand. We must navigate each one of these daily if we want to be truly successful in life. Here are the risks and how each of them shapes and impacts our lives.

- **Professional Risks.** Professional risks are those that we take with our careers and our ambitions. One of the best pieces of advice I can give to any young person is to have mentors and sponsors. Sponsors are people who use their clout to open doors for you or promote you, while mentors are people we build relationships with and take advice from. When we take risks early in our professional development it can be a very rewarding down the line. But before you take those leaps of faith, you need to make sure you have a supportive group of people in your life who are smart, experienced, and 100 percent team YOU!

- **Personal Risks.** Personal risks are those we take that deal with our emotions or feelings. You might not realize it, but these risks tie directly into how we deal with our professional risks. When you think of personal risk-takers, you might envision people who do things that most of us would consider reckless and possibly dangerous. Maybe so, but these kinds of risks are also a key ingredient to professional success. You really cannot have one without the other.

- **Relational Risks.** Relational risks are the scariest of all because they involve risking our heart. They involve baring ourselves to another: opening ourselves up to love, to rejection, to happiness, and to sadness. It used to be that people would take their chances by meeting people in person, one way or another, and then getting to know them. In our hyper-connected world, we no longer take those kinds of risks. Many people now choose their mates online by looking at a profile and swiping right or left. People do Google searches and background checks. We like certainty and think these things will protect us. While this can be a wise precaution, doing these things won't necessarily keep us safe. Worse yet, it also kills something of the mystique and awe of dating, courtship, and falling in love.

My point is that risks do not have to be a bad thing. Regrettably, I think many people have come to associate the word *risk* with failure. And that's too bad, because some of my greatest loves, joys, passions, and accomplishments have come from standing at the edge of the cliff and jumping, not always knowing what would happen when I did.

The most important takeaway is this: we encounter risks in every aspect of our lives. You may as well embrace them and realize that they are tied to your goals and aspirations. You get to your goals by asking questions, by making choices, by starting out with baby steps, then more calculated steps, which eventually become calculated risks. It all fits together. Too many of us get stuck doing what we think we must do instead of what we want to do. We miss so much of life and the possibilities it offers because we have limited vision. We seldom see more than a small window of what is directly around us. That's unfortunate because there are so many opportunities out there beyond what we can see.

Here's the key to having some sense of happiness and fulfillment: Life doesn't happen to you. You must believe in your heart that you make of your life what you want. No matter what you may go through, you are still the designer of your life. We all experience obstacles and curveballs, but you do not have to throw up your hands and accept these things as your fate. You get to call the shots, and you get to have life the way you want it if you have the courage to follow your heart, ask questions, make good choices, and take the steps necessary to win. Act deliberatively, focus, and understand that you must have a plan and a strategy. Have faith that you can and will succeed, if you are willing to step out of your comfort zone and then reap the rewards.

> **The most important takeaway is this: we encounter risks in every aspect of our lives. So, you may as well embrace them, and realize that they are tied to your goals and aspirations.**

## To Make Your Dream Come True, Write It Down

The prophet Habakkuk said, "Write the vision and make it plain." There is power in what we write, what we speak, and what we seek. We attract what we say, what we do, what we give. One of my mentors always used to tell me, "Sophia, a goal isn't really a goal unless you put it on paper." His point was *you can't just think about it—you gotta put ink to it.*

The ironic thing is that as much as we like to dream and talk about our goals, according to self-help guru, international speaker, and author Brian Tracy, less than 3 percent of Americans have written goals, and less than 1 percent review and rewrite their goals daily. Tracy lists five basic reasons why people don't set goals or follow through on them:

1. Their goals are too vague;

2. Their goals aren't quantifiable or manageable;

3. Their goals are irrelevant to their lives—in other words they don't have purpose;

4. They can't add a time frame by which to achieve the goal;

5. They're setting unattainable goals.

Tracy's assertion that only 8 percent of people achieve their goals is backed up by hard scientific data. According to a University of Scranton study on something we all know well—New Year's resolutions—a whopping 92 percent of people who set those resolution goals never achieve them. This study also shows a big drop off of keeping the resolutions once January 1 passed. Seventy-seven percent of the resolvers studied made it through a full week. Fifty-five percent stuck with their goals for a month. By June, six months into the New Year, only 40 percent of those who had made a resolution were still sticking with the goal.

Given how many people start out with good intentions but then ultimately fail, the researchers made some interesting observations. Here are the key things they learned about those few who stick to their goals, and why they succeeded where others, the vast majority, fell short:

1. They keep it simple—they start with the end in mind (*i.e.*, the goal).

2. They make it tangible—it's something they can achieve.

3. They make it obvious—everyone around them knows they are working toward that goal (for example, you want to run a 10K race, so you start training daily for months for the big race).

4. They build support systems around them (people who encourage, inspire, and celebrate their goals).

5. They set specific and challenging goals.

6. They recognize when they are off track and they get back on (they hold themselves accountable, and others hold them accountable).

7. They listen to music to focus or motivate themselves (think the theme from the movie *Rocky*).

8. They have great willpower, and they believe in themselves,

9. They write down their goals and post them so that they can visually see them daily (on sticky notes, posters, whiteboards).

A broad study conducted from 1969 to 1980 that addressed "goal-setting and task performance" results from a review of laboratory and field studies showed that in 90 percent of the studies, specific and challenging goals led to higher performance than easy goals, "do your best," goals, or no goals at all. Goals affect performance by directing attention, mobilizing effort, increasing persistence, and motivating strategy development. Goal setting is most likely to improve task performance when the goals are: specific and sufficiently challenging; have sufficient ability (and ability differences are controlled); feedback is provided to show progress in relation to the goal; rewards such as money are given for goal attainment; the experimenter or manager is supportive; and assigned goals are accepted by the individual. No reliable individual differences have emerged in goal-setting studies, probably because the goals were typically assigned rather than self-set. Need for achievement and self-esteem may be the most promising individual difference variables.[2]

As the old saying goes, *"A goal without a plan is a wish."* Put another way, "A goal without taking risks is just a dream." We know for a fact

---

[2] PsycINFO Database Record (c) 2012 APA, all rights reserved.

that people who write down their goals earn more money, have more success, and fare better in life. According to Virginia Tech professor Emeritus Dr. David Kohl, who through his qualitative research with rural businesses and supporting financial institutions, found that people who regularly write down their goals earn nine times as much over their lifetimes as people who don't. His paper also stated that:

- 80 percent of Americans say they don't have goals.

- 16 percent do have goals but don't write them down.

- Less than 4 percent write down their goals.

- Fewer than 1 percent review their goals on an ongoing basis.

**Here's my advice:** if you want to take a risk, you must have a plan. And the plan starts with a goal or dream. Then you must put that goal on paper. See it. Print it. Post it, so you can look at it and imagine yourself doing or being whatever that goal is. If there is something you want to achieve in this life, you need to use vivid, crisp, written language—even drawings—to help you SEE IT. You cannot achieve it or be it unless you first SEE IT. I used to do vision boards when I was a young professional. I had an inspiration space in my closet that I would look at daily. It helped to keep me focused on my dreams and goals. Looking back twenty years later, I can say with certainty that I hit most of my goals personally, professionally, although less so relationally (I wanted to be married with children). But for the most part, seeing my goals on paper made all the difference.

> If there is something you want to achieve in this life, you need to use vivid, crisp, written language—even drawings—to help you SEE IT. You cannot achieve it or be it, unless you first SEE IT.

## Manage Your Gifts

Risk-takers are almost always gifted people. Whether it be in sports, politics, education, business, or science. You might be thinking, *This is not me. I'm just an ordinary person, hardly gifted.* Know this: Gifted people are people just like you and me. The reality is, we all have gifts. The key is to know your strengths and weaknesses and work them accordingly. I knew, for example, that I did not want to practice law for the rest of my life. Was I good at it? Sure. But I was not passionate about it. I was passionate about writing, about politics, and about people. I knew that whatever I was going to do with my life (even now, I am still shifting, creating, and opening new doors), it had to allow me to use my gift of the pen and of my voice.

One of the first things I want to encourage you to do right now as you read this lesson is to ask yourself a simple question: What are my gifts? And then this important follow-up question: What will I do with my gifts? You must start there. You must be in touch with your desires and your passions in order to know what gifts you have and how you want to use them in the world.

The Bible talks about this in Matthew 25, the parable of the talents. A man and two others were given talents, or gifts, by their Master. One man got five and he multiplied them into ten. Another got two and gained two more. But this man was given one talent that he could use to grow. And he decided instead to bury the talent. He wanted to keep his gift safe. He wanted to hoard it as he feared his Master and thought he could simply return to him what was given. But when he presented his one gift to his Master, the Master became angry with him and rebuked him as lazy and unwise. Here's the point of the parable: when you are given a gift or blessed with talents, when you take the risk to multiply them, you will often get a great return. But when you live in fear of what you might lose, or when you hide your inner light and gifts from the world, you rarely get anything in return. You do not multiply your gift, and you have no return on your investment.

A talent given by God for you to sing, to compete, to build, to create, to paint, to blaze new trails; whatever the talent is, it is one you must multiply and share with the world. Our gift back to God is what we do with the talents He places in us. At the end of the day, all risk-taking is about is having the courage to fulfill your God-given potential. As I said at the outset, life changes, we change, and so do our goals and desires. The way, however, to stay on track is for us to set up plans and strategies that keep us focused on our core goals. I knew I was going to be an attorney since the second grade—because my mother told me that was my destiny. She wanted to be a lawyer. I became the vicarious life that she wanted to live. I stayed on track with my grades, with my focus, and I graduated college (the first in my family to get a four-year degree). I continued and went on to law school. I graduated, took the bar exam, and passed it. It was hard work, but I stayed the course because I had a goal. I took the risks, and I have most definitely reaped the rewards.

## Applying the Lesson to Your Life

The application of the lesson to your life should be clear. You set your goals and you write them down. You write them down so that you can see them. And you see them so that you can fulfill them. I do not know what your goals or dreams are, but I want you to give yourself some grace and some flexibility on your journey to achieving them. The application of this life lesson is that whether you are a great dancer, athlete, artist, writer, thinker, planner, or builder, you need to have a vision on how you are going to take that talent and make it your own. Think of all the people you admire. Think of all the successful people you know personally. What do they all have in common? They all have in common the positive power of embracing risks and being willing to take them to achieve their greatest hopes and dreams.

You can do this, too. You also have what it takes to become who you want to be or shift into who you always wanted to be. It's never too late. You can do it now. But you will need a strategy and you will need a laser-like focus on your goals to get them done, to make them a reality. And you need to stop procrastinating, putting it off for some other time, because, if we have all learned anything during this global pandemic, it's that we are not promised tomorrow. Life is short. Life is sweet. And life is meant to be lived in real time.

> You can do this, too. You also have what it takes to become who you want to be or shift into who you always wanted to be. It's never too late. You can do it now.

## Challenge Yourself to Take These Actions to Manage Calculated Risks

Here are some steps you can take today to start managing your risks and setting your goals as you figure out how to implement them and make them a reality in your life:

1. **Think big.** Don't hold back on your dreams. If you start early, you'll have a long runway to get to where you want to be and to adapt as needed along the way.

2. **Give yourself permission.** Allow yourself to do what it is you desire or are passionate about. It all starts with giving yourself the encouragement you need to follow your goals.

3. **Write down your goals and dreams.** Keep the list tight, focused, and attainable. If you are in college and you are gifted in technology and invention, stick with it. Find a career path that will help you to grow your talents and skills and allow you to thrive in that space. If, however, you are forty and you want to be a professional baseball player—that is not going to happen. But you can coach the local high school team or host a clinic for boys to learn about baseball. Maybe your childhood goal of being a professional baseball player is gone, but what is *not* gone is the "gift" you have of your knowledge of baseball. You can still live out your passion by helping others who share that passion.

4. **Know the difference between impossible goals and improbable goals.** When you think big, that is a great way to get yourself excited and interested in a goal or aspiration. That does not have to be what you ultimately do, but focusing on possible goals based on your gifts is a great way to get there.

5. **Understand the difference between personal, relational, and professional risks.** They all fit together, and they all impact your life and others connected to your life. Risks always involve other people, not just us.

6. **Trust your inner voice.** You can't let fear or worry or the naysayers in life shut down what you know you are meant to do on earth. You must practice the art of trusting your instincts and your gut. I have learned that my gut instinct is rarely wrong.

7. **Most of all, you must believe in yourself.** Surround yourself with people who believe in you, too. It's called building a great life circle or "Front Row," as I call it in my book *The Woman*

*Code.* Make a list of people who can help you get to where you want to be, starting today. Likewise, make a list of people who may be holding you back. Then set the appropriate boundaries to protect yourself and keep it moving. Let's go. You got this.

> *"If you aim at nothing,*
> *you will hit it every time."*
>
> —Zig Ziglar

# LESSON 4

## Know the Things You Need to Leave Behind in Order to Move Ahead

*"Accept yourself, love yourself,*
*and keep moving forward. If you want to fly,*
*you have to give up what weighs you down."*

—Roy T. Bennett, *The Light in the Heart*

## *Your Life-Balancing Acts*

One the most difficult things about living is having to let go. There will be people, experiences, and opportunities that come into your life after which you are never, ever, the same. Some of those experiences and people will be amazingly wonderful. They will open your eyes and your heart to the beauty of life and people, yet others will come into your life and cause you great pain. As I shared in Lesson 1, the family you are born into can be either a source of love, comfort, and support, or it can be a source of hurt, scorn, and shame.

Leaving things behind that no longer serve us well is never easy. Leaving people behind, even when they have hurt us or disappointed us deeply, is harder still. But we also must also be willing to leave behind beliefs, traditions, and thoughts that no longer serve us well. Your thoughts become your actions, then your character, and ultimately your destiny. Everything starts with a thought. So, you have to guard and keep those things that build you up and release those that hold you back. Life is 100 percent about how we balance the two. And it is always a complicated, layered, and challenging balance to say the least.

The best way to decide how we balance, however, is by first asking: what do I want? Self-reflection is always the way forward. We must always be willing to do the work to keep growing and to keep evolving into better human beings. That is why we are here after all: to be better, to do better, to love better, to shine our light in the world just a little bit brighter each day that we are blessed to live. If you can adopt these beliefs early in your life, you will be a blessing to others as you allow them to bless you.

In this life lesson, I want to share three core things with you that, had my twenty-year-old self, or even my thirty-five-year-old self, known, likely would have influenced some of the poor choices I made. There were some people I needed to leave behind me. In fact, I needed to run from them. There were some workspaces, some frenemies, and some "haters" that I simply couldn't see for who and what they really were. That's called having good peripheral vision, the ability to see things that are going on around you and to be able to make an honest assessment as to what you need to do with the information you have. I talked about this in Lesson 1 regarding the impact my family has had on my life. I now understand that I needed to move physically away from them years ago, and even more so emotionally.

When we are in young adulthood, grown and starting to spread our wings, it is important to cut the cord that ties us to family. That doesn't mean we don't love them, call them, check in, or visit. NO! What I am saying is that you must allow yourself the opportunity to form into your own person, with your own values, and your own belief systems. You do not have to cut people off (unless it's physically or emotionally dangerous to stay connected to them). There is a way to love people and to honor them—but at a respectful distance. As a Gen Xer, I was not raised that way. We were taught to stick it out, to tolerate, to look the other way even when people and things were not the best for us. And when it came to family, we felt obligated to stay connected even though these relationships were clearly not good for us.

Young people today have a different set of values; some I admire, and others I do not as I addressed in earlier life lessons. Knowing when to hold on and when to let go is never easy. In fact, it is downright complicated. The important thing to remember is that you must consider your mental and emotional health first. Some things are part of your history, but not a part of your destiny.

I know that is antithetical to everything we are taught in our socialization. But when you consider how someone or something impacts your mental, emotional, physical, and even your financial health, it informs you to make better choices. And life is 100 percent about making good choices, or at least choices that don't cause collateral damage to the rest of our lives and the lives of those we love.

In this life lesson, I want to break down into three parts the larger message of knowing what to leave behind so you can move ahead:

1. Choose your life mission.

2. Know your values and your value.

3. Know when to walk away.

As you journey through life, these three tools will help you to assess what to keep and what to let go of. There is no exact science to this; neither is there a formula that will guarantee success. But I promise you that, if you do not get this lesson down early, life will be difficult for you to manage because you will always be digging out of the rubble of drama that you allow.

## Choose Your Life Mission

> Some things are part of your history, but not a part of your destiny.

When I was in my early thirties, working as an attorney at a prestigious national law firm in Washington, DC, the firm hired a life coach for the women who were on the partner track. She was a great woman in her fifties, and I will never forget our first session. She informed me that we were going to be drafting a "life mission statement." I must admit, I was thinking, *What have they gotten me into?* But I stuck with it, and it was one of the most amazing things I ever did because it helped to propel me to where I wanted to be in life, and not where everyone else expected me to be. Writing out that statement made me refocus and reconnect with what I needed to recapture in my life, and what I needed to let go of career-wise so that I could truly walk in my gifts and in my destiny.

Choosing a life mission statement is simply writing down (remember, it's not real until we write it down) your goals and dreams in a coherent manner that helps you to accomplish them. My life mission statement, as I recall (this was back in 2006), was as follows:

*"My mission is to use my gifts of writing and speaking to uplift my fellow man and make a difference in the world that is felt long after I am gone."*

Let's break down that statement a bit. First, it starts with a mission—in other words, with an assignment, a vocation, a calling, or a challenge. You find your life mission by being honest with yourself about what you want from your life. What are you passionate about? What do you love? What makes you come alive? Tap into that and your life will have meaning and purpose.

For me—it was then and has always been—the power of words through my pen. If think back to grade school or high school, and my thirty years' worth of journals, writing has always been my gift, followed by speaking, lifting, and encouraging others. Being an attorney in a big law firm, billing hours, chasing million-dollar deals, and navigating gender and racial politics, frankly, made me miserable. I was not walking in my gifts. I was adapting to the wrong career and even dating the wrong guy for all the wrong reasons. I was drowning, and it was literally making me physically and emotionally unwell. I as living my mother's dreams, not my own. I was doing what everyone

**You find your life mission by being honest with yourself about what you want from your life. What are you passionate about? What do you love? What makes you come alive? Tap into that and your life will have meaning and purpose.**

else said I was supposed to do, not what I was called to and wanted to do.

So, how do you write this life mission statement? After you write it, how do you put it into practice? First, let me reiterate what I said in the Prologue: Life is all about being flexible. Knowing when to shift, to reinvent, when to pivot, and when to let go. Second, you must know that your life is worth having a mission and a purpose. Third, and most importantly, there is no specific formula for writing a personal mission statement. I had the help of a paid life/career coach, and you may not have that opportunity. However, the good news is that you can do this all by yourself using these quick steps to create your statement.

- Keep it concise—one sentence.

- Be honest and authentic. Don't lie to yourself.

- Ask yourself: What do I want?

- Write down what inspires you. What excites you and really gets your creative juices flowing?

- Include your values (I will break this down in the next section).

This last one is critical to your life's success because what we value creates our character, and character is fundamentally the essence of who we are.

When you have followed those simple steps, you can then begin to draft your mission statement. Keep in mind that it is not chiseled in stone. You can update or rewrite it on an as-needed basis to keep up with the changes in your life. As we discussed in Lesson 3 about taking risks, know that whatever you put down on paper will begin to manifest and take root in your life. Words have power.

What's important is to just start. Get something down that you can begin to put into action in your life. It doesn't matter if you're young, middle-aged, or older. You can let go of what no longer serves you and you can discover and embrace that which you deeply desire for your life.

My experience with the amazing life coach in my thirties helped to change my life dramatically by age forty. She made me sit with myself and really listen to my heart. She helped me to write down some *thirty-odd words* that radically changed my life trajectory, not just my career trajectory. That mission statement has created the narrative of my life. It was the turning point for me to be what I needed, for me to honor myself, and for me to walk in the direction of my own childhood dreams of becoming a successful writer, author, and public speaker. Has it been easy? No. Nothing worth having ever is, but I did not allow myself to get stuck in a career I hated, in a marriage with a man I didn't really love, or to be pushed by others in a direction that would have left me empty and unhappy, a place where too many of our fellow travelers sadly dwell.

> **Life is all about being flexible. Knowing when to shift, to reinvent, when to pivot, and when to let go.**

## Know Your Values and Your Value

If you read my second book, *The Woman Code* (stick with me here, fellas) you know that the first code of that book is to "know your value" or your worth. In this book, which is meant for anyone of any age, gender, or background, I want to expand that definition to include not just knowing your worth, which is critical for all of us (male and female, young and older, Black and White) but to understand and set out what your own values are.

I cannot stress enough how important it is for young people to know and define for yourself what your values are. You might be thinking, *What are values anyway?* Glad you asked. Values are simply what you live by. What you honor. What matters to you as a person.

In our ever-changing world of fast-paced technology, with Google searches, online dating, ghosting, texting, blocking, and unfriending, defining values is a little tricky. Values when I was a girl were universal: the importance of respect, courtesy, manners, and in-person verbal communication. To not treat others with those basic social conventions was to find yourself socially ostracized and isolated. Now, not so much. We type out whatever comes to mind without a second thought—things we would never say in person. We cancel people. We use outrage as an everyday weapon instead of working through hard things and having courageous conversations. We belittle. We demean. We post. We hit "reply all" to humiliate someone. Values are now very individual; personally subjective, versus socially objective, as they once were.

As I explained in Lesson 1, we are all products of our families and of our communities. Your faith also shapes your values. So do your friends and acquaintances. But at the end of the day, we must know what we value before we can form values about how we treat other people, how we treat ourselves, and how we show up in the world. If you want to have a good benchmark for how you learn what to leave behind so that you can move forward, it all starts with your code of conduct: what you will not compromise on no matter what other people think of you or demand from you.

What we value is deeply personal, but it is heavily influenced by many factors outside of self. If I were to list my core values (or code), honesty is at the top, being a person of integrity is next, and lastly being loyal to those I love and the principles I reflect to the world. In short, being authentic is what I value most of all. I detest fake people. They are taxing to be around. They operate on the surface of life, and I do not do surface well. Some might not be bothered by this, and that is certainly their prerogative. But I want something deeper, richer, and more meaningful every day. It's why I could not practice law in a big firm. The money was wonderful, but along with the firm came other expectations. I was not willing to make the tradeoffs, which meant I had to trade myself out the door.

For example, I had a sorority sister who was also African American and working in the litigation section of the firm. She was well-spoken and super smart. But she wore natural dreadlocks. She was very Afrocentric, as opposed to my more corporate dress code, my perfectly coiffed, straightened hair, and pearls. Yet, she was always professional, always well dressed, and an attorney's attorney. She was the real deal. Regrettably, that irked some of the old, gray-haired White men in the firm, and she began to catch flack for her hair because White, male corporate clients, and even fellow attorneys, did not think it was appropriate. This was long before The CROWN Act, which stands for "Creating a Respectful and Open World for Natural Hair" and is a law that prohibits race-based hair discrimination, began to gain steam throughout the country. She ultimately left the firm and went out on her own. The stress of always having to be as they wanted her to be was simply not worth it. Did this move hurt her career? Absolutely not! Today, she is thriving: married, successful, and wearing her hair however she deems fit. Like her, I made the same decision to leave the practice of law and pursue my life's passion of becoming a writer, an author, a speaker, and now a professor as well. We both knew we could not be our best selves in that environment, and we both had the courage to take a leap and move on.

You see, knowing your value, and knowing what and who you value, is a very important guide to knowing who values you, and what others value. It is a great personal alarm system that I believe God gifted us all, but we must work at it every day so that we can hear our inner voice. When we do so, we honor ourselves and live out our mission statement.

When you know who you are, it makes it a whole lot easier to navigate which things, people, and experiences you need to keep and those you need to put away or walk away from. Your values are your lamppost. They serve as the inner light that keeps you on track in your relationships, in your career, in your family, and throughout your life. Your values are that small inner voice that speaks to you faintly but insistently that something or someone is not quite right—that it's time to move on, to let go, and release the person, place, or thing you are afraid to let go of before it does great harm to your life and to those you love. I call it my alarm voice. Every time I have ignored that voice of warning, or the "red flags," I have lived to regret it deeply. Learn to trust your instincts because they almost always know the way.

> We must know what we value before we can form values about how we treat other people, how we treat ourselves, and how we show up in the world.

## Knowing When to Walk Away

Those who know me well understand that although I'm often in the public eye, frequently commenting online and in print, and appearing on television, I am a deeply private person. And I know, much to my delight, that this is a great source of frustration for my haters and detractors. Nevertheless, I am going to break that life code here in the last part of this lesson because people often learn best when they can see how someone else has erred or suffered by not making a good choice. Sometimes these unwise choices come about because they are based on emotion, or by simply being human and unwittingly trusting someone who meant to do them harm. It happens to all of us, and if it has not yet happened to you, keep living. It will.

I shared this story, briefly, in my first book, *Black Woman Redefined*, and I spoke about it once on national radio (*The Tom Joyner Morning Show*) when discussing how important knowing your value and worth is for young women. It is the great mistake of my life. The personal failing I never thought could happen to me. I was young, I was vulnerable, and I had not yet done the work I speak of now in dealing with my past and my childhood traumas. In not dealing with my unspoken, unhealed hurts, I allowed myself to get in too deep with someone who was a valued friend since college. He was a great guy, and I adored him—but strictly as friends. We reconnected at a friend's birthday party after college when he moved back East. At first, I did not know he was married. Eventually, he confided in me that he and his wife were having problems and he wasn't sure they would make it, and that he was sneaking off to see an old college sweetheart. I rebuked him, of course, told him that needed to stop. My mistake was in still providing emotional support and allowing myself to cross boundaries, which at the time I didn't even realize I was crossing.

As time went on, he revealed that he had feelings for me that he had been hiding for years. I was shocked and had been completely unaware of this. He shared how at social engagements and interactions he would watch me and long to be with me, thinking of me when we were apart. That was my first clue, a big red flag, to shut it down. My gut instinct (there's that word), every cell in my body, told me to run. It was totally against my core values, and what I valued was screaming at me to walk away. I did not.

Hindsight is 20/20, but I was coming through a bad patch at the time. I'd just endured a very bad breakup post law school with an Ivy League-educated, narcissist boyfriend who had been most unkind to me for all to see. This left me wary, and although I had dated some great guys afterward, I was shut down emotionally. Instead of coming across as the person those closest to me knew me to be—kind, devoted, and fun—many men saw me as cold and competitive. It was totally not who I was, and the whole experience was draining. My friend didn't see me that way, however. He got me. He liked me for who I was. Couple that with the fact that I had lost someone I loved dearly in college to cancer, and I was not making good choices relationally.

My fledgling career was not going where I wanted it to. I had the educational credentials, but I was a working-class Black girl with no money, no power, no support, and no one to protect me professionally in a White man's world at the time. It was like being chased constantly by a ravenous pack of wolves. I was lonely. I didn't feel loved. I wanted to be married. I wanted a family of my own. And I felt like I was drowning. I was simply ripe for the disaster that was heading my way. It was a fast-moving train that I simply did not know how to get off.

We connected emotionally in our unhealthiness. We had similar upbringings. Challenging childhoods. Both survivors of childhood sexual and emotional trauma. It was a perfect storm waiting to happen. I had some good friends who saw the train wreck coming and who did try to warn me. Despite their best efforts to help me break away, I did not listen. I was in too deep. Most of all, I did not know how to get away from this person who had pulled me into his drama-filled life. I became his lifeline at the expense of my own. This went on for several years, right out in the open, yet few people had a clue.

My self-esteem was being quietly destroyed. I was in love with someone I could not have. I should not have wanted to be with him in the first place because he was very bad for me. He was emotionally and at least once physically abusive. I was being controlled by a master manipulator. And all the while I felt duty bound to stay. Like all married cheaters—all of them—he played the game of being the victim while still being in the driver's seat. Everyone was expected to sacrifice but him. He wanted a mistress who was accomplished, attractive, and available, while keeping his unsuspecting spouse at home.

But thank God for good friends. One of my best friends, a married sorority sister in my church, saw me one day sitting in the back of the church devastated and sad. She reached out and invited me to lunch so we could talk. I told her everything, including that I wanted out, hoping that she could help me. And she did. I finally found the courage to break it off for good.

**Here's the point of my sharing this deeply personal story:** it took me years to forgive myself. And years to heal. I never quite trusted myself again, even after extensive counseling. It took me even longer to trust my feelings again. I had done this to myself because I did not have a healthy sense of knowing when and how to move on from something toxic in my life. I violated everything I believe in. I lost good, prime years of my life with someone who moved on with theirs and to this day is still married, now with adult children. Thankfully, we never saw one another again. God has been kind to make sure our paths never crossed. What I want you to take away from my experience is this: **DO NOT** ever connect yourself to a married person, or to a person who is abusive, manipulative, or otherwise emotionally unavailable to you. It will result in great pain, great humiliation, and great regret. Married people are off limits. And for those of you who may be LGBTQ+, this applies to you as well. Never get involved with a married person who is leading a double life—or on the "down-low," who is using you on the side to feed their true self-identity while living a lie that society or their career demands of them. Cheating is wrong. And it will not end well. It could literally cost you your life—look at the national headlines, and you'll see how these kinds of things can end with violence or death. Affairs are soul crushing and you may not recover. All married people are spoken for. If they want you, they should work on themselves first, ask for a divorce, become single again, and then come see if you want to date them; not the other way around. There are no exceptions to this rule. **None.**

This, of course, is just one example of something that is not good for you. There are many other such situations in life: The abusive boyfriend; the controlling and verbally abusive boss; friends who try to get you to use drugs, drink too much, or get involved in sexually damaging relationships; a family that refuses to face its demons and keeps pulling you down with them. Whatever the situation, you must know who you are and what you value. That will be the only thing that saves you from making reckless decisions and from people and situations that mean you harm. Never, ever, put yourself in the position of not knowing when to stay and when to walk away. The price is always higher than you will be willing to pay. The key to knowing when to stay and when to leave is to put wise people around you who will hold you accountable. And to hold yourself accountable to who you are and the values you live your life by.

## Applying the Lessons to Your Life

The way you apply the lessons to your life is simple: You must do the work in Lesson 1, 2, and 3, so that you develop the personal maturity and judgment you will need to make good

> The key to knowing when to stay and when to leave is to put wise people around you who will hold you accountable. And to hold yourself accountable to who you are and the values you live your life by.

life decisions. Knowing when to hold your cards, when to fold them, when to walk away, and when to run (as the old Kenny Rogers song goes) is not an easy thing to learn. But you can learn how to know what is not good for you by taking care of yourself first. If you are healed, if you are whole, this all works out. It's not that you won't make bad choices in life—you will. The goal is to make better choices by knowing what you really want and need. And you get in tune with that when you stop and actually listen to yourself.

Heres' my best advice on this: you need to keep those things and those people in your life who bring you joy; who feel like sunlight on your soul; who make you laugh; who love you and show you they love you by how they treat you; people who speak truth to you in love and who are there for you when you need them the most. If you can build a row of friendship and support with good people, honorable people, people who share your values (or, better still, who model good values for you when you are young), you will be okay. I promise. Keep the people who make you a better human being. Let go of those people and situations that cause you to go against your values and pull you down into drama. This is all on you, just as it has been on me. You

must be the one you need in your life. It makes all the difference.
Trust me.

After that challenging emotional ordeal at such a young age, at
such a critical point in my development as a young adult and as a
professional, I dramatically altered my behavior. I set firm boundaries. I was more careful to guard my heart without shutting down emotionally. I now never counsel married male friends, or even female
friends, who are married. I send them on to someone who can help
them, someone who has been married or is currently married and
who is a healthy role model for them to follow. I learned a hard and
painful life lesson for sure, but I also came out of it a wiser woman.
Everything I am sharing with you is to tell you that it is imperative that you be your own best friend. Your own best advocate. Your
own best protector. Your own best boundary setter. Your own best
everything. Self-care is more than just a day at the spa or a fishing
trip with the guys. Self-care starts with good emotional intelligence
about who you are and what you value. It really is that simple, folks.
Some of this life stuff is not that complicated. It's just good common
sense. And sometimes we just need to be reminded of what makes
sense in our own lives.

Having values starts with you loving and liking who you are. This
is critical. That is how you begin to develop a sense of what you want
from your life, and for others connected to your life. You grow up
when you know what you will stand for and what you will no longer
tolerate. Being your own man or woman is 100 percent about how
you treat yourself when others are looking, and when you are alone,
when no one looking. Sharing what you value, who you value, and
the sum of your values is what makes a life. A good life. A balanced,
happy, respectful, and well-lived life.

## Challenge Yourself to Take These Action Steps

I want to challenge you to take some steps right now to learn this life lesson well. Let's recap what we have learned so far in this book and how it applies directly to knowing what to keep and what to walk away from. The first lesson we learned is the impact of your family on your life and the importance of breaking away from generational "curses" that will otherwise continue in your own life. The second lesson we learned was about guarding and taking care of your emotional and mental health. The way you take care of your emotions and mental well-being is everything to the quality of life you will have. The third lesson we learned was about taking risks—smart, calculated, focused risks—and how risk-taking correlates directly to professional, personal, and relational success.

**You grow up when you know what you will stand for and what you will no longer tolerate. Being your own man or woman is 100 percent about how you treat yourself when others are looking, and when you are alone, when no one looking. Sharing what you value, who you value, and the sum of your values is what makes a life. A good life. A balanced happy, respectful, and well-lived life.**

In this life lesson you need to take all those lessons and put them into practice as you make the choice of what to keep and what to let go of. This is an everyday exercise in good judgment. Here are a few things you can do to develop and hone this skill well.

1. You need to understand that all of us are shaped by our families and the communities in which we grew up. If you did not get

a healthy dose of self-value and worth, or good old-fashioned values like manners, honestly, loyalty, faith, kindness, etc., you need to work on that now and start to learn how to value yourself and develop some core life values.

2. Connect your life to people who show up in the world as "helpers;" those who assist others, love others, build others, and flourish in their relationships with others.

3. Write down your life mission statement so that you know who you are and what you want.

4 Write down your core values and what you value. Keep them where you can see them often. Challenge yourself to live up to your highest ideals and values. Hold yourself accountable.

5. Develop what I call my "Love Council," which is the row of women and some men in my life whom I have known as long as thirty-five years, dating back to high school, and some for as little as just a few years. This is my group. My people. My girls. My row. I go to them with issues, I seek their counsel, their rebuke if needed, and I trust them with my well-being as they have proven themselves trustworthy. Everyone should have one of these groups. Mine has about twenty-five people in it, but the smaller "Kitchen Cabinet" group has about five people in it. I started this group around 2010. We host prayer calls, counseling calls, venting calls, whatever is needed. And it works. It works really, really well.

## *"All good things are wild and free."*

### —Henry David Thoreau

# LESSON 5

## Wander and Wonder:
## Life Is an Adventure—Live It!

*"Two roads diverged in a wood,*
*and I–I took the one less traveled by,*
*And that has made all the difference."*

—Robert Frost, from "The Road Not Taken"

## *Your Life*

People often confuse the words *wander* and *wonder*. They are very different but also very much connected. To wander is to seek. To explore. To go places others may not have ever gone before. To move sometimes aimlessly or purposely in wonderment. You see, wonderment, wondering, or imagining is to be awed. To consider. To see something or someone beyond what you see on the surface and to feel something more just underneath it.

If you were to ask me which I would choose: to wander about in my youth on a great adventure, traveling abroad with my backpack, exploring the world; or to live each and every day in wonder, curiosity, amazement, and joy—of course, I would want both. But, if I had to choose, I would select the latter. Because wonderment takes us back to the innocence and pure joy of childhood. A child is awed by simple things: releasing a balloon into the sky; seeing a dog walking down the street; unwrapping Christmas gifts; falling into a pile of leaves. Their delight and laughter makes everyone smile. Children— when they have been untouched, undamaged, unmaligned by life's difficulties, traumas, and tragedies—simply live in a constant state of wonder. While they may wander off from time to time and get into situations where they don't belong, children are pure, loving vessels. That is, until adults taint them with anger, doubt, fear, bitterness, worry, and hopelessness.

We were born to both wander and to wonder. I call them first cousins: they share the same roots, but they can take us on very different life paths. They are connected, but they are independent and not one in the same. So, it is critical early on that you truly grasp the difference between wander and wonder. As the old saying goes, "Wander often, wonder always."

This first section of the book has focused on early life formation and choices, and what I want you to take away from this fifth life lesson is that people who are truly fulfilled and successful human beings are intentional about living in that space of both wander and wonder in their day-to-day reality. That is the true key to finding the balance of happiness and success that we all so desperately crave. Unfortunately, the time in which we live makes it harder to find this balance. We have been conditioned to work in jobs that leave us feeling drained and unhappy; to drive alone in our cars; to come home and stay inside without saying hello to our neighbors, who we might not even know; to sit on the couch all night in front of the TV; to drink lots of wine before we fall into bed. We're constantly on our devices and jump when they buzz or ping and feel unnerved when they are out of reach. We have forgotten how to explore beyond our own homes or neighborhoods, beyond our own familiar circles. In doing so, we miss so much about life and about one another. We live in the familiar, safe, gray spaces. Hours and days and years pass, and we wonder where the time went. We live in between the raindrops, not wanting to get wet, and therefore never experience the exhilaration of refreshment and renewal when they splash on our faces and evaporate in the breeze.

In this brave new world of technology—smart phones, texting, FaceTime, WhatsApp, social media, and streaming live events literally across the globe—we have made the world seem smaller, more accessible from wherever we live, no matter how remote, how rural, or how urban. With the touch of a button, we can literally see the world. We can be open voyeurs with millions of others, and so we have become spectators of life instead of willing participants in life itself. We push keys while we sit and stare, stand and stare, or walk and stare at screens. We work all the time. We are on all the time. How far we have fallen from the adventurous spirt of past generations. Men and women alike who explored, sailed, traversed, built, traveled, chiseled, ploughed, walked, hiked, climbed, dug, and charted a course where others had dared not go. We Americans pride ourselves on the taming of the frontier, on the spirit and idealism of discovering new places, people, and things. We are inventors by nature. America put the first airplane into flight, and we put the first man on the moon in the twentieth century after others had only dreamed of space travel since the time of Galileo and da Vinci.

**We live in the familiar, safe, gray spaces. We live in between the raindrops, not wanting to get wet, and therefore never experience the exhilaration of refreshment and renewal when they splash on our faces and evaporate in the breeze.**

And for all that access, something seems amiss. Something has shifted, like a set of cascading dominoes. We are more isolated, despite all we have at our disposal to connect ourselves to others. We are more afraid, more worried, and much more stressed out. This leaves us more reluctant to venture outside of our comfort zones and into uncharted spaces. If you feel stuck, like your life is nothing close to an adventure, nothing close to amazement, wonderment, or new possibilities, I want to encourage you to reject that and to do anything and everything you ever dreamed of doing. It starts now and it starts, as I said in Lesson 3, with a plan. A plan that begins with you answering a basic question: *What would you do in this life if you knew that you could not fail?*

It's a big question. But if you can summon the courage to set aside some quiet time by yourself to dig deep and ask it, then you can answer it as well. This life lesson really depends on what season of life you are in as you answer the question. Are you in your twenties and just starting out? Are you in your thirties and forties, building your career and family? Are you in your fifties, an empty-nester looking for a way to rediscover yourself and feel relevant again? Are you in your sixties, not ready to retire, but wishing you'd chosen a more fulfilling career path? Wherever you find yourself, the key to living with adventure and wonder starts with you asking yourself: "What would I do with my life if I knew I couldn't fail?"

I know this may sound trite at first glance. Maybe you are dealing with illness, financial issues, or marital challenges. How can you live an adventure when you are just trying to survive, overcome real difficulties, and can barely make ends meet? Trust me, I get it, I've been there. I had to start over after losing pretty much everything I had at age forty-nine. As result of an accident, I had to give up writing, speaking, and corporate training. And that is how I made my living. As an entrepreneur, if I don't work, I don't have an income. For almost two years, I could not keep up. There was no paid leave, no disability allowance. I went from booming, making lots of money, and setting aside a good bit of it into savings, driving a sports car, having a beautiful home and nice things, to having to start all over when medical bills nearly wiped me out. So, I am not speaking some crazy, pie-in-the-sky words, my friends. I am speaking from what I know, from the life lessons I have learned.

We all have doubts, worries, and fears. This is just a normal part of our human condition. However, very few of us truly believe that anything is achievable if you plan properly and work hard. This is why so many people get stuck in a rut. They lose their ability to dream, and they simply stop feeding their sense of adventure, their sense of the possible, and of the idea that unexpected and amazing things can happen in their lives. From there, it is easy to lose hope and to slip into a bland routine of responsibility and necessity. I have learned through experience, born of much hardship and also much success, that the key to a fulfilled life is never giving up on yourself and in always having something to look forward to—an adventure, a trip, a newfound friend, a new love, a new puppy, a new child or grandchild—something that lifts your spirits and excites you, that keeps you daring to reach for more and to aim higher. That is the very meaning of living an adventurous life, my friends. Don't miss the importance of what I am saying: an adventure resides in your spirit. Living a big life. Taking risks. Exploring. Wandering this earth in wonderment. That is the beauty of the journey. That is the essence of why we are here.

As you read this life lesson, I want to encourage you to read with Lesson 3 in mind (Take Risks) because, although closely connected, they are different. In that lesson, I encouraged you to learn how to take calculated risks, to fail up (so that even when you fail, you win because you learn), and to make good life choices. In this life lesson, I want to focus on three things that will help you lead an adventurous life that allows you both to wander and to wonder at the same time:

1. Remember that nothing is impossible when you are young. You have everything ahead of you. When you get older, some things, as I mentioned, may at some point get beyond our reach, but then you adapt by creating something new to reach for, something that you can truly touch.

2. Creating a bucket list will bring you the adventure and wonder

you seek. Surprise yourself!

3. Remember, routine is the enemy of risk and reward.

Keep engaged and interested by seeing with fresh eyes the beauty, the awe-inspiring, the magical, all around you. Create mini adventures throughout the seasons of your life that sustain you through the hills and valleys. These things don't have to be expensive or involve extravagant planning. For instance:

- Get up early and walk or run through your neighborhood before you need to jump into your routine. Take in the splendor of the moon setting and the sun rising.

- Have a romantic candlelit dinner at home on the good china in the middle of the week to rekindle the spark in your marriage.

- Explore places you've never been in and around your city, as though you are a tourist.

- Spend quality time with your elders; sit with them, ask them about their lives, really listen and learn from their wisdom.

- Turn up your favorite music and dance.

- Climb a tree.

- Run through the sprinklers on a hot summer day.

- Eat lunch in the park instead of working at your desk.

- Have happy hour in your driveway on Friday evenings. Invite the neighbors and start a new tradition.

As I said at the outset, life is a great adventure filled with many joys and sorrows. If we can accept that going in, then we can make of life what we will. We can choose to make life incredible by looking at

> *"The key to a wonderful life is to never stop wandering into wonder."*
>
> —Suzy Kassem, *Rise Up and Salute the Sun*

things with a child's sense of wonder, as though everything is a new and exciting experience. Before long, we will realize that life is splendid and precious. And most of all, that anything is possible.

## Remember: Nothing is Impossible

Let me start with this: there has never been another you. You are fearfully and wonderfully made—a miracle, when you consider how mathematically hard it is for a child to be conceived and make it to full gestation. When you begin with this premise, life makes a lot more sense. Every one of us who walks this earth is an original—one-of-a-kind. When you think of all the stories throughout world history of mere mortals (us) achieving the impossible, it literally sends a chill down your spine, all those men and women who had dreams, who had vision, who believed in a purpose and defied the odds to make them all come true. The first thing you must accept, my friend, is that you—yes, you—are amazing! I don't care how you started. Or where you lost your way. Or what happened to interrupt your life adventure. If you still have the breath of life in your body, you have the breath of possibility within you.

What seemed possible to Mozart, Joan of Arc, van Gogh, Monet, Henry Ford, the Wright Brothers, Einstein, Gandhi, Marie Curie, Amelia Earhart, Jackie Robinson, and Shirley Chisholm seemed 100 percent impossible to everyone in their day. Yet they all pressed on, and they leaned in. They trusted their instincts (see Lesson 3) and they soared to heights unimagined. Each of these great men and women believed in themselves, and they took the adventure of a lifetime to change the trajectory and the humanity of mankind for the better.

When you believe that nothing is impossible, it makes everything possible. What may seem crazy to others may make perfect sense to you. Go with that. Trust that. It's the way to your greatest adventures. Make sure you have good, honest people around you who will encourage you along the way—people who will help you get to where you want to be and, more importantly, help you course-correct when you go in the wrong direction.

Remember, people with adventurous spirits don't just climb mountains, walk on the moon, backpack across a continent, or swim across the sea. Adventurous spirits create art, invent technologies, and create groundbreaking companies. They never stop learning, laughing, and loving. They use their inner light to shine the way for everyone else around them. And, more often than not, they do it against the soul-crushing weight of criticism, rejection, and in some instances outright hostility. They remember what most of us have long forgotten—to think for themselves and to believe in their gifts, passions, and their wildest dreams.

## Create a Bucket List: Surprise Yourself!

One of my favorite songs is "Say," by John Mayer, because it sums up life and because it was also the theme song for the movie *The Bucket List*, starring Morgan Freeman and Jack Nicholson. A bucket list is a deeply private and personal list of things you want to do before you, well, kick the bucket. It isn't

**When you believe that nothing is impossible, it makes everything possible. What may seem crazy to others may make perfect sense to you. Go with that. Trust that. It's the way to your greatest adventures.**

something someone else can really give to you. It cannot be found in one of those little wisdom books or canned checklists that appear everywhere online. You have to feel it and think about it deeply. However, if you haven't really considered this, here are some suggestions that might help you to start thinking about what you want to do with your life. My goal in this section is to help you figure out how to live your adventure by starting with that life mission statement I asked you to create in Lesson 3. That statement is the driver in how your adventures and explorations will play out over the course of your life.

1. **Write down your wildest and craziest dreams.** Remember, if you haven't written them down, they don't exist. What were your childhood dreams? All of us have a list of places we've always wanted to visit. Begin your list with these. For me, it's always been the Sistine Chapel in Rome, Italy. I want to walk where Michelangelo painted, stood, slept, and was touched by the hand of God himself with his gifts as an artist. I want to climb to the top of the Eiffel Tower in Paris, France. I want to see the Great Wall of China and walk it all.

2. **Start with some tangible stuff.** This means, the things you can check off your list easily, such as walking along the beach and collecting seashells. Or taking a gourmet cooking class and then preparing the meal for your family. Or going to New York City to see the Statue of Liberty.

3. **Think humanitarian efforts.** Building homes for people in remote areas of Brazil. Being a missionary to kids in Africa. Helping people get food, water, or clothing right in your local community, or starting a Food Mission Center. Teaching young girls about self-esteem or creating a baseball camp for boys.

4. **Immerse yourself in what you most want to experience.** Prepare your senses for your bucket-list adventure by wading into the sensations of what you'd like to experience. For example, I mentioned wanting to walk on the Great Wall of China but it's much bigger than that. I want to meet people from another culture, inhale the exotic smells, eat some awesome food, and learn how they dance, how they party, and how they celebrate life. Start locally and go to the Chinatown district in your city. Watch movies and read books about China. Go to museum exhibits that feature Chinese art and culture.

5. **Decide what is a must-do and move that to the top of your list.** Realistically, you won't be able to do everything (unless you're loaded and have plenty of time, money, and resources) so be focused and prioritize your list. Choose some of the most basic things that you presently like to do and some of the more tangible, immediate things you would like to do that are within your financial means and time availability.

6. **Get inspired.** Trace your ancestors—mine were enslaved in South Carolina, Georgia, and North Carolina. I have been to at least one of our ancestral homes and plan to visit the others. Talk to friends. I have a family friend who recently went to the Galapagos Islands. She saw the most amazing wildlife. Her photos were stunning. It's not a place I want to go, but it inspired me. I went to Sydney, Australia, a few years ago on business, and I know that I want to go back to see more of Sydney, then go to Melbourne, Fiji, Singapore, and even more places in that part of the world. Open your mind to new things and places that maybe you never thought of before. It is so life changing

> *"You must give everything to make your life as beautiful as the dreams that dance in your imagination."*
>
> —Roman Payne

to go to faraway places and meet people from those places.

## Routine Is the Enemy of Risk and Reward

If you want to live a life of adventure, fun, laughter, exploration, and surprises then you need to get rid of routines. I don't mean your morning coffee, or your evening exercise class, or your Saturday house cleaning, or your weekly grocery shopping. Those are necessary routines. I am talking about the mindless habits that desensitize us and suck the joy out of our lives. They are the routines that form into ruts where we wallow in regrets, hurts, losses, and grief that break our spirit.

I suffered a devastating loss when a man I was going to marry just up and left me. It rocked my world, and I shut down. And I mean I shut all the way down. Then one day, I looked up and realized I had let almost ten years of my life go by before I dared to open myself up to another meaningful relationship. I had fallen into a bad life routine. I was in perpetual mourning, operating on autopilot governed by destructive emotions. I kept up appearances, I kept living, of course, but, in hindsight, I was not living at all. It wasn't until I took a trip to Australia in 2018 that I began to come out of the fog—to break with my unhealthy routines of being just with my girlfriends on weekends, drinking wine, or staying in alone to watch movies, read, and listen to music.

I will never forget our descent into Sydney Harbor early in the morning after a seventeen-hour flight from the US. The sky was a beautiful, serene, azure blue mixed with purple and pink. You could see the maritime life in the ocean below, a whale swimming with what appeared to be other smaller whales or dolphins. I was awed. My senses awakened. My spirit lifted. I was literally on the other side of the world and in a different hemisphere. It was exactly what the doctor ordered to snap me back into living. I took pictures, I hiked, I walked the beautiful streets of Sydney at sunset. I sat by the harbor, ventured into the beautiful gardens there, and saw a koala and a kangaroo for the first time in my life. I felt a child's sense of wonder, and thought of my favorite childhood book, *Winnie-the-Pooh.*

My point is that before this trip my sense of adventure had died. My life had become routine. Drudgery. Stale. I had accepted my fate on some unconscious level and was just going through the motions of living. That trip opened me up. I started dating again. I reconnected with a wonderful man who became my best friend. He helped breathe life back into me, which I so sorely needed. So, take it from me, when you open your soul to big things, to small things, to anything new, different, and unplanned it revives your spirit and zeal for life. It works like a charm. Get away. Get out. Go seek and wander this beautiful earth and make sure you do your darndest to touch everything and everyone you can living in it.

> *"So shut up, live, travel, adventure, bless, and don't be sorry."*
>
> —Jack Kerouac,
> *Desolation Angels*

## Applying the Lesson to Your Life

Adventure is a spirit that dwells inside us. It is not necessarily an exterior event or trip. You can create small, meaningful, tangible adventures every day of your life by committing not to live a life of drab routine or a life of regret and feeling stuck.

You and you alone decide the quality of your life and the rhythm of your life once you get past the childhood part of your life. As I said in Lesson 1, you are not your family. You must begin to live by a mantra I adopted in 2018 when I walked the beaches of Sydney alone, with my journal and with my tea: Life is not what happens to me. *I am what happens to my life.*

It is never too late to have a fulfilling life. You have the power to change your fate. It is you who decide what comes next in your story. My story, undoubtedly like yours, is made up of all kinds of twists and turns; joys, and sorrows; loves and losses. But the best parts of my journey have been when I embraced the entire story and decided to teach what I have learned, and to keep living, loving, and laughing despite the things and people that hurt me.

When you live with a spirit of adventure, with a spirit of wandering and wondering, nothing is impossible in your life. Nothing. Because as long as we have the breath of life in us, whether we are old or young, we can still live out the adventure of our dreams.

*"All that is gold does not glitter,*
*Not all those who wander are lost.*
*The old that is strong does not wither,*
*Deep roots are not reached by the frost."*

—J.R.R. Tolkien, *The Fellowship of the Ring*

# SECTION II

## Manage Your Emotions Before They Manage You

*We're emotional beings by nature. To deny that is to deny our most basic humanity. Yet, if we do not responsibly manage our emotions in life, love, business, and relationships, we find ourselves isolated and alone. These lessons will help us to recognize and better manage our emotions and use them as powerful tools for self-care and success.*

# LESSON 6

## Reframe Your Thoughts: Build an EIQ Toolkit

*Respect yourself,*
*and others will respect you.*

## *You and Your Emotional Intelligence*

How we see people matters—a lot. It sets the foundation for how we engage them at work, in love, and in life. Our thoughts become our actions. Learning the keys to unlocking healthy interpersonal relationships is everything in how we succeed or fail at work, in dating and marriage, and in our day-to-day living. Dealing effectively with our emotions and responding properly to those of others is what I want to address in this life lesson. Emotional intelligence (EIQ) is a complex way of stating the obvious: it's how we manage our feelings, our strengths, our weaknesses, our moods, our perceptions, our stress, our anxiety, and how we perceive those same feelings and emotions in others. More layered, however, is how we define emotional intelligence from a psychological standpoint. Professors Peter Salovey of Yale University and John Mayer of the University of New Hampshire both define EIQ as "the ability to monitor one's own and others' emotions, to discriminate among them and use this information as a guide to one's thinking and actions."

Sounds a bit technical, right? It is and it isn't. Emotional intelligence is broken down into five categories by EIQ leadership and behavioral experts:

- **Self-awareness:** a constant consciousness about our own shifting emotional state and the emotional state of those around us.

- **Self-regulation:** the ability to respond to and control any change in our emotional environment.

- **Motivation:** the capacity to redirect our emotional state toward optimism and commitment so that we can achieve our goals no matter what emotions may be provoked by challenges or setbacks.

- **Empathy:** recognition and appreciation of the emotional experience of others to increase one's understanding of their perspective and point of view.

- **Social skills:** the ability to communicate with, negotiate with, and influence others through an emotional, not just rational, channel.

Thus, a big part of developing good emotional intelligence is being self-aware. You can't address or nurture or fix what you don't recognize in yourself. Psychologists call naming our emotions and how we feel about them "labeling," an important first step in dealing with our emotions effectively. Yet, even if we are honest in identifying how we feel, giving it a name can be hard—much harder than it sounds. For example, do you really know the difference between merely feeling tired and frustrated versus depressed and isolated? Do you know when you are truly feeling angry? Are you able to recognize that you have been suppressing your emotions for so long that you need to speak and release them? What about the many feelings we must manage when we are grieving a loss?

The truth is, all of us struggle to identify what we are feeling, and more often than not, we ignore those feelings. We stuff them down. It's just easier not to deal with emotions and feelings that we can't get a handle on. And sometimes, even if we do understand them, we don't know how to navigate them. Your emotions are your constant companion, and they go where you go: work, home, church. They are with you at play, on a date, while you are working out, or simply socializing with friends. We can never outrun our emotions, but the lens through which we process them is important to how well we manage them.

All of this may sound overwhelming, so I am going to help you reframe your thoughts and create an EIQ toolkit that works. It's not as complicated as you might think. This is information that I wish I'd had when I was twenty, thirty, or approaching forty because it would have allowed me to live a more peaceful and fulfilling life, but it is helpful no matter your age or stage. It is never too late to embrace good emotional health practices. Never.

Let's start with our words. Words matter. What we speak truly is the power of life and death, as the Scriptures say. For example, if you're experiencing a strong emotion—say, anger—while at work, take a moment to consider what this emotion is and what the outcome will be if you act upon it in that moment. But don't stop there. Once you've identified it, try to come up with two words that describe how you are feeling. You might be surprised that what you think is anger is actually something else. You are ill-suited for and frustrated at your job. You're not happy at home. You then realize that it is you who needs to shift and make a move. By doing something that simple, *stopping* to think, you will have uncovered the breadth of your emotions, and by doing so you will have unearthed a deeper set of emotions buried beneath the more obvious one.

Here's my point: you must always be aware of your emotional temperature. I know this sounds ridiculous, but it is not. By developing emotional intelligence—the ability to recognize our emotions and feelings—and, secondly, by being able to name them, we create a process of saving ourselves from words we cannot take back, and lots of trouble. Thinking before you speak and act may sound like an antiquated adage in the modern age of social media—Instagram,

Facebook, Twitter, etc.—but it is not. Good EIQ is the key to a successful personal and professional life.

Truthfully, one of our greatest tragedies as humans is that we've been trained to believe that sharing strong emotions is a bad thing and therefore they should be suppressed. More than that, our gender plays a huge role in which emotions we express, and what we say and think, particularly in the workplace or in our relationships. Women are socialized from the time we are girls not to be "bossy," not to talk too much, not to speak our minds, to be likeable and get along well with others, to be agreeable. Whereas boys are taught and encouraged to be rough and tumble, to speak up and take charge, to take chances, to trust their own voice. They are taught to compete and be "strong." On the flip side, they are taught that showing some emotions, like sadness, is "weak." Fortunately, we are becoming more cognizant of these old rules of socialization, and we've seen a great shift by media, corporations, politics, and academia toward empowering our daughters to be and do anything they desire. And changes in how we raise our daughters, inevitably will change how we raise our sons.

Expressing your emotions is an important part of being a well-rounded human being. However, this does not mean that you shouldn't think before you speak, that you shouldn't consider before you act. In other words, you must manage your emotions before they manage you.

So, starting now, be intentional about "reframing" your emotions, and how you react to and engage with others. Begin by asking yourself these questions:

> **Truthfully, one of our greatest tragedies as humans is that we've been trained to believe that sharing strong emotions is a bad thing and therefore they should be suppressed.**

1. Do you often react on impulse, or take offense, when someone criticizes you, even if it is constructive?

2. Do you often feel emotionally numb? In other words, do you not allow yourself to cry, or to be vulnerable, or to vent your frustrations so you can better work through them?

3. Do you go out of your way to avoid conflict, even when it might resolve a situation?

4. Do you avoid asking for what you want or need?

5. Do you often misread people's intentions toward you as bad when in reality they are not?

6. Do you not know how to protect your emotions in time of stress and challenge?

Answering yes to any one of these questions is a good sign that you likely need to work on building your EIQ. I am going to get into the "how," but first you must commit to learning to keep your stress and emotions in check. Be intentional and choose to do this. The good news is that by learning how to listen to your own emotions, and to see other people beyond their emotions, you increase your knowledge, your leadership skills, and your ability to persuade others to reach higher and be better, too.

By learning how to take a moment when frazzled, puzzled, unsettled, or angry—or unsure of what you feel—you are giving yourself time to process your emotions. By giving yourself the space and distance to assess other people's virtues, values, and strengths, you are allowing them the time to grow. And by thinking before you speak, and effectively factoring in the likely consequences of what you're about to say, you are giving yourself the grace to win at life. By simply pausing, you'll not only improve how you communicate with others, you'll also be able to pivot into something healthier. You will learn how to manage your moods, trust your intuition, make good decisions, and bring your life into balance.

Remember, there are no quick fixes in life. When it comes to change, there are two kinds of people: those who are willing to do the work and make improvements and those who are comfortable being where they are in life, even when they hate where they are. Change is hard, but if you are willing to make changes in small, manageable bites, it is less difficult and not as frightening. Having what I like to call an "arsenal of wisdom," or an "EIQ toolkit," handy makes working, living, loving, and playing much more enjoyable. People with a good EIQ have devoted, close friends, and they succeed at all they do in life. You can be one of those people, too. It's all up to you. The value of building up your emotional intelligence is like building up your muscles. You must work at it regularly before you see results. But by doing so, you become stronger, leaner, and healthier. To see results, you must use the toolkit, and work at it every day. Great leadership trainers like John Maxwell, Dale Carnegie, and others all talk about the importance of how most people think that a high IQ (intelligence quotient) or intellectual intelligence drives success. Sure, intelligence helps. But, if we look more closely at high-achieving people, we find that emotional intelligence drives their performance. Emotionally strong people circumvent common pitfalls (like people-pleasing) that derail success.

> *"There is no separation of mind and emotions; emotions, thinking, and learning are all linked."*
> —Eric Jensen

# EIQ Tip 1: Spot and Correct Your Negative Moods and Attitudes

Let's start with a premise: feelings aren't facts. They are just feelings. And if you can feel bad, I am here to tell you that you can also start feeling good. We all get down. We get depressed at times. We doubt ourselves. And we can get in a funk that isn't easy to get out of. The most important way to spot and then deal with your negative moods and attitudes about people, places, and situations is to face them head on. Do not ignore them. Do not push them down. Do not wish them away or think it will just pass. If you want to stay ahead of your dark side, you must fight it constantly with your optimistic side.

We talked earlier about how to spot and name your emotions. I'm starting with dealing with your negative moods and attitudes because I find that, particularly at this time in our history, we are dealing with a mental and emotional health crisis both in the workplace and in our families. As we discussed at the beginning of this chapter, depression, isolation, and a sense that we no longer belong to a greater community as a fellow citizen, has brought about a very serious challenge in how we deal with our emotions.

*"When dealing with people, let us remember that we are not dealing with creatures of logic. We are dealing with creatures of emotion...."*
—Dale Carnegie

So, let's get to it: you spot your negative attitudes, fears, and emotions by being in tune with your body. I talked in previous chapters about the critical importance of our physical health and our mental health. I am not a therapist. I am not a psychologist. But I am an award-winning corporate EQ trainer (executive coach). I have seen firsthand the impact that COVID-19 has had on the workplace and, in particular, on women and the emotional health of their families.

One of the first signs that we are spiraling down into a place of negative or depressed emotions and attitudes is that we begin to manifest physical symptoms: for example, we have trouble sleeping, we stop eating, or may begin to eat a whole lot more. These are just a few symptoms that are very common when we're dealing with things that we don't know how to talk about or manage. One of the first things that you must do, as I've said repeatedly, is to face it so you can fix it. When you spot it, you must address it. The good news is that we live in a time in which celebrities like Oprah, or athletes like Naomi Osaka and Michael Phelps, and even politicians like Congresswoman Alexandria Ocasio-Cortez, and law enforcement like US Capitol Police Officer Harry Dunn have talked about their bouts with overcoming depression, anxiety, sadness, PTSD, or other traumatic emotions. With this trend, we are beginning to create an environment in which we can be open and honest about such things and embrace professional therapy. But we still have a way to go, as men commenting online have been harsh about other men who talk about their feelings, take paternity leave (like Secretary Pete Buttigieg) and seek to deal with their emotions.

The next thing you must do once you identify your need is to come up with a plan on how you will work through these emotions; that is shorthand for reframing your thoughts. When I recognize that I am feeling down or negative, or find myself with a bad attitude, I stop, I get up, I take a walk. Or I pray, or eat a healthy snack, or get a fresh cup of coffee or tea. Sometimes, I just sit quietly. If I am really not okay, I will hop on my Peloton or stretch. Or I will pick up the phone and talk to one of my mentors or best friends, someone I know is a great example of having good emotional intelligence, and I just pour out whatever I'm dealing with, and they help me work through it. My point in sharing this is to get you to have people who serve as wise sounding boards in your life, as well as trusting your own voice.

There are four things that I want you to do when you recognize (remember, you've got to recognize first that you have a problem or none of this is going to work) that you're feeling negative or can't control your mood:

1. **Do not blow things out of proportion.** Keep it all in perspective. You are a human being and human beings sometimes feel negative or get down. Resist the temptation to replay repeatedly in your mind something that you feel you did poorly or that you didn't handle well. Instead, reframe your thoughts to: Okay, this happened. How am I going to change this or make it right?

2. **Be reasonable with yourself and be kind to yourself.** One of the worst things we can do is punish ourselves for feeling normal human emotions. Anger, sadness, doubt, and regret are feelings that every single one of us experiences throughout the various seasons of our lives. Acceptance is key, because once we accept that we're human, once we accept that we all have periods of darkness and negativity and things that we don't feel good about, we empower ourselves to shift and to do something positive with something negative.

3. **Help somebody else.** The best way to get out of a bad mood is to do something good for another person. You will not only lift your spirits but lift some else's and create a chain of goodness and grace.

**4. Do something that relaxes you.** Get outside, put on soothing music, light a candle with a beautiful scent—anything you enjoy that calms your mind and your spirit. This will allow you to again reframe and refocus your thoughts.

The Scriptures say, "Life and death are in the power of the tongue …" (Proverbs 18:21). While I would never argue with Scripture, I will say that if I were writing that verse today, I'd say the power of life and death are in our thoughts. How you think about things, how you see them through the lens in which you process them, sets the tone for your day, sets the tone for your professional engagement and accomplishment, sets the tone for how you date or how you do in marriage, how you love your kids, your family, and how you love your friends. How you think about a thing is everything.

## EIQ Tip 2: Manage Situational Stress and Anxiety

Situational stress is stress that brought about by uncomfortable or challenging situations we find ourselves in. In those moments, you need a strategy to get you through to the other side. If you're at work and your boss does something out of line that makes you want to erupt, you need an outlet so that you don't compound his or her bad behavior with your own. The key is to respond and not react.

Remember, there are no quick fixes in life. When it comes to change, there are two kinds of people: those who are willing to do the work and make improvements and those who are comfortable being where they are in life, even when they hate where they are. Change is hard. But if you are willing to make changes in small, manageable bites, it is less difficult and not as frightening.

Responding means we have thought it through, written it down, or talked it out with someone we trust first. Then we can address that person or situation that has us upset. We do that effectively when we get our emotions under control and not let them escalate during moments of stress, worry, and anxiety. I call it the "walk away therapy" and I use it often.

Daniel Goleman, a pioneer in the study of emotional intelligence, is quoted in the *Harvard Business Review* as saying, "The most effective leaders are all alike in one crucial way: They all have a high degree of what has come to be known as emotional intelligence. It's not that IQ and technical skills are irrelevant. They do matter, but . . . they are the entry-level requirements for executive positions." What Goleman is saying is that the leaders who lead best are those who know how to understand, empathize with, and navigate people. They aren't necessarily the kids who come out of college or law school or business school with a 4.0 average and record-high test scores.

In my experience, I have found that the most successful people in business and otherwise were the B and C students, the ones who, like me, were class presidents, leaders of organizations, the rebels, and the outliers. Yes, of course, some of these people were at the top of their classes, too, like the partners at my law firm, but then there are people like Bill Gates, Steve Jobs, and Mark Zuckerberg who dropped out—went against the grain—the creators, the dreamers, and the shakers. Many of the fraternity leaders, student-government leaders, and the like, that I graduated with in college and law school went on to be very successful in life. All of us were, and are, highly social and highly verbal individuals. We like people. People is what we are good at. Some of it has to do with having an outgoing, charismatic personality (see Bill Clinton or Barack Obama), but most of it is people being intentional about how they govern themselves emotionally day to day. For those of you who just might be shy—so was Bill Gates. They key is he tapped into his gifts, and he put good people around him who helped him build a company called Microsoft. Good EIQ is knowing what we are good at and what we are not, and then building a team around us to fill in the gaps so we can soar, and they can, too!

Back to stress, we all feel stress and anxiety, and this was particularly pronounced during the early stages of the pandemic. But even before COVID-19, stress had risen to new levels. We all know it because we all feel it. Even the youngest among us are dealing with stress, distress, depression, and even suicidal thoughts. The people who successfully get through that stress are those with good EIQ, and they practice the following strategies both personally and professionally to relieve it:

- **Exercise regularly—every day or every other day.** When you get moving, your stress-relieving hormones (endorphins) begin to flow, calming you and making you feel happy, strong, and positive.

- **Find a helping professional: a counselor, therapist, or career coach.** It is a huge emotion booster, sets you on a path to help you help yourself, and keeps you grounded and well. I talked about the life coach in Lesson 3 and how it radically changed my career and life for the better. I highly recommend it.

- **Establish a relationship with a mentor or people who can help guide you to professional and personal success.** Successful people never outgrow coaching or taking good advice. Sometimes, others can see what you can't.

- **Get adequate sleep.** So many of us struggle with insomnia or just not sleeping long enough. You must make rest and sleeping a priority. Don't think that cutting corners during the week and sleeping in on the weekends will help. It does not, you need to be consistent. Sleep is restorative, both mentally and physically, and helps you make decisions with a clear mind.

- **Drink water.** It sounds simple, but most people are not adequately hydrated. Make sure you keep a big container of water at your desk or keep count with a water-drinking app and stay hydrated every day. Dehydration is a growing health challenge for all of us. We don't drink enough basic $H_2O$, which is so vital to our bodies and our brains.

- **Chew gum.** Yes, you read that correctly, I said chew gum. Or have a fidget toy you can grab, or a stress ball. You would be amazed at how quickly these can calm you down.

- **Create a refuge.** Establish a quiet, undisturbed space that is just for you—a place you can go to, at work, at home, or in between and where you can grab some tea, light a candle, or just sit and breathe for a few moments.

## EIQ Tip 3: Build Empathy for Other People— Especially the Difficult Ones

Navigating people is never easy, particularly in the workplace. We have different personalities and come from wide-ranging situations, there are power differentials and sometimes hidden motives. We are all so complex—even on our best days. The key to getting along well with others, and influencing others positively, is to have a good EIQ. You bring others to your team and to your side by being trustworthy, honest, and authentic. Great leaders in the workplace and in business are men and women who are very much in touch with, and clear about, their own strengths and weaknesses. When we have a good inner knowledge of ourselves, our difficulties, and our challenges, we then develop that all-critical leadership skill called empathy. You cannot be a good leader if you do not have empathy. I call it the three F's: fair, focused, and flexible. You navigate difficult people by being someone who's not difficult yourself.

Empathy is something that more and more human resource officers and corporate CEOs and leaders in the Fortune 500 are spending a lot of time developing. They bring in renowned experts, like Dr. Brené Brown of the University of Houston, who have become international superstars talking about and advising leaders on how to be vulnerable, or how to lead with empathy, and how to pay attention to people's emotional needs in the workplace, as well as being able to recognize their talents and strengths.

Navigating difficult people is an art form. It's something I learned as a young law student reading the cases and studying how great lawyers like civil rights icon and Supreme Court Justice Thurgood Marshall, Justice Felix Frankfurter, and Chief Justice Earl Warren and others who won arguments that set legal precedent, or literally changed history, were able to do so. Each of them possessed something well beyond their intellect, beyond the facts. Each of these great leaders knew how to navigate the worst of human beings. They knew how to persuade, evade, duck, come back, hold their cards, fold their cards, and they knew when they could press forward or when they had to step back and wait for another day.

As a young Black woman from working-class roots, I learned quickly about the inequities of life, about those who mattered and those who did not. My freshman year of high school, I told my guidance counselor that I wanted to be a lawyer. I'll never forget her smirking at me, telling me I needed to pick something "more reasonable." She told me that the college prep course was not for me, that I would be more suited to going to a two-year junior college or a trade school, but never law school. I thought about her stinging words on the day I got my law degree in two and a half years instead of three, and when I passed the bar exam with one of the highest scores in the history of the state. But it didn't end with her. Difficult people are going to be around you your entire life: the naysayers, the doubters, the haters. They will always be there, and your job is not to engage with them, or to spar with them, or to go back and forth throwing mud and negativity. Your job is to have the skillset in your EQ toolkit to be able to not just withstand their barbs and their jabs, but more importantly, to be able to rise above and use their words as motivation to thrive and do everything that they say you cannot do.

Great people and great leaders, in addition to having great empathy, are humble. They aren't loud, they don't brag about themselves even when they've done something extraordinary, and they trust their instincts. They march to the beat of their own drum. And they keep marching no matter what anyone else says they can or cannot do. I can tell you that both being humble and understanding when speaking, and knowing when to listen, has been a game changer in my personal life and in my career. It is often tempting to take a swing at someone who has been unkind to you or, worse, tried to ruin your career or your reputation. But let me assure you that, if you learn the art of navigating, you will come out on top every single time. Here are my tips for dealing with negative people, difficult people, and people you simply don't like:

1. **Learn to build small bridges.** By that, I mean take baby steps with difficult people. Bring them a cup of Starbucks in the morning, find out what their favorite bagel is, leave it on their desk with a note inviting them to lunch. I have found that most people who are negative are people who feel isolated and alone and don't have a lot of friends. So, make friends, be nice.

2. **Keep an open mind and don't make assumptions.** As the old saying goes, when you assume, you make an ass out of you and an ass out of me. You can't really know what is going on in someone's life that might make them behave the way they do.

3. **Try to understand the why.** Haters didn't start out being haters. They have a back story just like you and me.

4. **Stop trying to change people, because you can't.**

5. **Take your power back.** Taking your power back requires you to first understand to whom or what you have given it away and why you did so. When you take your power back, you stop allowing your emotions, or other people's emotions or their actions to negatively affect you. And you begin to do those things that are emotionally healthy for you and balanced for you, and that make you feel safe and sure of yourself.

## EIQ Tip 4: Be Fair. Stay Focused. Be Flexible.

For this final tip, I want to go into more depth about what I call the three F's. I first came up with this formula when I was doing diversity, equity, and inclusion training for Fortune 500 companies such as Deloitte, Comcast, Walgreens, Ernst & Young, JC Penney, Land O'Lakes, Kimberly-Clark, Morgan Stanley, and Microsoft, among others. During my training, I interviewed people at both the C-suite and at senior management levels. When I was able to get access to them, I'd also speak with mid-level managers and lower-level workers. One of the things I continually heard from workers was that they felt that their bosses weren't fair, meaning they seemed only interested in the success of people whom they felt were on their level, or in their clique, or with whom they had some connection. One of other issues I frequently heard about, particularly from women, was that they needed job flexibility and that they were most excited to work for senior leaders who understood how to be fair, and how to be focused on what mattered in the workplace.

Let's take a deeper dive into the three F's:

**Fair.** What does it mean to be fair? A leader with good emotional intelligence understands that life is never fair. But when we're dealing with other human beings, particularly in the workplace, and even in our interpersonal relationships, fairness is all about how we make people feel. One of my favorite Maya Angelou quotes is: "I've learned that people will forget what you said, people will forget what you did, but people will never forget how you made them feel." Fairness, then, is simply treating everyone around us with the same respect, giving them the same hope, and offering them, as best we can, the same opportunities.

**Focused.** A good leader is focused on his or her team, on the task or the goals at hand, and is not given easily to distraction. We all know that distraction is the greatest enemy of success. How many of you have set out to do something or accomplish a task only to be distracted by minutiae—things that in the scheme of life don't matter very much at all? All good leaders with solid emotional intelligence have mastered the art of being focused. My staff hates me because I say to them at least ten times a day, "Focus!" When we're focused, we're destined for great things.

**Flexible.** Last but not least, the third leg of the stool. To be flexible is simple in theory but more difficult to put into practice. The reality is that most leaders are Type A personalities. And most Type A personalities like to have things their way, on their time, when they want them. Let me break the bad news to you: that's not a good way to lead. And it's an even worse way to inspire loyalty from your team, loyalty in your relationships, or respect from those you very much want to look up to you. Good leaders, good spouses, good siblings, good friends all know that they must be flexible, that it is not all about them. Likewise, it is not all about you. It's about all of us working together. People who are flexible are empathetic people. People who are flexible are humble people. People who are flexible understand that they're not always right and they're open to exploring new ways of doing things, ways of opening up to new possibilities both in their professional lives and in their personal lives. Flexibility breeds opportunity. Rigidity breeds contempt and resentment.

## How to Apply This Life Lesson and Challenge Yourself to Develop an EIQ

So, now you have some tools to put in your EIQ toolkit. The most important takeaway from this life lesson is that you have the power within you to control your emotions. It all starts with first acknowledging them and then understanding what to do with them.

Before I get to how to apply this lesson to your life, and how to further challenge yourself to develop an emotional intelligence quotient, let me say this: what you focus on in life will grow. If you focus on being someone who is positive, you will attract positivity. If you are someone who focuses on light, you will radiate light. If you are someone who is empathetic, you will attract empathy. And if you are someone who is humble, you will be lifted. The point is, emotional intelligence is simply another way of saying that we actually have power over our own emotions. Once you look at it from that vantage point, once you reframe your thoughts to the fact that you have control over yourself and what you say, what you think, and what you feel, the world suddenly opens. It can no longer be a dark place, or an uninformed place or lonely place. It can only be a place with possibilities.

I'll say this again: there is no quick fix to managing our emotions because emotions come and go every day; we're up one minute and down the next. Emotions are very unpredictable unless, we become predictable in managing them in our favor. Challenge yourself. For example, if anger is your Achilles heel, if anger is something that has been a modus operandi in your family or in the leaders that you've worked for, challenge yourself to be the one who does things differently. Challenge yourself to be the person who reaches out in compromise. Challenge yourself to be someone who doesn't get angry and instead be someone who listens to and who learns from others. We must remember that life is made up of little things, not big things, as I said throughout this life lesson. It's not about how smart you are, it's not about how much you know, it's about how you treat people and the impact that you and your energy have on them every day. Offer a simple smile. Lend a helping hand. Extend a caring heart. Give a word of praise. Share a cup of coffee and, in doing so, make a connection. At the end of the day, we are most alive as human beings in those moments when we connect with one another, and we feel respected and rewarded by one another. People with a good EIQ understand this, and they walk it every day. *Will you be one of those people?*

"Everything can be taken from a man but . . .
the last of the human freedoms—to choose one's attitude
in any given set of circumstances."

—Viktor Frankl

"Be content with what you have. Rejoice in how
things are. When you realize there is nothing lacking
the whole world belongs to you."

—Lao Tzu

# LESSON 7

## Don't Sweat Your Haters:
## Use Them as Fuel for Your Success

*"You can't be friends with
someone who wants your life."*

—Oprah

## *Your Reactions to People*

W e've all heard the expression, "Haters gonna hate." It's true. I hate to break the bad news, but you need to be ready for the fact that there are going to be people who simply do not like you just because you are you. There will always be those who are jealous and who will try to take you down. It doesn't matter how nice you are; it doesn't matter how good a person you are; it doesn't even matter how well you treat other people. Hate—or a better word for it, envy—is something that goes deep within a person. All envy first starts as admiration. I need to take you back to what I've

> **You cannot change other people. You cannot wish or will them to be better human beings. That can only come from within themselves.**

been saying since the beginning of this book: You cannot change other people. You cannot wish or will them to be better human beings. That can only come from within themselves.

My goal in this life lesson is to help you learn how to navigate the inevitable; and by that, I mean the inevitable jealousy, envy, hate, dislike, and all the other negative human emotions that we all

experience from time to time. And as we go through this lesson, let me tell you another truth: you will never understand a hater, so do not waste your time trying to do so. One of my mentors used to tell me, "Sophia, the best revenge is success." Boy, was he right. The most important thing to remember is that whatever reasons people may have to be jealous or to hate, it is not your fault. Haters hate because they are not happy with themselves or their own lives. Bishop T. D. Jakes, who is someone I admire and is a family friend and a mentor of mine, likes to say, "I've never had a hater doing better than me."

What he means is that people who are highly satisfied with their own lives, with their own relationships and careers, do not have the time or the energy to focus on what you're doing or why you're doing it. They simply do not have the energy to hate. Life tip: those are the people you want to be connected to in life.

The bright side is this: if you have haters, you're probably doing something right. You're out making a difference in the world. You're pushing the envelope. You're a mover and a shaker. You are a disrupter. You're not someone sitting on the sidelines being a spectator of life; you are engaged in the process of living. I know firsthand that the more successful you become in life, the worse the haters are going to get. Hate and jealousy are as old as the Bible. Two of the more profound stories in the Old Testament, in the Book of Genesis, deal with the issue of envy and jealousy. Take the story of Cain and Abel, two brothers both working in the field. Cain becomes jealous of the crop Abel has been able to grow and the favor he received from God. Instead of talking to Abel and asking him for a few pointers about how he, too, could raise such a lush and wonderful crop, Cain instead decided to murder his brother. Now, for those of you who are religious scholars or read the Bible and are familiar with this story, you know what happens next: God steps in and asks Cain where his brother Abel is. Of course, we know Cain's famous refrain, "I know not; am I my brother's keeper?"

The second story in Scripture that deals with the issue of jealousy and envy gone badly is the story of my favorite person in the Bible, King David. At this point, of course, David is not yet king, because Saul is the first King of the Jews in Israel. David is a shepherd boy, the runt of the litter, who becomes famous because he slew Goliath with a slingshot and some rocks. Now, once David takes out Goliath, he becomes a hero to all, and he experiences great favor in his life and love from the king himself. But, one day, the king hears a crowd cheering when the men return from battle and saying, "Saul has killed a thousand of his enemies, but David has killed ten thousand." Upon hearing this, Saul turns his anger and envy upon David, who is then a very young man and very loyal to the king, and, even more interestingly, is about to marry his daughter. Bear in mind, David did nothing to Saul but be loyal. All it took was for Saul to feel threatened by David, and that changed everything.

And so, the story goes, from that moment forward King Saul hated David and wanted to kill him. He literally hunted David for years—in fact, if you count the years that David had to literally run for his life, from his wedding day forward, it was about thirteen years before David himself became King of Israel. David eventually takes the throne when Saul dies by suicide on the battlefield because he defied God and went into a battle that God did not bless. The hater Saul is dead, and the person he sought to kill is elevated to king of the land.

So, what's the message of these two biblical stories that are thousands of years old? It is this: even people close to you, people in your own family (see Lesson 1), in your profession, in your circle, even your closest circle, may turn on you. Some will hate you to the point of attempting to damage your reputation, and, in extreme cases, literally take your life. Although it's my hope that you won't experience any of that, we know that, in our present social-media culture, there are people who have fights on Twitter, YouTube, Facebook, fights that have led to people's physical harm and/or their deaths.

As I've aged, I've come to understand that, indeed, all *envy first starts with people who want to be like you*. Let me explain what I'm saying. Most of the harm that will come to you in your life will be from people who are near you—your family, your friends, your spouse, your siblings. Yes, you will have people at your job, at your college, in your sorority, people who will not like you, may not want to associate with you, may believe that you think you're "all that." Let them have their opinions. Your job—your one and only job—is to keep moving forward. There will never be enough hours in the day for you to chase down every person who says bad things about you, who gossips about you, who hates you, and who means to do you harm. Of course, there will be times, trust me, where you will have to respond to people who are trying to do you in. I've had to do so and, if you live long enough, you will have to do so as well. Sometimes, it will break your heart; other times, it will be a great relief to your spirit. Although it's true, as the old saying goes, that you should never burn bridges, you must always consider whether you should cut someone off completely, or whether you should simply "untie" that relationship for the moment. These two things are very different, but we will get into that a little bit later in this lesson.

For the purposes of this life lesson, I am going to address three topics to help you. First, we need to identify when someone is being a hater to whom you must pay attention versus one who is simply being petty and should be ignored. Second, I want to address how to deal with true and dangerous haters, because it is not a one-size-fits-all response. And third, I want to give you another EIQ tool to pull from your toolkit from Lesson 6, showing you how you can use your haters as fuel for your success in life.

## The Definition of a "Hater" and Learning How to Spot One

If you follow me on social media, you have seen me post any number of times on Facebook, Twitter, and Instagram the phrase, "Go where the love is." Or you've seen me post, "Stay connected to people who feel like sunlight," or, one of my favorites, "You want friends who clap when you win." Or maybe you've seen me post a famous Oprah quote, "You can't be friends with someone who wants your life." What I am saying is, connect to people who like you and who are rooting for you to win, just as you need to do for them.

One of the things I talk about a lot, both in my books and in my national opinion columns, is "know your front row." My second book, *The Woman Code*, outlined a set of timeless values, virtues, and commonsense sisterly conduct that are important to how we develop into the person we want to be. "Know Your Front Row" is Code 17 and is the one that resonated the most with readers. Know your front row is simply another way of asking, "Who's in your inner circle?" Whom do you spend time with? What kinds of people do you have in your professional circles, in your relational circles, and in your personal and community circles? It matters a lot. You must answer that question, because whom you hang around, and whom you spend time with, dictates how many times in your life you're going to be subject to people who are petty, small minded, or who are just envious haters.

"Hater" is a label often used to refer to people who use negative or critical comments, or at worst, bad behavior, to bring down another person by making them feel bad, look bad, or by attacking their character. Haters are also good at gossip, at shaming, and defaming their targets. As my grandmother used to say, "Nobody trashes your name better than someone who's afraid you'll tell people the truth." Female haters usually operate in small, what I call "she-wolf packs"; they gang together and work to discredit their target behind their backs. Men are usually far more direct. Haters are usually people who have been simmering quietly about you in the shadows for some time. By attacking you, by bullying, or by gossiping about you to others who do not know you, they attempt to tear down your good character or reputation.

There are a lot of ways to define a hater, but we can put them into a couple of categories. First, haters often pick on people whom they perceive as being different from themselves. They focus on appearance—the person's weight, or their hair, or their looks in general. They might attack someone's intelligence, or where they grew up, or their accent, or their values and morals. Haters are narcissists. They have no empathy and never think about the impact of their words and their deeds on other people. Normal healthy people don't go out of their way to gossip about or tear down other people, and if they realize they've hurt somebody, they are very quick to apologize and try to make amends for hurting someone's feelings or for being unkind. Haters are energized by knowing they caused someone anguish.

Haters also tend to be bullies. Social media has created a breeding ground for this kind of behavior, with a marked uptick in online bullying, hate speech, unkind postings and the like. It's particularly problematic and damaging for teenagers. This new generation of Gen Y and Gen Z must deal with something that, fortunately, I didn't have to deal with as a child or even a teenager. Bullying wasn't allowed. It was dealt with swiftly by your teachers and by your parents, and you had to apologize if you were mean to somebody or unkind. That's likewise the case today, but schools and teachers are even more vigilant because of the dangerous and instantaneous online component that we did not have.

Keeping all of this in mind, when choosing with whom to spend your time—whether it be a friend, or a mentor, or a sponsor—you must choose wisely. So, here's what I've learned: choose people who choose you, those who ask how you are, who see you for who and what you are and the amazing gifts that you give the world. Choose people who let you be you, people who don't waste their time, or yours, trying to change you into a version of themselves. Choose people who feel good to your nervous system (as someone once said to me) and to your energy, because when people are in our space, as I said at the outset of this book, they put energy into that space, as we all do.

> **Choose people with whom you can let your hair down, and with whom you can breathe easily.**

Choose people with whom you can let your hair down, and with whom you can breathe easily, people with whom you are comfortable to speak freely. Choose people you do not have to perform for or pretend to be something or someone you are not. Choose people who are good for your mental health, for your spiritual health, and for your physical health. Choose people who want to see you win and, as I said earlier, clap for you when you do. Be on the lookout for one of the most characteristic traits of a hater: the wish to control you. Haters are controlling people who do not feel good about themselves on their own merits, and who can only acquire this feeling when they are attacking, belittling, or demeaning another person who is doing far better in life than they are.

What if one of these haters has made their way into your circle? How can you spot them? Pay attention to something as simple as who applauds your successes. Do you have that "friend," or, better, "frenemy," who congratulates you but simultaneously tempers their words with a little bit of shade? This person might say something like, "Congratulations on your promotion, Mr. Big Man!" Or, "That's a nice engagement ring, but I'd never wear something like that." Or,

"You lost a lot of weight. I bet you think you're hot stuff now!" In other words, there's always a nasty, unsupportive, unkind undertone in response to your accomplishments while everybody else in your circle and your front row is excited to see you doing so well, happy for and with you, throwing parties for you, or sending notes of congratulation. Be aware of the few who are never happy or supportive. You need to get them out of your row—quickly.

Just a note about social media. I have a personal Facebook page, which I reserve for family members, close friends, sorority sisters, and people I went to school with—in other words, people who know me, like me, and whom I like in return. As someone who is a public figure, I have less control over my public page, obviously. I look through it from time to time to see who's following me. And it's hilarious, because I find a lot of people following me whom I don't like, and who I know don't like me, but, boy, they sure are following my every thought, my every post, my every tweet. One of the things you'll find out about people who are haters is that they are desperate to see you fail. They talk about how much they don't like you, or how bad a person you are, while at the same time looking at everything you post and sharing those posts with others because they are obsessed with seeing you fail. We all have those people around us at our jobs, in our families, in our circles. And there's another type of hater I want to talk about that's much

**Choose people who choose you; those who ask how you are, who see you for who and what you are and the amazing gifts that you give the world. Choose people who let you be you, people who don't waste their time, or yours, trying to change you into a version of themselves.**

more dangerous. This person is actively trying to block you, ban you, disparage you, and hurt you. The question is, how do you deal with those people?

## How Do You Deal with a Hater (Online and in Life)?

Dealing with a hater can be tricky, but there is a strategy that you can employ that helps get these pesky people out of your life with very little risk to yourself or damage to your reputation or your livelihood.

There are two kinds of haters. Let me address them more clearly here. The first is the kind I deal with every day on social media as a public figure. Unfortunately, this type of hate has gone to a new level for many of us with high profiles. Since 2012, I've needed physical security at all my events and when I travel because I've received death threats. It is expensive and a personal burden to my freedom. However, on at least two occasions, having security likely saved me from physical harm at large public events, where the stalkers could track my whereabouts, go to the hotel, and confront me. I no longer advertise where I will be or share my location until after I have left and returned home safely.

So, let's get into it. Let's deal first with online hate and stalking, because they both fall into the category of people who do not like you and who want to cause you distress. You have several options with online haters: the first is, you can ignore it. Walk away. You don't have to respond, react, or engage with negative, unkind, or offensive comments. This is the easiest thing to do unless it persists. The second thing you can do, which is something I highly recommend, is use your block function and report the harassment, bullying, or stalking. Cyberbullying is a federal crime, something not everybody knows, and is covered by federal regulations. In addition, many states have separate regulations of their own. Another thing you can do, which may seem strange, is to just be kind and defuse the situation. A lot of times on social media, particularly around hot-button issues like politics, religion, race, and gender, people just want to be heard. So, try to lower the temperature by listening and trying to find a place where you can agree and then respectfully agree to disagree.

Now let's turn to dealing with the second kind of haters: those at our job, in our social circles, or, God forbid, in our church community. Step one, as I mentioned, is spotting them first. And, once you spot them, you must deal with how to confront them, have a courageous conversation with them, and perhaps decide to remove them from your life. A courageous conversation is one in which you are brave enough to talk from your heart and reveal your feelings in order to resolve conflict, and to be open to the other person's feelings as well. Remember what I said at the outset of this chapter—sometimes we must cut and burn the bridge, and other times we simply need to step back and understand that perhaps the friend or colleague is not a hater. It may instead be that they have some trouble in their lives and their hate is a cry for help. I have had friends who were close to me, who loved me, who would do anything for me. But, at some point, when they felt their lives were stalling, when they found themselves in a place they didn't want to be, and every time they turned around, I was winning an award, I was on television, I was writing a new book, I was traveling around the world, they became haters, looking at someone else's life and wishing that it was theirs.

If you choose the course of confronting someone you feel is a hater in your life, I strongly suggest that you take someone with you as a witness to the conversation. Having a friend nearby, if you think the confrontation could be difficult, is a wise choice. And often having a third person there who has both of your best interests at heart can be a helpful way to talk things out and resolve any conflicts.

This is a situation that does not call for texting. You need to muster up some courage and have a face-to-face conversation, no matter how difficult. Do it over a cup of coffee or a glass of wine. You might be surprised to discover that the negativity you've been getting from the person now sitting across from you has nothing to do with you, and everything to do with someone who is unhappy with themselves. Any shots they're taking at you is really a reflection on them, not you. People who feel good about themselves do not engage in gossip, they don't put other people down, they don't get on social media and engage in character assassinations and social media wars; they're too busy living their own best life. The person who is criticizing you might be in pain. Sometimes, people lash out because they have other life struggles, and they think your life looks like sunshine and happiness twenty-four hours a day. Of course, we all know that no one has a perfect life or is happy all the time. I don't care how rich you are, how big a celebrity you are, all of us have problems, all of us have struggles, and all of us need a village of good, positive people around us to help us get through.

> People who feel good about themselves do not engage in gossip, they don't put other people down, they don't get on social media and engage in character assassinations and social media wars; they're too busy living their own best life.

## How to Use Your Haters As Fuel for Success

As we close out this life lesson, I have two experiences I want to share with you that I think illustrate the point about how you can take the harm a hater tries to do to you and use it as fuel for your success. There is no greater revenge in life than success. You beat your enemies by coming out on top. Let them watch the doors they closed, or the gossip they spread, end up being used by you as a pathway to your joy, to your ingenuity, to your resilience, and to your standing on top of the heap of wannabes with a big smile on your face.

The first story I want to share is about someone I had never met and had no relationship with. It happened when I was invited to be a keynote speaker at an event celebrating Women's History Month in Seattle, Washington. It was sponsored by major companies, among them Boeing, Amazon, and Microsoft, and held downtown at the Bill and Melinda Gates Symphony Hall. I had just returned from Sydney, Australia, where I had been on a panel of women talking about the election of Donald Trump and what that meant to the lives of women in the United States, as well as women around the world. Although I knew I would be jetlagged from all the travel and the major time difference, I was super excited about this trip because it was my first visit to Seattle, and I had been wanting to get in front of the sponsoring companies for a long time as a speaker and to get my book *The Woman Code* into their corporate employee resource group and their women's groups. All was well when I arrived, and people were kind and wonderful to me. I was shown to the green room with some of the other speakers for the evening. As the keynote, I was the last speaker. As I was waiting to take the stage, I asked to speak with the woman I had been in touch with over many months about this engagement. I wanted to introduce myself and thank her and her team for all their assistance with logistics in making this happen, especially since I was coming directly from Australia.

When the woman (let's call her Jane)—who was an older White woman (in her sixties)—finally arrived in the green room, she had a scowl on her face. She didn't say, "So nice to meet you, Miss Nelson, welcome." She didn't even say hello! Not only did it take me aback, but it also stopped everyone in the room in their tracks. It got worse. Jane addressed me in a very disrespectful way in front of my mother, in front of a group of women I'd never met, and proceeded to advise me that I would need to cut my keynote and keep it short because she had some seven or eight speakers lined up before me. I was puzzled, and frankly a little shocked, so I waited for my contact, Sharon, to come into the room. And before I could say anything, she had already heard from some of the other speakers how disrespectfully I had been treated by Jane. I'd given literally hundreds of keynotes over the years, and I had never been treated with anything other than respect, graciousness, and hospitality by my hosts. The keynote is the featured speaker, so Jane's behavior made no sense on any level. Along with insulting me, she made other people feel uncomfortable, and I couldn't for the life of me figure out why.

I called my publicist, Monica, and told her what was happening. She said, "Telling you to cut or abridge your keynote is a violation of your contract. Pack up your things and go."

I replied, "No. I'm not going to do that. I'll never give her that kind of satisfaction, and I don't want to let the audience down, or the amazing ladies who helped to get me here. I'll just suck it up and we'll move on. I'll get through this."

As my turn to speak came up, I stood on the side of the stage waiting for Katie Perry's "Roar" to start, which was my cue to come to the podium. I overheard Jane and her colleague, "Allison," talking. Allison told Jane that she really owed me an apology, and that her behavior toward me had been inappropriate. Jane said, "No, she needs a comeuppance. I've googled her. She's a diva. She thinks she's all that."

Remember how I told you to watch out for those people who say *you think you're all that?* In reality, *they* think you're all that, and they resent it because they think they should be where you are. I found out later that apparently Jane was angry about how much I had been paid, that she thought my honorarium was too much and that it was inappropriate. (For the record, I gave them a 50 percent discount off my Speaker's Bureau rate because my friend Sharon wanted me to come.)

At the end of the program, after two standing ovations and the event trending on Twitter, Jane came up to me with a sheepish look on her face and said how amazing I was and that she had just had a bad day, but she hoped that we could go to the reception together and have a great time. Even though I was exhausted, I wasn't going to miss the reception. The representatives from all the corporate sponsors were going to be there, and I absolutely wanted to exchange business cards with them so that I could have my team follow up once I got back home to Virginia. Even before I could get out my business cards, the Microsoft representative approached me and said, "We loved you, and we want you to come and talk to all our women. And we want to buy copies of *The Woman Code*, so please contact me." And guess what? It turns out that her best friend was the infamous Jane.

Once the event was over, it got back to me that Jane tried to blackball me by telling people at every single company that sponsored the event not to hire me. Reflecting back again on the wise words my grandmother once told me, "Nobody trashes your name better than someone who's afraid you'll tell people the truth," I knew that this situation was the living embodiment of her words. I was mad. And I was going to put this lady on blast on social media because I felt her conduct was racist, and that she was just completely out of line. She never would have treated a prominent White woman in such a manner—ever. A few powerful women who were there that night reached out to me when they had heard what Jane was doing, and they were appalled.

So, here's what I did. I called a mentor of mine who was a former Fortune 50 executive in the tech sector who had recently retired. I knew that she would know the players, including this woman. I told her what had happened. She listened, then she said, "Sophia, you have a big platform. You can put this woman on blast. She's got a reputation that precedes her, and everyone will believe what you say because this is what she does to people. She's just not a nice person. Or, we can go around her." She offered to call one of the senior vice presidents at Microsoft and connect us for a meeting in Washington, DC.

I chose the latter course, and the rest is history. I was able to do business with Microsoft, speaking at their big East Coast women's event in 2019, and I have made some of the best connections and friends one could possibly have. Here's the moral of the story: I didn't let that woman's insecurity, anger, or jealousy stop me. I went around her, and I did it successfully. She would have to see my face on a big flier and see all the emails going back and forth about how I was going to be doing this and that with one of the world's truly great companies. I won. She lost by being petty, and everyone around gave me kudos for how I took the high road when she went low.

The next story is more personal, and I shared it exhaustively in Code 9 of *The Woman Code*. I had befriended someone at a ladies' retreat overseas, a woman who happened to be one of my Alpha Kappa Alpha sorority sisters. She was also a woman in ministry. Married, a mother, a very smart, very attractive, very accomplished woman—just the type of positive person you want to be around. I truly looked up to her as a role model at the time, as I was dating seriously and hoping to be married myself. We became quick and fast sister friends. We talked all the time and bonded even though she lived on the West Coast and I live on the East Coast. What I didn't know was that this woman was already speaking ill of me to others and telling people she was friends with me only because I was well connected, and she thought that would help her get a publishing contract and get on television and major media.

As you can imagine, when people have those kinds of motives the friendship will fail, and it will fail quickly. Without getting into all the gory details, everything came to a head, and the friendship blew up. And instead of just being respectful, walking away, and moving on, this woman engaged in a full-fledged, open, hostile, vicious character-assassination campaign against me, the likes of which I've never seen before in my life. And I've been in law and politics since I was a teenager.

Not only did she engage in a public character assassination, but she also enlisted many other women (some of them my sorority sisters) who had never met me. She even tried to attack me to Bishop T. D. Jakes and other powerful ministry leaders who were having me speak on their major platforms. As it turned out, although she was a minister, no one was inviting her anywhere to do anything. That really made her angry. So, she struck like a cobra, telling people we stopped being friends not because of her conduct, but because I was "in love with her," and that I "wanted her." The people who knew the facts of what actually happened (an argument over some books), really came through and pushed back on her vile narrative. Thank God my reputation precedes me, and a lot of good people not only stuck up for me, but they told her to shut her mouth and leave me alone because it was her, not me, who was going to come out of this looking bad.

Things got so terrible that I hired my old law firm to send her a formal cease-and-desist letter. It was truly an ugly experience, and to this day I can't tell you why it happened. We haven't spoken a word to each other since 2012. I took this awful, hurtful, truly stunning experience and turned it into an example in *The Woman Code* to help other people understand that there is never harmless gossip, that it can destroy lives.

In both these cases, I ran across petty, small-minded women who found themselves at midlife and were not happy with where they were. These were women who thought, *Who the hell does she think she is?* One of them texted a dear friend of mine, "Well, if she can do it, I can certainly do it." They want what you have. They want the glory—but without doing any of the work you put in or experiencing any of the sacrifices or hardships. That's a hater for you. A hater is always going to take the shortcut. They don't want to do the work and they hate that you have and that you are reaping the benefits and rewards.

As I said at the outset of this lesson, haters have always been. Haters will always be. If you can hold on to that truth, then you'll be successful at everything you do because you won't take it personally. Because haters hating on you is never personal. It's always about them wishing they were you.

> *"Learn to use the criticism as fuel*
> *and you will never run out of energy."*
>
> **—Orrin Woodward**

# LESSON 8

## Control Your Anger
## Before It Controls You

*"If you are patient in one moment of anger,
you will escape one hundred days of sorrow."*

—Chinese Proverb

## *Your Ability to Exercise Self-Control*

My grandmother had many words of wisdom to share with me. She used to say, "Anger is one letter away from the word danger." Controlling our anger is important but difficult, and let me confess at the outset that I haven't completely figured this one out either. However, having lived for over five decades, I do know something about how to spot my anger and manage it before it erupts into an uncontrolled fire that I can't put out. Painful experience has taught me that when I let my anger get the best of me, or when I let my anger lead the conversation, or when I let my past anger and resentment take over the present, I am not only setting myself up for failure, but I'm going to end up doing great damage to people I love and care about.

Anger is one of those tricky emotions: at times we need to express it, and at others we need to hold back from expressing it. What a contradiction, right? How can it be that, in one instance, I need to get my anger out, to let people know how I'm feeling, to tell them that something they've said or done has hurt me, has caused outrage in me, and that I need to let them know it before that anger boils over. But then there are times when my anger needs to quiet itself, to settle down so that I can sit with it and then later express it when I am not upset, emotional, or in a state of outrage.

Unfortunately, we live in a rage-a-holic culture. Gun violence is worse than ever (for the record, I am a gun owner and Second Amendment proponent). Domestic violence is through the roof. Our first instinct is to curse one another and cancel one another and berate one another rather than talk. We are an angry lot in the twenty-first century. The goal of this lesson is to see what tools we can put in our

EIQ toolkit to deal with anger, to manage it effectively, and to try to operate from a spirit of collegiality and respect.

I want to touch on three points in this life lesson: **First,** discerning the difference between being angry and feeling something else that we haven't dealt with. **Second,** facing your anger so that you can fix it. And **third,** managing our anger effectively.

## Is It Anger or Something Else?

Just like any other emotion, anger is normal. I really want to underscore that anger is a necessary, healthy human emotion. When we are angry, it's our body's way of telling us that there is either pain or danger ahead, whether that danger is emotional or physical. When we become angry, it is our emotional response alerting us that something is not right, that someone has violated a boundary, that someone or something has triggered something in us that we must let out.

I said earlier that we are clearly addicted to anger, to rage, and to some very unhealthy ways of interacting with one another. But I want to emphasize that you are allowed to be angry. All of us have felt anger, whether as a passing annoyance with our children or spouse, at the office, or in our social circles. That is normal, everyday, human being stuff. All of that is okay. Annoyance is not anger. Upset is not anger. Hurt is not anger. Disappointment is not anger. But left unaddressed, all those emotions can lead to anger.

What we must keep an eye out for is what lurks deeper. That darker anger that has been sitting below the surface

> *"Anybody can become angry—that is easy; but to be angry with the right person, and to the right degree, and at the right time, and for the right purpose, and in the right way—that is not within everybody's power and is not easy."*
> —**Aristotle**

like a Titanic-sized iceberg, where you can only see the tip, and not that dangerous block of ice lurking beneath. If you run headlong into that, it will ruin you and everyone around you. If you find yourself frequently fighting, screaming at people, throwing things, engaging in full-fledged yelling matches, then you need to stop and tap into what is really bothering you. Someone who is angry all the time has something deeper bothering them.

Your body is hardwired like a complex computer, with wires, motherboards, plugs, ports, and modems constantly at work. When your computer is about to crash, you usually get some early warning signs. It is slower to boot up. It takes forever for websites to load. Finally, it crashes. When we let anger sit, it simmers. And little by little it starts to cause small but noticeable malfunctions in our day-to-day lives—until we crash. Don't ever let your anger sit so long, unattended, that it takes control of you.

We've all been stuck in traffic when we need to get somewhere. We've been frustrated at work. We've had to deal with bullies. We all have triggers. There will be few days in your life that you will not find someone or something that makes you what I call "situationally angry." Situational anger is different than allowing anger to be an everyday part of your life. Situational anger is a response to a specific situation in life.

We control anger by first understanding that anger starts in the human brain, not in the heart. Our brains generate thoughts, and our thoughts control what we say, what we do, and how we react. The brain is at the core of all we do. I'm not going to get all nerdy and wonky on you here. What I am going to do, though, is refer back again to an amazing book, *What Happened to You? Conversations on Trauma, Resilience, and Healing* by Oprah Winfrey and Bruce

D. Perry. I learned so much from that book about how the brain controls everything about my life—and yours: How I receive things. How I understand things. What I remember. How my emotions are expressed. Which traumas stick with me and which ones I have buried so deep I don't remember them. You can control your emotions, as I explained in Lesson 2. And the good news is that you can control your anger once you learn to spot it.

Anger comes from a variety of sources. Here are a few common triggers:

- Personal problems in your relationships with your spouse, your family, or with your children.

- Physical health limitations, whether chronic or short term.

- Emotional stress that you don't know how to talk about.

- Financial stress or mounting bills you cannot pay.

- Unresolved conflicts.

- Grieving a loss or being in mourning.

If you know the source of your anger—for example, grief masquerading as anger—you know you need to get some help or use your EIQ toolkit to work on it yourself. The hardest part is always understanding what you are feeling, as we covered in Lesson 2. The next step is what to do about it once you know what's really bothering you.

## Facing It So You Can Fix It

There's a great line in the movie *Brokeback Mountain,* where the main character played by Heath Ledger tells the other

> *"It is wise to direct your anger towards problems—not people; to focus your energies on answers—not excuses."*
>
> —**William Arthur Ward**

man he is involved with, "If you can't change it, you gotta stand it." Most people live their lives right there, in that epic line. We stay in what we cannot stand because we do not see a way out, a way to change things. And we die a thousand quiet deaths from feeling stuck. You just keep living a helpless life until you die.

But instead, flip that perspective of life on its head and say to yourself: "You have to face it before you can fix it." When you know what hurts, or what is wrong, or what you need, you are empowered to change your circumstances. You can change your destiny. I know this. I have done it a few times.

So, how do we face something and fix it? We do this by finding a way to work through it, or to work around it, or to get beyond it, because we know that not all things can be fixed; some things just are. My best advice, based on decades of experience trying to address those things that I am truly angry about, is to do the work. Get ahold of your emotions or they will take hold of you. I used to spend my time trying to figure out why I was angry, snapping at people, being short-tempered, being grumpy, and generally not nice. But I was looking only at the surface when what was really bothering me was beneath it.

One of the things that I struggled with for years is that on the surface I seemed to be a successful, happy, healthy woman. But what I didn't realize, what I didn't own until it got so bad I had to get psychological help, was that I had been carrying deep grief for two events that had happened early in my life that I hadn't talked about with anybody. I didn't want to face what had happened, because I knew that if I faced it, that if I ever spoke the words out loud, that I would have to deal with it. This is where most of us get stuck. We know that we need to deal with it. We know what it is that's bothering us. But we know that if we own it, if we lean into it, we're going to have to be accountable for it. And most people just don't want to do that level of work. And it's hard work, which requires daily vigilance. And for those of us to who are in older generations, we've been trained to just get on with it, to suck it up, thinking that eventually things will work themselves out. That is wrong. That is unhealthy thinking. And it's a good formula for a life of misery.

You must love yourself enough to get what you need to heal what has hurt you. Anger comes from trauma. Anger comes from neglect. Anger comes from not taking care of your soul landscape. Here are some steps I would recommend you take to work on facing your anger issues, or more importantly, the *underlying cause of your anger:*

- **Know your triggers.** This is huge to facing and alleviating angry encounters or outbursts.

- **Know when to ask for support or help.** Sometimes, fixing or working through things requires help from others we love, trust, or who are professionals.

- **Know when to speak and when to walk away.** I have gotten into a great deal of trouble in my life by not always knowing when to walk away.

## How to Manage Your Anger Effectively

As we wrap us this lesson, let's talk about how you manage your anger effectively. **First**, you must know what anger is. **Second,** you must know how to spot it. **Third,** you must understand that anger is just what's on the surface, and that there's something much deeper that you must

*"Anger is just anger. It isn't good. It isn't bad. It just is. What you do with it is what matters. It's like anything else. You can use it to build or to destroy. You just have to make the choice."*
—**Jim Butcher**

face so you can fix it. When you're able to do those three things, you are ready to fix or manage your anger issues. Remember what I said earlier, though: some anger is normal, everyday irritation. The key is to learn the difference between the two. When we're talking about managing our anger effectively, what we're really talking about is emotional intelligence. Yes, anger is normal; it's something every human being feels. Taking your anger out on others, however, is not normal and not healthy. You must know the difference.

One of the best books I have ever read was by Dr. Don Colbert, *Deadly Emotions: Understand the Mind, Body, Spirit Connection That Can Heal or Destroy You.* In this book, Dr. Colbert takes us through how our emotions and our physical wellness are intricately linked. For example, we carry around anger for years, we don't talk about it, or maybe we don't even recognize that we are angry. In response, the body overproduces a hormone called epinephrine, which causes us to be in fight-or-flight syndrome all the time, which wears down the body's systems. The next thing you know, you have a heart attack, or you get some fatal disease. Dr. Colbert's main focus in the book is on people dealing with deadly emotions stemming from trauma; for instance, people who've been sexually abused or are victims of domestic violence. He offers techniques they can use to face their emotions so they can fix them, and then manage them so their health is not negatively impacted.

Below are some steps I've taken in my own life, as well as those I've compiled in my journal over the years from counseling, from life coaches, and other resources. I know they will help you to manage anger more effectively, even your basic situational anger, and to get control of your life. But before I get into these steps, let me say this, because it's very important: another way of saying I'm angry is saying I've lost control. Let that sink in for a moment. We get upset and we get angry when we feel we've lost control of the narrative, of our emotions. All of us must exert some kind of control over our day-to-day lives or our lives will be in chaos. We will live in anarchy. We must wake up a certain time, we must go to work a certain time, we have to come home and fix dinner, or make sure that the kids are cared for, or check in on our aging parents. We must have an order and a structure to our lives.

Here are six steps to help you get control of your life. If you follow them, they will really help you to feel less out of control, and you will feel more powerful in ways that are constructive, productive, and more emotionally healthy.

1. **Think before you speak.** As Mark Twain said, "When angry, count to four, when very angry swear."

2. **Express your anger—once you have calmed down.** You must get it out. Don't go to bed angry, as my nana used to say. And don't hold grudges. Say what you need to say.

3. **Exercise regularly.** It's a natural dopamine high for your body. It calms the systems, and it calms the soul.

4. **Use humor to get through.** I look at funny TikTok prankster videos or some funny memes each day and just laugh out loud. When I feel upset or angry, I find something to laugh about.

5. **Have a good therapist or life coach.** If cost is an issue, use a meditation app, or one of the online mental-health resources that are free or little to no money.

6. **Learn how to defuse conflict** by not attacking someone, but instead using what my therapist calls "I statements." Instead of saying, "You did this, or you did that," which is confrontational, say, "I feel this way when X happens," or, "I feel bad when X happens."

*"For every minute you are angry,
you lose sixty seconds of happiness."*

—Ralph Waldo Emerson

# LESSON 9

## Get Out of Your Own Way

*"Emotions are built on layers. Beneath hatred is usually anger; beneath anger is frustration; beneath frustration is hurt; beneath hurt is fear. If you keep expressing your feelings, you will generally move through them in that order. What begins with "I hate you" culminates in "I'm scared. I don't want to lose you, and I don't know what to do about it."*

—Mark Goulston, *Get Out of Your Own Way*

## *You Against You*

**W**here to start with this life lesson . . . First, what does it mean to get in your own way? I mean, it's something of an oxymoron, right? How does one get in his or her own way? Well, it happens more than we are often aware. Getting in your own way is simply sabotaging your own success, or sabotaging your desires, or not being open to wise counsel when it is offered by someone who means you well. Or worse, being someone that must have it your way or it's no way at all. All these things are what I like to call self-microaggressions. We often talk about the behavior of others and how their behavior impacts our lives positively or negatively, but what about your style? How do you lead? How do you connect with others? How do you resolve conflict?

This is one of the most important life lessons I can possibly teach you. I had to learn it myself too many times, and often with great regret. The key to not getting in your own way is simple: you surround yourself with honest brokers, people who care about you and your success and who will correct you when you go in the wrong direction. Successful people know how and when to take a hard look at their own leadership styles, at their own communication styles, at their own engagement with other human beings and then adjust as needed. Successful people also do not shrink away from doing the work of understanding what character traits they may have that can be too aggressive, or even offensive, to other people. Looking in a mirror is never easy, but it is required. Getting out of your own way requires honesty, humility, and lots of self-reflection. You must be willing to consider not just what draws people to you but what may also repel them from you.

Life is a wonderful adventure if you can first master yourself. People will do what people do. And life will throw you curveballs, but at the end of the day your toughest critic is you. You against you. You in control of you. You learning how to manage yourself effectively. You being open to being "coachable" about your behavior when it does not line up with your values and character. And most of all, learning that you are responsible for what you say, what you do, what you think, and what you put out into the universe.

Let's face it, we live in a culture now that really likes to place the blame on others. And if we're all honest, we all know that this is destroying not only our civil society, but our civil order, and it's having a real impact on our families and our relationships one with another. As I mentioned at the outset of this book, there comes a point where we must be accountable for self. And that is what this life lesson is all about. We need to have the emotional intelligence that we learned about in Lesson 6 so that we have good self-awareness radar that helps us to not do damage to ourselves.

> **Life is a wonderful adventure if you can first master yourself.**

In this life lesson, I want to cover three quick tools to help you better navigate yourself. Who you are, what you want, how you feel, where you are strong, and where you need work. Once again, these are great tools for your EIQ toolkit that we discussed in Lesson 6. They are:

1. Seeing the blind spots.

2. Building a great circle.

3. Being coachable and using soft power.

Another way people get in their own way is through self-sabotage. People do this for many reasons. I'm not a therapist or psychologist, so I'm not trying to analyze anyone. What I do know, however, is that when we are not whole, when we have not done the work on ourselves, and if we have not faced our own traumas, we are going to be self-destructive. What life experience has taught me is that most self-defeating, self-destructive behaviors come from fear or feeling that we are just not quite good enough. It doesn't matter what degrees we possess; it doesn't matter what titles we may hold; it all goes back to what we learned in the beginning of this book. How we feel about ourselves and our initial view of the world based on our experience with our families and how we were raised is something we carry with us for the rest of our days. We are in a constant battle, most of the times silent (just me against me and you against you), and we wrestle with our demons, and we try to overcome them the best that we can. The key to staying out of our own way is to spot those demons and put them down for good.

I think, if we are honest, we all indulge in self-destructive behavior. We're aware of it most of the time, but what we do is we make excuses for ourselves, and we blame it on other things, or other people, or we say that it's somebody else's fault. That is not the person that you want to be. Be a better person. Be someone who faces your internal challenges. Be someone who dares to break the bad habits that most people just succumb to over time and learn to live with for better or worse. Successful people have certain traits (as I mentioned in the emotional intelligence life lesson) that are a common thread for people who are leaders in industry, who are trailblazers, who are inventors, and who are the movers and shakers in our society. That common thread is they have great EIQ. They know well how to self-evaluate, and they know how to get out of their own way. They are not afraid to be vulnerable, to ask for help, or to do something different to get what they want and where they want to be in life.

Self-destructive behavior has different levels. The first level is often the small things that we do in life that really don't help us, but they don't hurt us either. However, they can impact others around us in negative ways. For example, I am a checklist, routine kind of girl. I like order. I like structure. I like to tick things off my "to do" list. And I do not do well with people in my space who are disorderly and disorganized. That's me being rigid. That's me being stuck in some old ways that make me feel comfortable and in control. It works for me. But I know it turns others close to me off. So, I have learned to modify my behavior to be more flexible and accommodating

And then there are the big self-destructive behaviors like addictions: alcohol abuse, drug abuse, sex or porn addictions, dishonesty, not keeping your word, never finishing what you start, poor financial management, and on and on. These types of behaviors really do lasting damage to our lives. And to the lives of those we marry, our children, our parents, and those who love us. If you are not in control of yourself as an adult and you don't know how to make good choices, you will find that you have many tough days ahead. This lesson is designed to help you get and stay out of your own way by identifying the things you need to do to keep moving forward in life in a positive direction.

## Seeing the Blind Spots

How do you see a blind spot? How do you see something that is not readily visible? In theory, you cannot. But with practice, you can. Let me explain. From a physical standpoint, our eyes have a blind spot within the back of the retina. That blind spot is permanent. However, when we're talking about our lives, we have blind spots that do not have to be permanent. Blind spots refer to our lack of awareness of the things that we're doing in our life that are not healthy or productive for our life, or worse. those connected to us. The goal is to have a growing and deeper awareness every day of those things we need to develop that help us uncover the blind spots in our lives. It's simple: it's called self-mastery. Specifically, it is mastery of those things in your life that are not helpful and that are likely holding you back from greater success, greater love, greater connection, and greater fulfillment.

Here's the thing you must remember: it's virtually impossible to achieve change in our lives without first having clarity on where those changes need to be made. Put another way, you can't spot your blind spot unless you discover what it is that you can't see. I know this sounds confusing, but stick with me for a moment, because it really isn't. What's most important here is that you must have a process. I've talked to you about process a lot in this book, because from the first life lesson of this book to the very last one that you will read, everything we do about being the one that we need to be is about the process of self-discovery, the process of growth, the process of putting away old things, and the process of healing from trauma. Once you do all of those things your blind spots become glaringly obvious.

Here are a few quick things you can do to help you better navigate the blind spots in your life. Take a professional assessment test like Myers-Briggs Type Indicator, Gallup's Clifton Strengths Online Talent Assessment, or the VIA Character Strengths. These tools explore your strengths and help you maximize your potential. There is also one other tool that a good friend of mine does that I introduced you to in the first section of this book called Essential Colors. It really helps you to tap into your emotional side. How you think. How you lead. How you love. How you give.

I mentioned the word "clarity," and having clarity requires us to do an assessment. I mentioned at the outset of this book that we all need to write a life mission statement. The purpose is to help you break your life into a wheel, or think pie wedge, if you will, with all the parts of your life. So, for example, your wheel might contain relationships, career, finances, family, goals, hobbies, and most certainly health, which encompasses physical, mental, and emotional health. When you break your life down into these categories, it forces you to look at each area of your life and to decide whether you are thriving in those areas or if you are stagnant. Most of the time, when we are getting in our own way, it is because we either feel that we're not worth it, that we can't do it, or because, somehow, we are afraid of it. Fear is a very big part of why we self-sabotage and self-destruct. Even people who appear on the surface to be wildly successful have big blind spots in their lives.

When you lay out your "life wheel" on paper (remember to write it down), however, it allows you to see the bigger picture. This exercise requires honesty—not fear, not resistance, just honesty and hard truth. You must do some reflecting on the things that bring you happiness, and joy, and those that do not. Give yourself a rating from one to ten. For me, my biggest area of struggle right now, where I keep getting into my own way, is in my emotional health. Meaning, I am exhausted because I have so much going on in my life that it is hard to enjoy it. This turns into frustration, because I am not free to do the things I want to do at this season of my life. And that frustration builds into a lack of focus and being short-tempered with my loved ones and it goes downhill from there. My blind spot, a big one in my life, is that I have not yet mastered "personal time" to a degree that it keeps me emotionally, mentally, and physically well. Many of us Type A personalities live this way 24/7. I penned this book because I no longer want to live that way, and I don't want you to ever start living that way.

I became aware of this glaring blind spot in my life a few years ago. And even more so as the pandemic hit, and we all found ourselves being locked inside with a lot of time to sit with ourselves, with our families, our neighbors, and in our communities as we became dependent on one another. The way that I was able to face this big hole in my life was that I had to go back to that life mission statement that I had written so many years ago. I had to dust it off, make some adjustments to it, update it, and then get the clarity I needed around my life. To make the shift to a healthier emotional space, I had to own that I was in my way—not other people or things. I had made a choice to stay exhausted, overwhelmed, and stuck in a bad life cycle of work, always bailing others out. I am still a work in progress, and this book has been very cathartic for me in that process, but I uncovered the blind spot of poor self-care, and now I'm working to fix it in my life every day.

> *"This magical universe is so faithful in waiting for us to get out of our own way. No matter how long you have gone astray, when you take action, the universe moves to support the act. Move in the direction of your goals and watch the magic flow."*
>
> —Steve Maraboli

## Building a Great Circle

One of my mentors used to say, "Stay away from 'yes people.' Yes people will lead you to the water and let you drown." She was

100 percent spot on. A big part of getting out of your own way is to assemble an array of successful, loving, kind, honest, focused, deliberate, unflinching truthtellers in your life. All good leaders—indeed, all successful humans—surround themselves with people who help them to not only see their blind spots but to navigate through them.

You can build up a strong row of supporters and mentors, sponsors and coaches, but first you must be open to help and willing to ask for it. And you must invest in personal and professional relationships. If you do not invest in people, they cannot invest in you. In other words, you must do the work to let people get to know you; to let people earn your trust and likewise you earn theirs. When you do this, you create what I call your "front row." The front row is composed of the people who sit at the very front of your life. These are the people that you must empower to not just be there to celebrate you, or to clap when you win, or to be cheerleaders in your life. Yes, of course, you need that, too, but these people must be empowered to check you before you wreck you. The people in my front row have my permission to set me straight when one of my blind spots has rendered me dumb, ridiculous, out of control, or on a dangerous path to self-destruction.

I have shared many stories already throughout this book of the guiding principles of my life: faith, loyalty, hard work, empathy, mentorship, kindness, and love. What you need to ask yourself as you seek to build a great front row is: What are my values? What is my life code? Because like attracts like. What you give out is what you get back. I have so many people approach me after presentations and ask, "How did you do it? How did you get such amazing men and women in your front row?" My response is simple: I was not afraid to ask people to mentor me professionally. I am great at taking advice. I believe in being "coachable." And, most importantly, I model what I want to receive in my life. I am very intentional about that.

You will not be successful at attracting the right kinds of relationships if you are selfish and unwilling to do the work. Relationships are hard and often complex. And they must be nurtured. I was a big note writer and card sender in my college and graduate school years. Former President George H. W. Bush was the person who told me, in 1992, to start a Christmas card list. He told me about the power of the pen (remember this is in a pre-Internet world, however I still encourage my students and others to write thank you notes and mail them, the old-fashioned way). I listened, and a Christmas card list that started with 25 people in 1992 is now over 1,100 in 2021.

Here's my point: you need to have a process to avoid getting stuck in your life blind spots and, as a result, getting continuously in your own way. I have a checklist, or, better said, a "row checklist" that will help you get what you need, and who you need in your circle, and is another great addition to your EIQ toolkit. Remember, all good things take time. There is no magic bullet to anything in life. You must do the work. It starts now. Copy what follows and put it on a wall, a corkboard in your dorm room, or in your workspace—somewhere prominent that you will see every day—and then work at it every day. I promise you, the blessings will be enormous.

1. **You attract what you are.** If you have some unfocused, unkind, uncaring people surrounding you, you need to do a self-check. All the successful people I know have good people around them because they are good people, too. You must prune your row from time to time, just as you do the trees in your yard. You cannot grow unless you are you are willing to cut away dead branches and dead weight that no longer blossoms in your life.

2. **Do not engage in pettiness or gossip.** If you are sitting at a table with people who tear down others, understand that you will be next on the menu when you get up from that table. Gossip is a cancer of the soul. Haters will always speak hate when they envy successful people. Do not eat at their table or drink their poison. Connect your life to good people, who speak well of others, and who are too busy to engage in petty gossip and meanness.

3. **Find and cultivate new social circles.** That means you must get connected to people who share your life outlook and values. Sometimes it is easy to get stuck. Venture out to meet people who have similar interests. Maybe they like to cook, as you do, or travel, or ski, or sample wine, or read and discuss interesting books. You will make some of your best connections simply doing what you love. Don't let work or school be the only way you make friends.

> *"A life of growth means a life of exhilarating discomfort."*
>
> —**Dave Hollis**

4. **Check their energy.** I've said this before, and I am going to keep saying it. Check their energy and then check how it impacts your energy.

This may all seem hard or uncomfortable—but it isn't. You just must do the work required as outlined by the above checklist tips. We talked earlier about that old monster called "fear." Fear is what keeps us stuck. Fear is one of the big underlying causes of why we get in our own way time and time again.

Let me close out this life lesson by saying that you can do this. You can decide right here and right now to stop self-sabotaging your life and your relationships. Get rid of stubbornness. Get rid of arrogance and embrace that much better quality, humility. Accept that you will make mistakes and missteps. You are human, and all humans make mistakes. The key to this life lesson is seeing what you do not see about yourself by putting in some guardrails. By that, I mean: good friends who will help you; good personal and mental-health habits that keep you on track; and a mindset of excellence that makes you want to be all that you can. Stop limping through life because you don't have the faith in yourself that you can change and be better. You can. It starts with spotting and removing those blind spots.

## Being Coachable

*Being coachable* is a phrase that I learned from one of my best friends, who is a therapist. She taught me this phrase probably about a decade or so ago, and I remember it stopping me dead in my tracks. I thought to myself, *Be coachable. Man, that's good!*

Think of it like this: every sports team has a coach, right? If you've ever played organized sports in grade school or high school or college you've had a coach, maybe even a team of coaches. Their job was to help you to bring out all your talents, all your strengths, and help you to develop leadership skills, team player skills, and to help you move on to achieve great things on and off the playing field.

Successful people are coachable. I touched on this a little bit in the previous section when I was talking about developing a strong circle of people in your life. But this is a little different, because there are many ways that we can learn to be better. The question is, will we? When I say be coachable here's what I mean specifically. Let's say that a woman named Anna is having challenges in her romantic relationship. She and her significant other are at an impasse, and have stopped being able to communicate effectively or even talk to one another civilly. But she has these great friends who have known her and her partner for most of their lives and who really want to see them succeed in this relationship. The friend comes to Anna and says, "You know, Anna, you have a really bad stubborn streak. If you would just put aside your pride, listen a little bit better—really listen to hear and not to just cue up your response—you would have a much healthier, happier, and fulfilling relationship."

Now stop for a moment. This is where the rubber meets the road. Anna has two choices when someone in her row, that she trusts implicitly, approaches her and says, "Here's something you need to work on." The first choice is to ignore the advice and tell the person that she doesn't know what she's talking about, or worse, place the blame on her significant other and take no responsibility. Unfortunately, many people do this without really thinking it through. The second choice is for Anna to humble herself, take in the advice, sit with it for a while, pray about it, and then come to the correct decision—which is that she needs to work on her pride and that her stubbornness is going to be her undoing. In the moment, she needs to choose to be more vulnerable and open with her partner and hearing their heart and responding to what they need.

That is being coachable. It means you take good counsel and follow through on it for a positive outcome, or you take a positive step in a better direction of your life. In a nutshell, being coachable boils down to these two important points:

- You actually listen to wise counsel when it is offered, you weigh it, you trust the source who offered the counsel, and you move forward wiser.

- You invest in yourself by hiring a life coach, attending seminars, or explore other leadership tools that help you to grow or change.

## Using Your Soft Power Skills

**Successful people are coachable.** Your personality should not be a hammer. Being "tough" in the sense that you are abrasive and combative is as ineffective as it is unhealthy. Soft skills are far more impactful. We use them when we want to persuade people to follow us, work with us, or hear us. They are skills like empathy, kindness, touch, connection, and shared experiences.

When we talk about soft power, I am talking not just to women here—men, listen up. The word *soft* has no gender connotations or otherwise. It is an EIQ word—soft is the opposite of hard. It means you still have power, but you utilize it in a way that is situational. Part of what gets most people in trouble is that they do not know how to handle other people at work or in life with soft skills. They perpetually get in their own way because they have huge blind spots that have everything to do with their lack of soft emotional intelligence. You develop soft skills by doing the following:

- Being open to feedback.

- Communicating with those close to you regularly and authentically.

- Emphasizing teamwork on the job and at home.

- Doing the work of investing in building positive relationships.

- Stepping outside of your comfort zone.

- Being open to learn new things and engage new people.

- Adapting to workplace and life changes.

And you deploy these skills when you can tell that someone is in need, in trouble, or when they just want human guidance and care. Soft skills are the superglue of life. A major problem that threatens to unravel our society is that it seems everyone is angry about something and digging in without seeing any point of view other than their own. People yell at one another. They often make unrealistic demands without giving an inch themselves. They push, and punish, and if they feel especially aggrieved, they campaign to "cancel" people out of their livelihood. That is not only breaking apart our society, it is breaking our souls. It can only be changed when we find the courage to change and get out of our own way.

"*Those who are comfortable taking chances know that the best way to grow is to reach beyond their grasp. Their sense of direction comes from the heart. They don't shy away from surprise; they might even seek it out. And they seldom die with regrets. In the end we regret not what we have done but what we have not done.*"

—Mark Goulston, *Get Out of Your Own Way*

# LESSON 10

## Do No Harm, Take No Shit

*"How many more of us are faking the facade? How many more of us are pretending to be something we're not? Even better, how many of us will have the courage to be ourselves regardless of what others think?"*

—Katie McGarry, *Dare You To*

## *Your Self-Respect and Worth*

I know the title of this life lesson may make some of you bristle. Please don't. It's just me being me—authentically me. And it's one of my favorite sayings on my T-shirts and coffee mugs. If I'm being honest, I'll tell you that it's my new life mantra in my fifties.

When you have lived more than a half-century, everything begins to change around you. And, more importantly, in you. If you are living as an evolving, growing human being, you understand and you respect that there is a very distinct rhythm to living: we are born, we grow up, we go to school, we become adults, we continue school or we earn a living (or both), we couple, we travel, we explore, we settle, we start families of our own, we become part of a community. We live, we love, and eventually we die. It's the same for us all. No matter where we grow up, no matter what our socioeconomic status is, no matter what our family looks like, or even what color or gender we are, life goes pretty much according to that basic script.

The good news is that each of us gets to decide what part we play in the script of our lives. We get to make some choices. Some good and some not so good. We get to play various roles. Sometimes the villain. Sometimes the victim. But the ultimate goal must be to be the victor—to win, to finish strong—to leave things and people better than we found them. As I have aged and gone through so much loss and profound disappointment in my life, I have learned what truly matters and what does not. One of the things that truly does matter is how we treat other people and how we allow them to treat us. Because, at the end of the day, all we leave is the love we gave to others, and what we take with us is the love they gave to us in return. Hence the words: *I will do no harm, but I will take no shit.*

In this life lesson, I want to take you through a few truths I have learned in the hope that you will grasp three critical takeaways:

1. Protect your personal peace at all costs.

2. Respect other people's peace and humanity.

3. Never let people get comfortable disrespecting you—ever.

If you can embrace these three, you will do well. You will make great friends. You will find great loves. You will connect with yourself. You will connect with other people. And you will eliminate a whole lot of drama from your life. I promise. I had to learn all three the hard way. I want you to benefit from what I have learned so you can make better life choices. We cannot do better until we know better.

As we move into the next sections of the book, we are turning from those foundational life lessons I talked about earlier—how to recover from the impact of dysfunctional families and childhood traumas, how to practice good mental health as an everyday priority, how to take risks and live adventurously, and how to manage your emotions and feelings. Now we're taking a look at how the way you treat others, how they treat you, how the people you allow in your life, and how the people who allow you to be part of theirs determines a lot about the course your life.

These life lessons will be a bit shorter than the previous ones, but their message is every bit as powerful and practical as the earlier life lessons. The foundation of any house is its strength. It is the same with our lives. Our foundation is our family. Our foundation is our health and wellness. Our foundation is our ability to take risks and balance them with wisdom. Our foundation is to make life a great adventure and to wonder as we wander. Those core foundations help to build our character, our reason, and our emotional intelligence.

But we cannot live our lives well if we do not first engage in self-assessment. The first step is to understand that we are all made up of energy—all of us—and that your positive energy helps to make others positive. Likewise, your negative energy can make people feel negative. We all impact one another whether we know it or not. That's the "do no harm." I am accountable for how I treat others, as are you. I am likewise accountable for any harm I do regardless of my intentions. And when I am made aware of my harm, or insult, or insensitivity, I must seek to offer an apology or make amends where it is possible to do so. So, let's start with a simple truth: all of us cause harm, whether unintended or intentional. And from time to time all of us cause a bit of drama. It is important that you accept this fact because it is not debatable. It simply is. We humans are messy at times. We are frail. We mess up. We stumble. We fall. We cause those we love—often those we love deeply—great pain. Sometimes, we cause that pain by happenstance, or out of ignorance, or even neglect. And at other times, we can be spiteful, mean, thoughtless, distant, and unkind. The trick to this thing called life is to own our part when we get it wrong. And to be very intentional as best we can, for as long as we live, to do no harm to others.

The flip side of this equation, however, is more challenging: how to avoid others doing us harm, and when to draw a line in the sand. That's the "take no shit." As I mentioned in Lesson 1, our families are the foundation of everything we learn and know up until we become adults and can make our own choices. Your family is going to hurt you. The person you like, love, date, or marry will hurt you. Even your children will disappoint you and maybe cause you pain at times. That is all normal. It is all just part of being human, but what each of us possesses is the ability to set boundaries (remember those?) and we get to decide how we want to allow other people's energy, attitudes, quirks, and challenges to impact us. **Bottom line:** when I say "take no shit" I am simply saying Y-O-U are responsible for your own happiness, peace, joy, and life—never place that power in the hands of someone else. Ever.

**The good news is that each of us gets to decide what part we play in the script of our lives. We get to make some choices. Some good. Some not so good. We get to play various roles. Sometimes the villain. Sometimes the victim. But the ultimate goal must be to be the victor.**

## You Are Responsible for Everything in Your Life: Protect Your Peace at All Costs

Your peace is everything in life. If you are young, it may not seem that way now, but trust me—it is. Peace is a subjective term, but it is one we can all relate to. Each of us has that small inner voice that warns us when someone or something is violating our space, our solitude, our sanity, our peace, our humanity, our soul landscape. We know when our peace is disturbed. And, once disturbed, peace can be a really hard thing to get back. Peace is a very sacred place. Peace is more than just the absence of noise or upset. Peace is a place we go for safety, for respite, for rest, and to recharge when we are overwrought or down.

For starters, a good way to protect your personal peace is for you to be very intentional about who and what you connect your life to. I mentioned earlier that we are all energy. And we give off energy. We all have that family member, friend, or colleague that we hate to see coming. We get an instant headache. We don't want to pick up the phone. We want to avoid them and their energy at all costs. I call it

"Pig Pen syndrome." You remember Pig Pen from the *Peanuts* comic strip? He's quiet and doesn't seem to bother anyone. But he has a cloud of dirt constantly swirling around him. There's a great episode in which Pig Pen gets cleaned up and puts on a suit so he can go to the party with the other kids, but when he arrives at the door, they don't let him in. Why? Because no one recognizes him without his cloud of dirt and dust trailing closely behind. Here's my point: Pig Pen is a metaphor for that person in our lives who is always in chaos, who is always bringing drama, and always sapping our life force, our energy, our peace and quiet. You must be careful to avoid these kinds of people who constantly have stuff swirling around them. Your job and mine is to be accountable for our own peace and well-being. You do that by spotting these kinds of people and situations early—before you get sucked in—because it is hard to get out once you have fallen into patterns of allowing people to disrupt your peace to meet their needs.

> Relationships where there is little peace and accord ultimately splinter and break apart. People stop speaking. They stop caring. They simply disconnect for their own peace of mind.

Relationships where there is little peace and accord ultimately splinter and break apart. People stop speaking. They stop caring. They simply disconnect for their own peace of mind. I am old school; I am a ride-or-die kind of girl. But many of my family and friends have commented that in the past several years they have seen a dramatic shift in me. One friend called it "worrisome." Another went on a text rant on me for being "selfish" and like the "rich young ruler" in the Bible because I dared to say I was exhausted and drained from taking care of my sick parent alone for almost two years, with little to no help from my only sibling, while running a business, writing books, teaching, doing the things I want to do in this life, and trying to take care of my own health and wellness. Being a caregiver is difficult at best, even under the most optimal circumstances. None of us can do it alone.

People asked where the "old Sophia" had been hiding. What happened to "the immovable rock" who was always there? Let me translate that for you: *Sophia, why have you stopped being there for everyone, all the time, no matter the cost to yourself? Sophia, how could you do this to us? Don't you know your role in this family is to fix it when we mess up? Sophia, you are not entitled to any peace or a life of your own. You are a single woman with no children, you have no life, so we are your life.*

This was my life until I realized one day that, during the pandemic, not one member of my family checked on me or asked me how I was doing. My friends, yes, the family of my making, yes. But the people I was tending to, doing free legal work for, paying for counseling for, cooking for, taking care of, lending money to, and on and on, did not seem to give two damns about me and my well-being. I was not protecting my peace. I was putting it on the sidewalk to be trampled upon. I was allowing myself, once again, to be seen as non-human, as a "rock," a tower of strength for everyone else to recharge, to get their power from.

Once I realized what was happening, I got angry. And I got vocal. I made clear to all takers and users that the game was up. I demanded there be some family counseling. I made it clear that, if there were not changes, I was out—for good. I started to pay attention to my body and to my emotions—I started having serious heart flutters and palpitations. I hadn't cried in a decade or more. I had become a robot of a human, operating on autopilot. I had learned to survive the trauma, but I had no peace in my life. I was being gravely impacted by all the emotional stressors of my family and my life. After all the years I had endured, pushed through, been long-suffering, forgiven the unforgivable, and tried to practice "WWJD" (What would Jesus do?)—it had all finally caught up with me. I started journaling and speaking to a life-coach-therapist who helped me to pinpoint what was missing in my life—peace. I had none. I had no moments for me. No respite. No love. Just constant drama, constant personal insults being hurled at me, constant rejection and unkindness.

**Your job and mine is to be accountable for our own peace and well-being.**

It was slowly destroying me. I had to take my power back to get my peace back. I had to let some people go. I had to cut some people off (including family) and I had to start taking care of me first.

## Respect Other People's Peace and Humanity

All of us are good at knowing what we need to protect our peace of mind. We all know how we want to be treated: with love, with kindness, with respect. Yet, how often do we consider how we are impacting others?

My paternal grandmother once told me, "Always offer something before you ask for something. Always treat others as you want to be treated." She was, of course, borrowing from the Golden Rule in the second part of her advice. But the first part, offering before asking, always intrigued me. Offer something before you ask for something. What a maxim to live by. I think her point was you should go to people full, not empty. Have something to sow into someone before you ask them to sow into you. This is a good rule to live by because what inevitably ends up happening is that we try to go it alone, tough it out, and then we get depleted. We reach for someone or something (drugs, sex, alcohol, work, etc.) and we slowly drown. We have nothing to offer. When something or someone good comes our way, we aren't ready to receive them.

We live in a cruel world, as I said before. Bullying. Cancelling. Unkindness. Violence. All these things have increased in spades in the last decade with the growth of social media platforms and social media users. And since the COVID-19 pandemic erupted worldwide, we have seen an increase in domestic violence, suicide, and mental-health challenges. I am no therapist, but common sense dictates that we are becoming an increasingly angry, isolated, self-centered, and unpeaceful people.

Just look at the January 6, 2021, insurrection at the US Capitol. No matter your political persuasion, we should all agree that beating and brutalizing police officers and threatening the lives of elected officials is unacceptable. This just would not have happened in my grandparents' generation (the Greatest Generation of World War II) or in my parents' generation (the Baby Boomers, who marched for civil rights and women's rights). There was a code of conduct of how you treated people in public and in private. You had to communicate face-to-face, or by handwritten letter, or even a short phone call. You didn't have immediate response. Things moved slower. Life on a day-to-day basis was more peaceful. And people, for the most part, were peaceful as well.

Don't get me wrong—violence, cruelty, anger, and unkindness have always existed, and regrettably always will exist. But now we can be all those things from a keyboard, on smartphone, tablet, or laptop. We can do instant harm and cruelty with our words anonymously with a small avatar as our image. We can put people on blast.

We can call people out. We can expose embarrassing intimate images when someone breaks up with us and feels entitled to do so. We can take videos of unsuspecting persons and share them unauthorized. We can go onto platforms like Facebook and create groups that foster hatred, bullying, racism, and worse. Or we can go on YouTube and attack people we've never met, whom we do not know, and take their image and make the most hateful videos about them. I know, I have been a victim of this many times.

In a world like this, how do we protect and respect other people's peace and humanity as we work to guard our own? It's called character. It's called doing unto others as you would have them do unto you. It's that simple, really. We must start owning our own behavior. We must start removing the speck from our eye, as the Bible says, before we try to judge someone else for what is in theirs. We do this by thinking before we speak. We do this by communicating how we feel. People are not mind readers. Say what you need to say.

Here's the reality of our twenty-first century lifestyle: according to a 2015 Microsoft study, the human attention span has shrunk down to eight seconds. That's right, only eight seconds. People now generally lose concentration almost instantly, highlighting the effects of an increasingly digitalized lifestyle on the human brain. Microsoft found that since the year 2000 (or about when the mobile revolution began), the average attention span dropped from twelve seconds to eight seconds. What that means is that we are operating on a hairpin, a trigger, and on the surface. We no longer go deeper. We no longer listen to hear. Instead, we have kneejerk reactions, responding in outrage and vapidness.

The question is, how do we rewire how we think, feel, and speak to one another? We do, as my nana said, by offering something. By checking in on people we love. By asking, "Are you okay?" We protect other's peace and wellness by being guardians of our own. A healthy, happy, fulfilled you is a loving, kind, empathetic you. A drained, bitter, unhealed you is a dangerous you. Not just to yourself, but to everyone connected to you.

## Never Let People Get Comfortable Disrespecting You

> We protect other's peace and wellness by being guardians of our own. A healthy, happy, fulfilled you is a loving, kind, empathetic you. A drained, bitter, unhealed you is a dangerous you. Not just to yourself, but to everyone connected to you.

My favorite code from my second book, *The Woman Code,* is Code 3: "You Teach People How to Treat You." It took me a long time to learn the meaning of that truth. It is always easy to point the finger at others, to lay blame, to see the faults of others. Yet, we rarely own the even deeper truth—that we control everything that ever happens to us when it comes to how we let people behave in our lives and in our presence. Let that sink in.

You and you alone decide what you allow. You and you alone decide everyday what you will tolerate and what you won't. My best sage advice to you as I sit looking back from the seasoned perch of my fifties is that you must start this process of setting hard and firm boundaries early. It is the process of self-love and the process of self-worth. The best gift you can give yourself and your sense of peace is to never let people get comfortable disrespecting you or taking from you. If you do not, life will be hard.

I had a lot of people in my life who got very comfortable disrespecting me because I gave them permission to do so. Family members who were cruel, unkind, and cold could always count on a birthday gift or Christmas gift. When they needed money, I readily gave it. I would lie to myself and justify my stupidity as being "Christian" or "good." I was so programmed by the dysfunction and trauma of my life that I let people treat me any old way they wanted as I continued to try and win their affection or make them be nice to me, to like me. I know some people reading this will be shocked. Because the confident Sophia Nelson the world knows is nothing like this at all.

> A man who loves you, who wants you, and who adores you pursues you. He courts you. He chases you. And he is excited to be in your presence. He doesn't ghost you like a thirteen-year-old boy. He knows how to talk to you as a man talks to his woman. He doesn't miss an opportunity to tell you how special you are and how blessed he is to have you in his life.

My last serious relationship was constantly on again, off again. I had to finally stand up for myself. I had to walk away from someone who was cruel and controlling. I kept allowing his disrespect, sometimes subtle, sometimes loud, because on the face of it this man is handsome, very accomplished, my equal in every respect, and I loved his family and I wanted to be married. I wanted it to work. But he would say, text, and write the most ugly, demeaning things to me, even when I was being supportive and loving to him. I would always take the high road and allow myself to be talked into why I should overlook his "immaturity" (at well over forty years of age) and wait for him to see how good I was for him, how kind, how *blah blah blah*.

That is the "taking shit" part right there. We all do it, particularly us women folk. We refuse to hear the alarm bells. We refuse to see the selfishness. We refuse to see that a man who loves you, who wants you, and who adores you pursues you. He courts you. He chases you. And he is excited to be in your presence. He doesn't ghost you like a thirteen-year-old boy. He knows how to talk to you as a man talks to his woman. He doesn't miss an opportunity to tell you how special you are and how blessed he is to have you in his life. If a man is not doing this, ladies, let him go. He is not into you, and he will only end up disrespecting and hurting you.

I had to finally realize that I kept dating the same kind of man over and over again (except for a few really good ones in my twenties and thirties that I let get away). I realized that I was the common denominator. Me. I was doing all of this to myself because I didn't respect myself.

I let this this weak man, who liked making me feel less than to cover his own inadequacies, hurt me again and again. I was never good enough. There was always an excuse. I was getting too old. I couldn't have babies. I wasn't docile enough. I was too vocal. *Blah blah blah.* I allowed this clown to act this way in my life for years. Then a good male friend, who is married with grandkids, took me aside after watching us together as a couple at my birthday party, and said, "He doesn't deserve you. He is not worthy of you." My friend wanted to punch his lights out. And he was not the first friend to tell me that. But he was the first male friend to tell me that, and I knew it already. He had been showing his true colors for years. But here's where the rubber meets the road: I am responsible for my life, for my peace, and for my happiness. I had let this relationship keep going because I was not walking in peace. I was not walking in healed wholeness. I was still a little girl looking for her father's love and approval; seeking but never finding it in all the wrong men.

Here's what I want you to take away, whether you are a man or a woman, younger or older. You and you alone decide how people treat you. Yes, they may be bad people, or unkind or selfish people. That's not your issue. Neither you nor I can control other people. Period.

> Never tolerate disrespect. The more chances you give someone, the less respect they'll start to have for you. They'll begin to ignore the standards that you've set because they know another chance will always be given.

What we can control is the boundaries that we put in place. We can set limits on how much contact we allow, under what circumstances, and for how long. We can choose to go where the love is and run toward people who feel like sunlight, who truly like us and want to be in our company. I have started to do that, and it is such a balm on the soul. I don't know where you are right now in your life's journey, but I want to gently nudge you to do the same. You are worthy of love. You are worthy of kindness. You are worthy of peace in your life.

I got rid of some people, cut others back a few rows, and, in dating, I spend time only with men who like me a lot, and who like to laugh, who like to dance, who like to talk about politics, life, and drink good wine. Men who aren't looking at my credentials, but who care about how I show up in the world. Men who are confident, communicative, and not into playing sophomoric games. I took my power back these past few years. I did the work, and I am still doing the work, so that the second half of my life can be a life of peace, of purpose, and of being connected to people who do me no harm, and from whom I know I will have to take no shit.

## Applying This Lesson to Your Life

This life lesson is simple: protect your peace at all costs. It is the only thing you have besides your heart that is truly yours. You protect your peace by knowing who you are and who you are not. You protect your peace by setting personal boundaries and limits. You protect your peace by carving out a daily regimen of peaceful things and safe spaces. You protect your peace by letting the people in your life know what you will stand for, and what you will no longer accept. People respond to what they receive from you. I started this lesson by saying we are all energy. We are a bit like a two-way radio frequency. We give and we get. When you stand your ground, and you treat others with kindness and respect, you will attract the same into your own life.

What you cannot do is continue to walk down a road of distress and stress because you let people run wild in your personal life, in your business, or in your interpersonal relationships. People who break their word. People who do not follow through. People who lie. People who are in your circle, but who are really haters. You must root these people out quickly. Set a standard of excellence and watch people come up to that standard. If they do not, those are not your people. Your character is more valuable than anything you possess. So, guard it. Honor it. And make sure that the other people in and around your life honor it, too. And when they do not, you must exact consequences. You must speak up. You must make sure that they know clearly that what was said or done is not acceptable to you.

Life is reciprocal. You must work to treat others with the same respect you desire. You must work to give as much as you take. You must offer something before you ask for something. The way we do no harm is to be thoughtful, to care, to ask the people we love what they need. All of us are in this thing together. It *does* take a village. We are that village of friends, family, caretakers, and co-workers. We must do better by ourselves and in turn by one another.

## Challenge Yourself to Take These Actions

When life hits you hard, it can be a tough pill to swallow. But if you really want to have a good life, you can't spend it being distracted, creating drama, being reactionary, and wondering what in the hell happened to you. No, instead you must cut to the chase and cut the crap out of your life. Sometimes less truly is more—oh, how different my path might be if only I had boiled it all down to: Do no harm, Take no shit.

Here are a few things I suggest you challenge yourself to consider doing as you navigate this life lesson:

- **Boundaries are not brick walls that we erect to isolate ourselves.** They are protective measures that we put in place to protect ourselves from distractions, harm, or other intrusions. Challenge yourself to make a list of limits and boundaries you know you need to set and with whom.

- **Share your expectations with others.** By sharing what we need, want, and desire we clear up miscommunications and we avoid a lot of harm. People will either lean into what we want or they will run away. Give people a chance to truly know you as you know yourself.

- **Practice saying "No."** It is a complete sentence. Say it with respect but say it firmly and don't feel guilty. We will get to that more in a later lesson.

- **There are five types of boundaries: physical, emotional, sexual, financial, and intellectual.** Physical boundaries are space related—how much space do you need? Financial boundaries deal with your budgeting, lifestyle, and spending. Sexual boundaries deal with intimacy and how we feel about it. Emotional and intellectual boundaries go back to our families, our traumas, our belief systems, and how we manage them with others. Challenge yourself to know each of these and ask yourself what you need. Then connect with people who get you, who support you, who like you, and who want to see you win in life.

> *"Stand up for yourself.*
> *Never give any one permission to abuse you."*
>
> —Lailah Gifty Akita

# SECTION III

## Protect Your Peace, It's the Passport to Your Soul

*Every human has a soul. It must be nourished, watered, and replenished daily. These lessons help us to take care of the inner self, the part we most often neglect.*

# LESSON 11

## Practice the Art of Surrender: Release What You Cannot Hold

*"The moment of surrender is not when life is over. It's when it begins."*

—Marianne Williamson

## Your Ability to Give Up Control

My favorite spiritual hymn is "I Surrender All," and I love the CeCe Winans version. If you are familiar with the words, you know that it is a priceless refrain of setting aside pride, and just giving it all to the Lord. It is a way of understanding how small we are as humans in the big sea of life. It is learning how to submit yourself freely, and how to be humble. It is a pronouncement of loving something you cannot see; of trusting in what you cannot touch. It is a sacred pause that calls on us to live daily in a holy presence.

My favorite lines are: "All to Him I freely give. I will ever love and trust Him. In His presence daily live. All to Jesus I surrender. Humbly at His feet I bow." It does not matter whether you are Christian, Jewish, Muslim, or Hindu. Faith is something we all need in our lives. And faith is 100 percent about surrender. As the Bible says, "Faith is the substance of things hoped for, the evidence of things not seen." Faith, then, is about hope. And it is the hope of what can still be.

I have found that it is only when I can release control and surrender my feelings that I experience the fullness of faith, of hope, and of peace. Peace is so lacking in our time because we are always racing around, being busy, and never truly being still. The art of surrender means to stop fighting yourself, stop trying to control everything and everyone, and get out of your own way. This is difficult. Being a "control freak" is a term we throw around a lot, but the reality is we live in a time in which trying to be in control has overtaken our lives. Control is the opposite of surrender or release. Yes, there are times when we need to control things, when we need to be on top of something, or guide something, or be a leader in something. But control in our personal lives can get tricky. Control is different from setting boundaries, which we talked about in earlier life lessons. We set boundaries to protect ourselves, while control is something that, when taken to the extreme, can cause a whole lot of problems in our lives and sometimes in the lives of others.

It is when we can surrender ourselves, release ourselves, and free ourselves from the things that worry us, challenge us, or even break us, that life truly gets fuller and richer. When we submit to the natural flow of life, we have a lot more peace. For a long time, I believed that I would have everything I wanted in life if I could just control everyone around me; if I could just control what people did and how they did it; if I could just control every situation; if I could just keep things neat and in order. You might think this, too. However, quite the opposite is true.

It is only through surrendering that we can let go of our fears, of our doubts; only then can we fully and truly see what it is that we desire—who we want to become deep down inside.

I talked earlier about taking the Essential Colors personality tests. If you remember, I told you how devastated I was to learn that I was a Gold and not a Blue. Gold is the Type A personality—very successful, very much in control, an orderly "know it all" who appears to have it all together and doesn't understand why people just don't follow their orders. Blue, by comparison, is kind, empathetic, giving, caring, and free-spirited. Blues love to have fun, love to laugh, and love to explore. I hate the Gold in my personality. It's been the dominant force in my life—my whole life. And as we talked about in Lesson 1, it started with my family. I didn't have many choices growing up. I was the first born, so I was supposed to do things right and follow the dreams and visions my family had for my life. And I did that, and I did it well. Perhaps too well. But the truth of the matter is, in my heart and in my soul, I am true Blue. That is a part of me that very few people know, and it's the part I love the most about myself.

**It is when we can surrender ourselves, release ourselves, and free ourselves from the things that worry us, challenge us, or even break us, that life truly gets fuller and richer.**

My goal in this life lesson is to help you honor the true you. And that can never be accomplished by being so busy, so rigid, so controlling that you forget to live your life

Another way of saying to surrender is to let go. Just like giving up control, letting go is one of the hardest things that we ever have do. It starts from the time we were babies with our favorite blanket or our favorite toy. We like to hold on to things. It makes us feel secure, in control, even when what we are holding on to is no longer good for us, or meant for us to keep. But if you can learn to surrender and let go, you'll find that you will attract more things to your life— the right things, the right relationships, the right desires, and, most importantly, you'll develop a deep sense of gratitude. Because when you learn to let go of something or someone that no longer serves you, you are saying to God, or to the universe, or to whomever you pray: As hard as this was, I'm thankful for the path that surrendering opened to me.

I want to give you three principles that I think will help you learn to surrender and let go. If you can add them to your EQ toolkit, you will be a better leader, a better friend, a better boss, a better spouse, a better parent, a better colleague, a better sibling, a better human being.

1. Letting go of control

2. Learning to be present

3. Practicing radical gratitude

Believe me, holding on too tight will destroy you and everyone you love. **Bottom line,** the art of surrendering and letting go of control can bring you a greater sense of peace, more freedom, and more joy in your life. As I said at the outset of this lesson, we all have a little control freak in us. We are living in a time where things move so fast that we all feel exhausted and out of control most of the time. We are all overly attached to our successes, to our achievements, to our jobs, to our material possessions, our homes, our cars, our boats, our vacation homes, and our sense of security. And there's nothing wrong with wanting to feel secure. There's nothing wrong with wanting to have something to pass on to your children and grandchildren. But if there's one thing I've learned over the course of my life, it's that we rarely, if ever, are in control of anything. The sooner you realize that, the happier you're going to be. So, let's get into it.

## Letting Go of Control

Holding on to something, whether it be unfounded fears, bad habits, mindless routines, unhealthy relationships, old dreams, or even a belief about "the way things should be," can keep you stuck in the wrong places in life. We often mistake getting stuck with being in control. They are very different. Whenever we think we're in control, we feel less vulnerable to change, to the normal ebb and flow of our lives. But in truth, no matter what we attach ourselves to, the need for control can have detrimental and devastating effects. When we hold on to things and dig in our heels even though we know intuitively that we should let go of them, we are causing chaos in our lives and not at all the control that we seek. And, unfortunately, we get stuck. And we often stay there. We get stuck because we stop listening to that inner voice. We stop asking ourselves: What do I want? What do I need? What do I have to look forward to in my life?

It happens slowly at first, like the frog in the boiling pot of water. As it heats up, he doesn't realize he is adapting to the temperature, which will ultimately lead to his death. He succumbs to his deadly circumstance quietly. Whereas if you place a frog in a pot of boiling water, he will jump out, immediately sensing the danger. We are a lot like the frog. If we are in touch with our surroundings and what is good for us versus what is not, we flee. We pivot. We shift. Sadly, so many people, some of you reading this book, have accepted that life is over for you long before you physically die.

Letting go of control goes back to the blind spots we discussed in Lesson 9. You first must recognize that you're trying to control everything before you can release control. Surrendering, by the way, does not mean giving up. It means that you let go of fighting yourself. You get out of your own way. You stop using your precious energy to fight against what you know in your heart is best for you. You go with the flow of the current.

I have had to learn this lesson too many times. Sometimes, I have worked against my own best interests by thinking I could control a situation instead of letting it play out and take me where I was supposed to be. Sometimes, what looks like a loss in our lives is a win. Sometimes, what we thought we could never bear to lose or let go of is the opening to what was supposed to be ours all along. What I am trying to tell you is that when you try to control people or things— you suffer. And you ultimately make others you love suffer. Here are a few steps you can take to identify when you are being controlling and how to release some of that control and let go, so that you can take hold of something far greater.

1. **Have self-awareness.** You must know when you are too attached to someone or something, or to an outcome at work or in your relationship. This is a sure sign you are being controlled or trying to control something.

2. **Practice being open to new experiences and to new people.** When we are open, it's hard to control because we do not have the strings to pull, or the power advantage in new, unfamiliar experiences. We can only sit and be part of them.

3. **Surround yourself with good people.** This one is going to keep coming up in every single life lesson. You need people in your life who empower you, coach you (see Lesson 9), and who will call you out when you are being overbearing or controlling.

4. **Get therapy or coaching.** Being too controlling or too rigid is a sign of something deeper: fear or trauma. In response, you close yourself off, and, as a result, you block your blessings, your joy, and your peace.

> *"There are only two ways to live your life. One is as though nothing is a miracle. The other is as though everything is a miracle."*
>
> —**Albert Einstein**

## Learning to Be Present

Being present in our modern times is difficult at best. We are busy, harried, and hurried. And we are always thinking about our next deal, our next relationship, our next purchase, our next everything. How can we ever truly be present?

Of all the complaints I hear from colleagues, family, and friends, exhaustion is the number one. As we all had to adapt to a new way of living and working during the height of the COVID-19 pandemic, we had to take on more responsibilities, not fewer. We had to balance work, family, education, children, and health. If the data is any guide, we have all taken a hit in our emotional well-being. We are all drained, and many are lonely. Some of us are even angry, fighting back, protesting public health mandates and travel mandates. And all of that is bubbling up just below the surface of our lives and our interactions with one another. It restricts us from being free, from surrendering. And it ties us up in knots emotionally that end up making us frustrated, uptight, disconnected, and lost.

Not being present means you miss the most important things in your life. While you might be in attendance at your kid's ballet recital or soccer game, if you are checking your work emails you are not really present. Do you really feel your spouse's warm embrace or are you brushing it off as you rush out the door? Do you make time with your friends and family? Do you wander and wonder—just because? Do you let yourself laugh out loud? If you do none of these things, you miss small moments of immense delight.

All of this radically changes when you face your mortality and that of those you love. It wakes up your soul. It literally stops you and forces you to be present, to be in the moment, to cherish what you have instead of chasing what you do not have. It makes you ask the hard question: What happens when my mother is gone? Or my father? Or, God forbid, a spouse or a child?

If you want to live your life on purpose, if you want to master the art of surrender, learn to be present. Because all your busy, all your doing, all your working will not go with you when you die. A great example is the eulogy of the late four-star general Colin Powell, delivered by his son Michael in November 2021 at the National Cathedral in Washington, DC. Michael Powell did not talk so much about his father's storied career and many professional accomplishments: the first Black chairman of the Joint Chiefs of Staff, secretary of state, national security advisor, and on and on. He talked about the father who, although he was a busy man, a great man, found time to be present with his kids. To kiss a son on his cheek before he deployed for the first time to war. To sign report cards. To give hugs. To be by their bedsides when they were sick. To be a role model and mentor not by his words but by his character. He taught them to do good and to be good. Colin Powell's kids loved him. His wife of fifty-nine years loved him. They loved him because he was present. He made the time. He put in the work so that when his time in this life was over, he left a legacy of love, grandchildren, and honor that followed him.

These tips will help you to be more present:

1. **Let go of your past.** Carrying old wounds, trauma, and resentments robs of you of your life force. They rob you of the ability to see what you have now or who you are now. If you had a bad childhood of violence, trauma, and unhappiness, that is the lens through which you saw your life. But now you either must change that lens or you will stay stuck there. So many people are lucky enough to find happiness in a marriage partner and be blessed with children. Yet they never embrace and accept the blessing because they are still stuck in their own pain and unresolved traumas. You must work at letting go of your past or you will never take hold of your present.

2. **Learn to "be" instead of always "doing" something.** I had to learn this, and it's hard. For example, listen to music—without

watching TV or doing the laundry or working on your computer. Just listen. Take a nature walk without thinking what you're going to do when you get home or making a phone call while you're walking. Just walk and look at what's around you.

3. **Be intentional.** I have a prayer partner, and every morning we talk between 8:30 and 9:00. We are what they call "dosing" partners. Dosing is slang for sharing your feelings, praying, and connecting in a meaningful dialogue with another person. In doing so, you get a dopamine high just as if you were eating chocolate, finishing a run, or doing something that makes you feel emotionally satisfied. It forces you to be present with yourself.

4. **Practice meditation.** While you will gain immense benefits from disciplined, guided meditation, even starting your day with a few minutes to stop, focus, and breathe will help you to be more mindful and present. Have a ritual that you follow daily or weekly that connects you to peace, to quiet, to reflection, to affirmation. Only ten minutes a day can be life changing.

## Practicing Radical Gratitude

> *"Be thankful for what you have; you'll end up having more. Concentrate on what you don't have, and you will never, ever have enough."*
> —Oprah Winfrey

Gratitude is the superglue of life. Gratitude removes us from the past and keeps us in the moment, in the present, in the now. But the best thing about gratitude is that it has an ever-greater impact on our future, and on everyone connected to us. When we can be present enough to acknowledge the little things in our lives, and to focus on the moments of our lives that bless us, we unintentionally create a practice of radical gratitude. Adopt an attitude of gratitude and change the way you feel right now. Gratitude is merely a vehicle to focus our attention on everything positive in our lives.

What is gratitude, anyway? Gratitude is the ability to be present. It is the ability to see the silver lining in even the most challenging of circumstances. As I talked about in the "Be Present" section of this life lesson, you cannot stay stuck in your past and thrive. You must be in the moment you are in, yes, with one eye toward the future, but with your whole self present in the moment right in front of you. Gratitude is another way of saying be positive. Be thankful. When we can focus on the good, we are able to create and attract more of the same.

Radical gratitude, however, is different. It is a way of living, every day. It is a routine of focused humility that allows you to be a warrior for thankfulness. This is not easy to do in a world of so many distractions and so much white noise. It goes back to what I said in Lesson 3 about making a choice. We must choose gratitude. We must choose joy. If we don't make a choice, we will stay stuck in a life of unhappiness, resentments, and restlessness.

Here are a few tips that I use:

1. **Begin each day with a grateful heart.**

2. **Adopt an attitude of gratitude by keeping a twenty-one-day gratitude jar.** Every day for three weeks, write down something for which you are grateful and put it in the jar. Do family gratitude challenges, teach your kids how to be thankful. Walk it out with them. We did the twenty-one day gratitude jar when my nieces were young and I still have the notes we stuck in each day. It was a really great way to teach them how to give thanks for something every day.

3. **Be mindful of what you think about and feel.** Because what you think about you become. Your feelings are "blind spots" so mind them. Be present on what is good in your life, on what is loving in your life, or what you are still hoping and dreaming about. That is how you walk in gratitude.

4. **Be thankful for what you have, and you'll end up having more.** This is the most important of all. Concentrate on what you don't have, and you'll never have enough. Gratitude turns what we have into enough. Gratitude unlocks the beauty of life, and the ability to witness the miracles around us that we often miss.

**Bottom line:** If you will but live your life through the lens of radical gratitude, I promise you will discover the gateway to all of life's abundance.

> *"Surrender is a journey*
> *from outer turmoil to inner peace."*
>
> —Sri Chinmoy

# LESSON 12

## Trust Your Intuition— It's Rarely Wrong

*"There is a voice that doesn't use words. Listen."*

—Anonymous

## *Your Ability to Trust Yourself*

Have you ever felt something deep down inside, but you didn't quite know what it was? Ever have a hunch or déjà vu that turned out to be spot on? Have you ever known the moment that you met someone that they were going to be good for you—or bad for you? Have you ever been in a situation at your job, or as a student, or in some social setting where you somehow knew that you weren't in the right place, at the right time, with the right people? If you've ever felt any of those things, that's your intuition.

Intuition is that small voice that comes from a place deep inside us. Let me tell you from first-hand experience that every time I've gone against that small voice, that red flag, that glaring stop sign, I've been sorry for it later. When you have these intuitive moments, you don't need other people to validate them. What you need to do is to have a process whereby you evaluate it and then make the right decision according to your gut, period. It may sound a little crazy in this day and age, with all the information we have at our fingertips, to trust your gut. But believe me on this one, folks, when you live long enough, you learn that that voice inside you is there from experience. It's there from learning life lessons the hard way.

By the time we get to middle age, life has usually done a number on us. Many of us get stuck, as I said in the previous life lesson. But we rely on our gut instinct more because we have lived enough life to know what we know even before we know it. Meaning, sometimes, the best answer is the first one, the one we feel in our gut. Although most of us recognize that our inner voice has value, the problem is that we often have no idea how to effectively tune in to it. By tuning in to it, I mean that you have to be on the same energy frequency as your inner voice. Remember, I said earlier that we are all energy. All of us. We operate on frequencies of peace, love, joy, noise, rancor, stress, and so on. So, when that small voice says, "Pay attention, Sophia, something isn't quite right here," I have learned to stop dead in my tracks and pay attention. Fast.

You must know when to hear your own voice, to trust yourself. And to trust yourself, you must love yourself enough to listen to your own voice when it rears itself to the surface of your consciousness instead of always feeling compelled to heed the voices of others. When I look back on my life, I recognize so many missed opportunities I had to hear that small voice, and not be deaf to what it was trying to tell me. Of course, hindsight is always 20/20, and so my hope is that, by sharing this with you now, particularly those of you who are under thirty, you can learn to tap into your own energy, your own power, and your own intuition. You'll be doing yourself a big favor for your life down the road.

What, exactly, is intuition? Well, it's a combination of several things: your instincts; your senses (sight, smell, touch, and hearing); and, most importantly, your lived experiences coming into play with a big red flag telling you to stop, pause, and pay attention. By lived experiences, I mean the experiences we had growing up in our families, our emotional experiences, and how we process those things that have happened to us, in us, and

> *"Trusting your intuition means tuning in as deeply as you can to the energy you feel, following that energy moment to moment, trusting that it will lead you where you want to go and bring you everything you desire."*
>
> **—Shakti Gawain**

around us. Intuition isn't about logic. It's about knowing something deep inside, something that connects your subconscious with your conscious. Intuition is more than just a feeling; it's the ability to sense something coming at us, or around us, before we have a way of understanding exactly what it is.

One of those times I will never forget has to do with a job I took against my intuition, which was screaming at me, "Don't do it!" When I was leaving private practice, I was offered a position as general counsel to a huge defense contractor. This is not uncommon when you are based in Washington, DC, and doing the work I did as an attorney in defense, national security, and intelligence contracting. The opportunity seemed great at first. Friends I had who worked at the company said they were looking to build their diversity with women, and particularly with people of color. It seemed like a great opportunity to blaze yet another trail. I was all in, and yet that small voice inside me was nagging, screaming at me to STOP, evaluate, do my due diligence, and to be wary of any company that was full of White men over forty, only two White women in the executive ranks, and zero people of color. Yet, I went against that voice, much to my chagrin. After all, the pay was amazing, the stock options were incredible, and I was going to have a vice president title as well—all of this before the age of forty. After considering my other options, I decided to go with this company and accept their offer. It was close to my home, so my commute was not bad at all, and I was really excited about this new opportunity. That is, until I actually started working there.

Within my first few weeks, I knew I had made a grave mistake. It was a toxic workplace—not fit for women, and certainly not for a woman of color. These men made no bones about their displeasure at my being hired. And they made everything difficult. I was fired in my first month of working there. Of course, I hired an attorney and was paid a hefty settlement for the way in which I was treated, but it took a year. And it took a huge emotional toll. It was the singular event of my professional career that drove me out of the workplace into an entirely different space, working for myself and building a successful consulting business. It wasn't something I likely would have done, but since I had done it successfully about six years earlier, prior to going into big firm law practice, I already knew what to expect. I decided that I valued my emotional well-being and peace much more than a big paycheck and stock options.

Here's the lesson for you: when that small voice inside you hesitates, or says stop, or nags at you, listen. Investigate. Explore. Consider. And do your homework about that person, place, or thing, before you leap headlong into a situation that will cause you great harm. I now pay close attention to and heed that inner voice because every single time I have dismissed it or not paid proper attention to it, I suffer. I will never do that again. Ever.

I want to give you four tips on how to better harness your intuition to your advantage. It is a process of learning to trust yourself. Here are my top four intuition builders. If you can make them daily habits, you will avoid so many things you really do not need to subject yourself to. They are as follows:

1. Shut up and listen.

2. Trust yourself.

3. Be mindful of your attachments.

4. Practice good situational awareness.

## Shut Up and Listen

It sounds simple, but it's hard to do. We are constantly in motion; our phones are constantly pinging. We're always doing instead of being. So how do you learn to shut up and listen? And more point-edly, how do you listen to yourself, listen to your soul, listen to your inner voice? It requires that you learn you. Learn your moods. Learn your emotions (see the chapter on your EIQ toolkit). And, most of all, learn to spot the red flags that can only be caught if we are in tune with our own warning system.

I know that some people like to make fun of meditation, or just learning to be silent, but they really shouldn't. The world's greatest leaders, entrepreneurs, and even sports greats like Lebron James prac-tice it. You can use apps like *Calm* or *Headspace* to guide you. There are also moving forms of meditation like yoga, stretching, running, swimming, and walking (without music), as well as other ancient practices of getting still and quiet. When we allow ourselves to hear our own thoughts, we are harnessing our power.

Research in this area has made phenomenal findings into just how the brain works. Specifically, a series of studies at Leeds University in the United Kingdom has revealed that intuition is a very real psy-chological process whereby the brain uses our past experiences and cues from the self and our environment to make instant decisions that happen so quickly they often don't register on a conscious level. Think of it like this: your body, mind, and soul work together inter-nally to tell you what you need to know before you have even given it an intentional thought. The human brain has two distinct operating systems, left brain and right brain. One is the instinctual brain—the right brain—and the other is the analytical brain—left brain. The instinctual brain is where our intuition comes from. I trust my right brain—my gut—now, because I allow myself to get still and feel what I feel. Our analytical brain often shuts down the inner, expressive, emotional side. So, you must be intentional here, and slow down and listen to your own inner voice. Here are few quick things you can do to get quieter and hear your own thoughts:

1. **Be intentional.** Create space early in the morning before life starts to move. You must give yourself the time and the space emotionally to hear what you are thinking.

2. **Pray.** However you pray, to whomever you pray, do it often and with deep reflection so you can hear what you need from inside of you.

3. **Get with nature.** This is the most clearing, healing thing we can do. Walk in the country. Sit by the ocean. Find a peaceful park. Listen to the rain. Get into the practice of being silent and still by connecting with the beauty of the natural world.

> *"There is a voice inside of you that whispers all day long, 'I feel this is right for me, I know that this is wrong.' No teacher, preacher, parent, friend or wise man can decide what's right for you—just listen to the voice that speaks inside."*
> —**Shel Silverstein**

## Trust Yourself

How many of us truly trust ourselves?

Trusting yourself is an important leadership and life tool that few of us are ever taught. In fact, most leadership training and even relationship coaching deals with interdependence and counting on others, which is necessary and healthy, of course, because we all need each other. But the bad news is that people will fail you. People will have good intentions and let you down. You need to get comfortable trusting your own counsel as well as seeking consensus from people you trust and who you know have your best interests at heart. Once you take wise counsel, which I highly recommend, then you can sit with that inner voice, get still, and balance their wisdom with your own intuition.

Self-trust means that you honor your own thoughts and voice. You put your needs and your emotional safety first—which is what this entire book is all about. When you trust yourself, you extend grace to yourself, and you practice self-kindness and radical self-love. You learn that some things in life must be based on facts and others on feelings. You learn to manage life with grace. You learn to call people into your peace and not react to their chaos. Trusting Y-O-U simply means that you value your own experiences, your worth, your knowledge and your power.

Here are some tips on how to better learn to trust yourself:

1. **Speak kindly to yourself.** We always heap praise on others, and tell them that we love them, that we are proud of them. But we often reserve our worst criticism for the person we see in the mirror every day. It's vital to learn the art of being kind to yourself.

2. **Look at your past track record of wise decisions.** In other words, if you have been making good decisions, seeking wise counsel, and ultimately weighing the power of your own voice, then you can do it again and again. It's as simple as setting up a process, a process that allows you to move forward each time you must choose or decide, a process that allows you to hear your voice first, and then to hear others.

**3. Keep promises you make to yourself.** Keeping fidelity with yourself is huge. It enables us to keep our promises made to others as well. It honors self-care. It honors your soul. For example, keeping promises such as, I am going to take a walk every day, or, I am going to go to the gym every day; I like to putter in the garden on the weekend; I like time spent with friends outside of my family circle. Whatever it is that you need to do to honor you—do it.

> *"Follow your heart, listen to your inner voice, stop caring what others think."*
>
> —**Roy T. Bennett**, *The Light in the Heart*

## Be Mindful of Your Attachments

Attachments are a really big thing in life. By attachments, I mean the people we are connected to, the things we hold on to—even when they are clearly no longer good for us. The Dalai Lama put it like this: "Most of our troubles are due to our passionate desire for and attachment to things that we misapprehend as enduring entities." What he was saying is this: we get attached to people, places, or things that we misunderstand as being permanently with us, or joined with us, when we are simply holding on to something that was never meant to be ours. It was never meant to last forever. If there's one thing we all have in common, it is that we want to feel connected. We want to feel whole. We want fulfillment. We want happiness. We want joy. However, in that quest to feel loved and connected, we often hold on to the wrong people or stay in the wrong career. It happens a lot.

The reality is, however, that when we pin our hopes on someone or something that may no longer be good for us, we're setting ourselves up for a very big failure. By trying to hold on to what's familiar, we

*"Intuition is the compass of the soul."*
—**Anonymous**

miss out on what could be fantastic. We limit our ability to experience joy and happiness right here in the present. Remember being present? When you are present you can see things clearly past those pesky blind spots that we talked about in Lesson 11. Another thing we must be careful of is attachment to our feelings. Feelings are dangerous because they change so quickly if they are not deeply rooted in something real and lasting. **Here's the bottom line:** as I mentioned in the previous life lesson, when we stop trying to control the world around us, we give ourselves the freedom to fulfill, to love, and to live more fully. That's why letting go is so important; letting go is how we release those things that no longer work in our lives, that are no longer healthy for us.

An attachment can be something, for example, like death. Let's say we lost a loved one, and we haven't grieved properly. We haven't grieved in a way that's healthy so that we can go through the stages of mourning. Listen, it's not a simple thing to let go of an attachment. That's why it's called an attachment. An attachment is something that is close to us, it's connected to us, and, in a way, it's bound to us. Letting go of an attachment isn't a simple, one-time thing where you just say, "I'm done." By the way, the favorite vernacular of the twenty-first century is to say, "I'm done." No, you're not, unless you go through the process of releasing something properly. Otherwise, it's like pulling off a bandage on a wound. If the wound is not yet healed, you're going to have to reapply yet another bandage. Letting go of attachment is critical to hearing and feeling your intuition freely. It will allow you to hear that small voice that says to you, "This is the wrong way," or

"That's the right way," or "This is the wrong person," or "This is the right person, go for it!" Here are some steps to letting go of your attachments to better help you call in your intuition:

1. Own it. Admit that you are attached to a set of feelings or a person in an unhealthy way.

2. Ask yourself why you keep doing it over and over, attaching to the wrong things or people.

3. Shift away from the attachment and instead focus on caring for yourself. Do the work to find out the answer to #2 above.

## Practice Good Situational Awareness

Situational awareness is your ability to assess who is around you, what's around you, and how it's going to impact you or not. The ability to see what's around you, to be able—the minute you walk into a room—to assess those in that room. This is tool great leaders use to be effective with their emotional intelligence. This is another tool for your emotional intelligence toolkit. Situational awareness is something that every single one of us has the capacity to develop and use to our advantage.

The way to develop good situational awareness is by being mindful of your surroundings. It requires you to slow down. It requires you to listen before you speak. It requires that, every time you enter a new environment, you must take a moment to identify what's in your immediate vicinity, what's across the room, and, again, who is in the room. It's the ability to take notice of other people within your environment who may bring you harm or cause you stress. It is your mind's way of preparing you for battle, or for business, or, in the best-case scenarios, for relationship and connection. Intuition and situational awareness are first cousins.

Go back to that gut feeling you get when you walk into a club, or a place of business, or any environment, that feeling your intuitive brain picks up before you do. You feel it instantly. Trainers in the martial arts who teach self-defense teach you first to develop the skill of situational awareness. I am a Krav Maga student. Krav Maga is a system of self-defense that focuses on cultivating self-defense skills beyond regular physical combat or weapons training. It focuses on intuitive development and response. Or, said another way, situational awareness.

When we work to develop situational awareness, we are focusing on two unique skillsets: the intuitive and the predictive. For example, if you have a boss who is always angry and rants at the team during project meetings, you can pretty much predict well in advance of that meeting what things trigger him or her and how to manage them before it hits an eruption point. The key here is that you can predict the behavior because it's expected. But your intuition is what lets you know when this person is going to go off, so you mitigate it in advance because you already know it's coming. Make sense?

Here are some quick tips you can put into practice that will help you to develop this very important emotional intelligence tool:

1. **Pay attention to your surroundings.** Practice being "in the moment," cognizant of your surroundings, your senses fully engaged.

2. **Watch people without staring at them.** People-watching is something we do to evaluate who is in our space or near us.

3. **Pay attention to people's nonverbal cues.** What does their style of dress tell you? How are they acting, breathing, engaging, or not?

**4. Beware of distractions.** Limit distractions in and around you. Distractions are dangerous. They take your eye off the things you should be focusing on.

**5. Trust your gut feeling.** This one will come up repeatedly because your body picks up on energy from other people around you. Trust your gut. It's rarely wrong.

**6. Be strategic.** When you are in a situation that can pose a threat or you have to decide how you will get out of there: What will you need to do to make this stop, make it better, or fix it? Being strategic requires you to ask questions and then create a plan.

"All things can be deadly to us, even the things made to serve us; as in nature walls can kill us, and stairs can kill us, if we do not walk circumspectly."

—Blaise Pascal, *Pensées*

# LESSON 13

## Manage the Expectations of Yourself and Others

*"You are your own worst enemy. If you can learn to stop expecting impossible perfection, in yourself and others, you may find the happiness that has always eluded you."*

—Lisa Kleypas, *Love in the Afternoon*

## Your Expectations from Life

**E**xpectation. What a word. It is one of the few in the English language that is rife with many different and somewhat paradoxical meanings. On the one hand, we are told that expectations are good things to have for our lives. After all, if we don't rise to a standard, if we don't strive for excellence, if we don't expect something from ourselves—such as expectations for our education, for our relationships, and for how we live our lives—we're like a rudderless ship lost in the sea at night. On the other hand, we are told that having expectations is a problem, that when we expect things of people, or from our careers, or from the people we work with, we will always be left feeling a sense of disappointment. Because, after all, people rarely live up to our expectations of them just as we rarely live up to our expectations of ourselves. That makes very little sense, right? How can expectations be both good and bad? Well, they most certainly can be.

We all have expectations of what we want out of life and who we want to become. One of the keys to happiness lies in managing our expectations of people, of relationships, of ourselves, and of life itself. One of my biggest pet peeves is the phrase: "If you don't have expectations, you can never be disappointed." What a crappy, gloomy, pessimistic view of life. We want to believe that the way we treat others will be the way we are treated in return. Unfortunately, this does not always happen. So what? That's life. And part of the beauty of life is learning from our bad choices, our missteps, and our mistakes. It's how we grow wiser, smarter, kinder, and more empathetic.

As we said in Lesson 1, expectations start early in our lives, in our childhood. Think of all the stories you've read about how people, throughout history and in our own time, who experienced enormous pressure to follow in a father's footsteps, or to be more like their big brother the football star, or their sister the beautiful cheerleader. Or to become doctors, or lawyers, or engineers, or whatever their families expected from them, and how they spent most of their lives trying to live up to those expectations. The problem with expectations of that kind is that when you are constantly trying to measure up to someone else's dream, or someone else's life, sooner or later you're going to become resentful, angry, and distraught. You'll feel like you're missing something. And you are, because you're allowing someone else to take away the power of your own choice, your ability to determine your own life.

Trying to please other people is like chasing a moving bus. You will never catch up. One expectation once fulfilled will become another, and then another, and another still. Everyone in your life is going to have different hopes for you. There is nothing wrong with your family seeing talent in you as an artist and steering you to art school or noticing how fast you are when you run and steering you to join the track-and-field team at school. But social pressure is difficult to resist, and family pressure the most difficult of them all. Expectations become toxic when they override your own desires for your life. In reality, probably almost all of us have had to deal with overcoming the expectations of our family and our friends. Even our colleagues at work can sometimes expect things of us that simply aren't humanly possible or within the realm of what one person can realistically deliver by themselves.

By trying to please everyone, we end up pleasing no one—including ourselves. That's why most people don't live the lives they want. They do what's expected of them. And nobody knows this better than me. It took me decades to realize that I had not been living on my own terms, and that I was constantly meeting others' needs and others' expectations to the detriment of my own joy, happiness, and fulfill-ment. Expectations from others, and even sometimes from myself, made life harder, less enjoyable, and much more tumultuous. I want to save you from wasting precious years doing this same thing.

Here's what you need to understand about expectations: the rea-son we go about trying to meet everybody else's plan for our life, or to do what they want us to do, is that what we really are trying to get from them is love and respect, and we are trying to fulfill our own desire to have them both see and appreciate us. The key is for you to show love and respect for yourself by taking control of your life, by making your own choices, by standing up for yourself, trusting your intuition, and by developing a strong emotional IQ. Most of all, you need to believe in your own power and that you know what's best for you. In other words, you need to be the one you need.

**By trying to please everyone, we end up pleasing no one—including ourselves.**

Here are three things you need to understand about expectations:

1. Expectations can be a good thing.

2. Expectations can be the root of suffering.

3. Expectations lived in balance give us the best that life has to offer.

Let's start with the fact that all of us must expect some things from ourselves and others or else there will be chaos in our society, in our families, and in our places of business. What does it mean to expect, anyway? Well, according to *The Merriam-Webster Dictionary,* expectation means two things: First, it is a strong belief that something will happen or be the case in the future; Second, it is a belief that someone will or should achieve something.

One of our jobs as parents, aunts, uncles, grandparents, and mentors is to guide those entrusted to us on a good pathway in life. That means offering good advice, setting a good example, providing emotional and financial support, giving unconditional love, and being willing to speak truth and suggest correction in their lives when they make mistakes. What is not our job is dictating the terms of someone else's life or trying to manipulate and control others into doing and living life the way that we see fit. Unfortunately, this happens a lot in families, and it does extreme and lasting damage to the person who is the recipient.

## Expectations Can Be a Good Thing

My mother did a great job of setting the bar high for me. She gave me encouragement and she always taught me that I could do and be anything I set my mind to. She made it clear as far back as I can remember that I was going to law school, and that I was going to make something of my life so that I was never dependent upon a man for my financial well-being or otherwise. Looking at that expectation now, through my adult woman lens, I can say that her dream for me was accomplished. Yet, it was at a great cost to me personally. I touched on this somewhat in Lesson 1, but it is worth reiterating here, a bit differently.

My parent had a worthy goal for me to accomplish. Her intentions were pure. She was in a bad marriage. At the time she had no education past high school. She did not want her only daughter to have the same fate. I get it. I appreciate it. But the fate that has played out for me, and millions of accomplished women like me, is that we attained great success at great personal cost. Millions of Gen Xer women, and even more so Black Gen Xer women, are successful professionally, yet single, never married, and with no children. That's in part the subject of my first book, *Black Woman Redefined: Dispelling Myths and Discovering Fulfillment in the Age of Michelle Obama*. A good friend of mine, author Melanie Notkin, went even further, writing an entire book dedicated to this phenomenon: *Otherhood: Modern Women Finding a New Kind of Happiness*. In her book, she writes, "More American women are childless than ever before—nearly half those of childbearing age don't have children. While our society often assumes these women are 'childfree by choice,' that's not always true. In reality, many of them expected to marry and have children, but it simply hasn't happened."

Here's my point: the expectations placed on a generation of women born in the 1960s and 1970s was to not be like our mothers and grandmothers. Our mothers wanted us to be educated and independent. They wanted us to be free. They wanted us to be strong, smart, savvy, and fierce. In many ways, they wanted us to live the lives that they couldn't. And so many of us became just that. But the price we paid was a big one. We had to sacrifice marriage, children, and the emotional connection and partnership that all human beings crave. And men of our generation, by and large, were not yet comfortable with wives who worked outside the home and had careers. With a few rare exceptions, they had not been conditioned that way. Look at Kamala Harris, the first woman vice president of the United States, an early Gen Xer just a few years older than me. She did not get married until she was fifty, and she has no biological children. She is a stepmother to two young adults from her husband's first marriage.

Vice President Harris's career thrived because she could devote herself to it entirely. Just as men do, only they get to have wives who keep the home fires burning and raise their children. If you listen to speeches she has made talking about her mother, and how she was raised with her sister, she talks a lot about how her mom raised her to be strong, independent, and full of confidence. It worked. And it worked well. Her daughter broke barriers.

So, expectations are good. They are important. And they help shape us from the time we are small children well into early adulthood. But it is so important to note the costs of expectation. My mom had a great vision for my life, which I fulfilled. What she could not know, and never considered, was what I would have to endure and what I would ultimately lose. Law school was hard. It was expensive. I did not come from a family with money and means. I worked hard for everything I got. Trying to live up to my family's expectations of me, and their pride in my accomplishments, was like a heavy weight around my neck. I constantly had to lie, deny, and smile to keep up, when all I ever really wanted was my pen, my books, my guitar, and the love of a good man, some cute babies, and to grow old tending my garden in the country. (Remember, I told you that in my heart I am a mushy, romantic, homebody, softie, introverted Blue.)

> *"I'm not in this world to live up to your expectations and you're not in this world to live up to mine."*
>
> —Bruce Lee

Many studies show that it's good to have high expectations when it comes to your life and your relationships. Who wants to go through life with low expectations? We all need something to strive for and work toward. It makes life exciting and challenging. In short, it is healthy to have expectations of accomplishment, success, and personal happiness. More importantly, in our relationships it is important to have hopes for and expectations of finding mutual respect, affection, intimacy, and quality time. Being in a healthy relationship means you are getting your needs met by a person you love and trust, someone with whom you can be yourself. Otherwise, you will end up in sad, broken, unhealthy relationships where people treat you badly. That is not what you want or what you need in your life. Expectations can be very good. They can be life changing, but they also come with a cost if we don't set boundaries and manage others' expectations of us well.

## Expectations Can Be the Root of Suffering

Sometimes, we miss the greatest gifts in life because of the expectations we have of the way things "should be." We are so wedded to the checklist in our head. For example, as little girls we expect to have the lives we read about in fairytales, and later in romance novels and rom-coms—yet we often can't see what is right in front of us. We look at social media and see beautiful people post about what appear to be their perfect lives on Facebook and Instagram. For men, it can be the expectation of an adventurous life or playing professional sports. All of that can come true if we work for it and want it bad enough. The challenge, however, is that life, more often than not, does not always go the way that we planned. Life, as they say, is what happens when we are making other plans. Life is what happens when our expectations of the way life was supposed to be don't work out the way we envisioned.

The important takeaway is that if you dwell on what you lost, or on what you did not get, or on who walked away from you, you set yourself up for a life of victimhood and sorrow. Unmet expectations take a heavy toll on the mind, body, and soul. The Bible says in Proverbs 13:12, "A hope deferred makes the heart sick, but a longing fulfilled is a tree of life." It's the perfect summation of what happens when expectations (hopes, desires, vision) are not realized. Expectations, as I said, can be good for us, but unmet expectations can devastate us forever if we don't move past them and take hold of new dreams.

In a nutshell, unrealistic expectations most often lead us to a dark place of disappointment. Too many people, particularly in our age of gadgets, social media, and online dating, are obsessed with finding the perfect mate, and having the perfect career. As a result, they become increasingly frustrated when their expectations are not met. This is one of the unfortunate pitfalls of having too many expectations, not so much with our own personal goals in life, but in relation to other people and in certain circumstances that are simply beyond our ability to control. Remember that you cannot control other people.

If you're feeling lost or broken because you did not meet some of your expectations, or maybe even all of them, I understand. For a long time, the grief I felt over not being able to have children almost took me out. I was deeply depressed about this for more than a decade. I just hid it well, even from myself. I wanted children so badly. I had their names picked out. I started collecting things for a set of twins I was praying for (a boy and a girl) as early as college. I had two boxes made, one pink and one blue, and I put trinkets, clothes, and toys in them. I had vision boards. I was so ready to be a mom from the time I was thirty-two until my early forties. When it became obvious that motherhood wasn't going to be in the cards for me, I shifted to thinking about adopting. I went through the process, and then I considered that I would be a single parent and the sole breadwinner.

How was I going to do it all? Be a mom in the way I wanted (hands on) and work at a big law firm as a partner. I just didn't think I could do it all. I let fear stop me. I also had some health challenges that made getting pregnant difficult and pressing. The fertility doctors urged me to make embryos with my then boyfriend, or to harvest my eggs. This was the early 2000s and technology wasn't what it is now. I simply froze emotionally. I didn't make a decision. I was afraid of making a wrong choice out of fear. And in doing so, I made a choice, one I regret to this day. Please do not let fear or regrets stop you as they did me. What I want you to take away from this section are the following nuggets:

1. Don't dwell on what you once expected for your life. Lives change. People change. Learn to adapt your expectations for yourself and grow with them wisely.

2. Unmet expectations can be dangerous. Do the work of healing when something major you expected to happen in your life does not come to pass.

3. Don't put your expectations on other people until and unless you have had a conversation with them and agreed on a set of values and expectations for each other. People cannot agree to or act upon what they do not know. Communicate your expectations early and often, and make sure the other people in your life are on the same page so that they can know what to expect from you, too.

> *"Treat a man as he is, and he will remain as he is. Treat a man as he could be, and he will become what he should be."*
> —Ralph Waldo Emerson

Don't let expectations ruin your life. Simply readjust your expectations as required in life to keep things moving forward in a positive way.

## Expectations Lived in Balance Give Us the Best that Life Has to Offer

We are back where we started. *Expectations.* What a word.

We see that it has both positive and negative connotations. But here is what you need to know as we close out this life lesson: expectations are necessary, and they can be wonderful when we keep them in perspective and in balance with everything else in life. Yes, we should expect things from life—good things, happy things, fun things. But sometimes, the best way to get what we want is to just go into everyday life with an open mind. This allows us to fully immerse ourselves into enjoying life without the pressure of having to measure up to preconceived notions. When we have unrealistic ideas for people, and ourselves, we place ourselves at a greater risk of getting disappointed and hurt. Maybe people have let you down in certain aspects of your life, but it's unfair to yourself to give such people so much power over your life. It's the same with our own expectations. Think of how we beat ourselves up for decades because we did not end up where we thought we would or should. It happens. The most important way to respond is to keep going, keep moving, keep finding things to look forward to. By maintaining an accurate awareness of your own worth, you become able to better determine what is and is not truly expected of you. And what is not yours to offer or deliver.

It's all about balancing what is yours to carry and what is yours to cast off.

> **Expectations are necessary, and they can be wonderful when we keep them in perspective and in balance with everything else in life.**

The key to this life lesson, and every life lesson in this book, is to live your life in balance.

I want to end this lesson with some nuggets of wisdom I have learned about properly managing my expectations about myself and about others. Use these and add them to your EIQ toolkit. They will help you, I promise.

1. **Expectations are a natural part of living.** The goal is determining your expectations for yourself as opposed to others' expectations for you. They must be in balance.

2. **Life is not fair.** We rarely get everything that we want. And if we do get something we want, we rarely get it when we want it. Go with the flow. It all lines up in the end.

3. **Good things come after unmet expectations.** One of my favorite scenes from the movie *Gone with the Wind* is the one in which Scarlett O'Hara has lost everything—her child, her family home, her husband. Instead of giving up on life, as anyone under those circumstances would, she says, "After all, tomorrow is another day." She is correct. Good things can still happen even after we have lost everything.

4. **Everybody is not like you.** I had to learn this enlightening truth many times before I really got it. Everyone will not love like you, give like you, care like you, be loyal like you, help like you do. The faster you can grasp that one, the better your life will be.

5. **Negotiate expectations in relationships.** And most important of all: state what you want, what you need, and what you expect in your dating relationships, your family relationships, your marriage, as well as at work. Allow others to do the same.

It is not all about you. It is about navigating and negotiating expectations so that everybody is on the same page. Remember: say what you need to say. And let others do the same.

*"Today expect something good to happen
to you no matter what occurred yesterday. Realize the
past no longer holds you captive. It can only continue to
hurt you if you hold on to it. Let the past go.
A simply abundant world awaits."*

—Sarah Breathnach, *Simple Abundance:
A Daybook of Comfort and Joy*

# LESSON 14

## Beware of Distractions

*"You can't do big things if you're distracted by small things."*

—Anonymous

## *Your Ability to Focus on What Matters*

Distractions. Those pesky things can really derail your life if you aren't super focused and very intentional about your hopes, plans, connections with other people, and most of all, the pursuit of your dreams. And sometimes it's simply keeping on top of your day-to-day tasks. I believe the great challenge of our time is both time management and *soul management*. By the latter, I mean prioritizing what matters in our lives. We have put things over people. We have put success over family. We idolize our so-called connections when what they really are is disconnection. We are constantly being interrupted and disrupted by pinging, ringing, vibrating telephones, and we embrace every interruption as some sort of emergency. In truth, these create more distractions—the real threat, the real danger, that should have us sounding the alarm bells.

Let me explain. The twenty-first century is the era of multitasking. Multitasking has been sold to us as the ultimate achievement, a superpower. We've been led to believe that this is the ultimate way to win in life; the way without any consequences. The lie is that multitasking somehow allows us to perform several tasks simultaneously, increasing our capacity to do and to have more. But it's not true. Multitasking almost always results in exhaustion, frustration, and even emotional burn-out because we continually push the envelope further and further until it rips. The truth about multitasking is that it distracts us (there's that word—distraction). Instead of focusing on one thing at a time so that we fully complete each task, as previous generations did for millennia, we now are engaged in a shell game of moving back and forth among several tasks in quick succession, never giving deep, full attention to any of them.

I call it "capacity overload." I literally find myself walking around saying out loud, "I am overstimulated;" "I am overcapacity." "I need a minute." And I will stop what I am doing, or walk out of the room, and catch my breath. Literally.

Doing too many things at once is simply not good for your mind, your body, or your soul. True, we are strong creatures, but we are also fragile. Paradoxical, right? Yes. We push ourselves to the brink now. We don't take rest or respite. We do work. We do more work. And we do more work after that. What that means is we are never truly present; that we are always thinking and moving in our minds, if not actually in our physical being.

Distraction is another way of saying *interrupted*. Or the inability to give your full attention. My team hates this topic because I run around saying "FOCUS" all day. I bought them T-shirts with the word "Focus" emblazoned in bedazzled bling (sorry, fellas). It was my attempt at being both lighthearted and quite serious about what I want them to accomplish each day. I have noticed a direct correlation in my business between bookings and billings and focus. If my team was focused, they were able to follow up and follow through on speaking requests and corporate speaking engagements. If we were all over the place, trying to design websites, redesign materials, create content, create classes, work on book sales, etc., we ended up being distracted, frazzled, and very unproductive. I also noticed a high burnout rate from my senior staff because I am a good multi-tasker, or at least I like to tell myself I am. But the truth is, too much multitasking presents real challenges for us all.

Here's the thing about distraction and interruption: we are all energy centers. We flow and move in an energy force field. I have very fast-paced, fast-moving energy. I am like a whirlwind when I get wound up. I can do a lot in a very short period if I am focused and uninterrupted. When I have to stop and take my attention off working on a project, or having a conversation with another person, I interrupt my flow—whether it's for forty-five minutes or fifteen minutes—and it takes time to get back to where I was. The bad news is, like all of you, I often cannot get back to where I was or what I was doing, and then I must start over. Then I get frustrated. Then I start yelling. And I get all spun up because I am off-center and off my game.

By being distracted and allowing for interruptions, we unconsciously begin to foster a culture of broken concentration, lost social threads, stunted conversation, and unimaginable stress. When we're constantly losing the thread of what we're trying to do, it becomes difficult to define and pursue our most passionate goals. The next thing you know, we get stuck. We forget and abandon new ideas before they have a chance to develop. This is a challenging way to live life and not one I recommend. So, my first piece of serious advice in this lesson is that you take being focused seriously, and finish what you start before moving on to something else. It requires discipline and self-control—but the payoff is infinite.

Before I get into giving you some more EIQ tools, I want to acknowledge that, because we in fact do live in this robust, wild digital age, we will need to multitask from time to time. But we also need to learn the skill of deep focus and finishing what we start. We need to balance the new mandatory art of multitasking with the age-old need to focus. Distraction is the great enemy of connection. And we have all allowed our devices to run our lives. They are an unwelcome, but much courted intrusion into our lives. And if we do not course-correct soon, our lives, our work, and indeed our society will crumble.

We human beings are simply not wired to multitask 24/7, to always be on or on call. We need to turn off. We need to step back. We need to be truly connected to other people. We need to give our brains a rest. We need human touch, engagement, and love. Research shows that we have entered a cultural phase of

> *"Your results are the product of either personal focus or personal distractions. The choice is yours."*
> —**John Di Lemme**

what is called, "toxic positivity." Again, paradoxical, yes? How can something positive be toxic? Well, toxic positivity is a new phrase that means dismissing our negative emotions and instead responding to distress with false reassurances (like my least favorite church lady saying, "I'm too blessed to be stressed.") rather than stopping and assessing what we need from a place of empathy and caring. Our devices, our obsession with social media, and the shortened human attention span (because of all this instant media) have gone a long way toward causing us to live life on the surface. Distraction is something we invite.

This toxic positivity is another way of saying "fake." By being distracted so much of the time, we have learned how to divert and lie, not just to others, but most of all to ourselves. It all comes from being uncomfortable with our negative or unaddressed emotions. Such diversion is often well-intentioned, but we all know that the road to hell is paved with good intentions. Not dealing with what ails us, or concerns us, or is otherwise distracting us, can cause deep alienation and a feeling of disconnection from everyone around us. We have learned to hide in plain sight.

So, what's the answer? Simply put, slow down. Learn how to focus on what matters, once again. Parents, set boundaries with the devices your kids use. Put them on a schedule, make sure that every day they spend quality time with siblings and family: talking, engaged in old-fashioned conversation. Talk about the news, talk about their interests—just talk. And once you have checked your kids' devices and distractions, check your own. You must set an example for your kids. YOU. Show your spouse some attention. Make your relationships a priority, not by being busy, exhausted, and overwhelmed, but by showing your community what it means to rest; what it means to be focused on what truly matters in life; what it means to walk out self-care and to devote yourself mind, body, and soul to your relationships. And not in a crazed, foggy, emotionally exhausted way that only ends up hurting people, leaving an unhappy you, and a trail of badly broken relationships.

> *"Work is hard.*
> *Distractions are*
> *plentiful. And time is*
> *short."*
> —Adam Hochschild

The way forward will not be easy. We are literally addicted to distraction. But we must fight back by making a choice to devote our full attention to life. I think it is fair to say that at no time has man had so many shiny, new things to distract him from his true purpose: a life of wandering and wondering, a life well lived.

## Don't Get Distracted with Your Goals

Successful people are focused. They have mastered the art of filtering out the unimportant and embracing the useful. They know how to get rid of people who are toxic, or who drain the soul with human messiness, gossip, or drama. Successful people attract who and what they are: other focused, devoted, smart, connected people. That is why they win. Whether at sports, business, in education, or otherwise, successful people do not do distraction. I had to learn this the hard way. I lost so many years being connected to soul-draining, toxic family members and frenemies, and sometimes good people who fell hard on hard times and needed a friend, and because of my own issues, I always felt compelled to save them.

I wised up in my forties. I realized that I was not responsible for other people's choices or their bad luck. I was not supposed to fix broken people, or worse, invite them into my business to work for me. I got burned on that one many times—until I finally learned to stop.

Winning at your personal and professional life requires that you focus; that you surround yourself with good people, honest brokers, and people who can help to get you where you want to go. To do that, you have to prove yourself worthy. You must practice good discipline. You must be honest with yourself about the things in your life that you want to pay attention to, versus the things that you must pay attention to. In a culture of constant multitasking and interruption, you must practice the art of being intentional. All successful people do so.

Being intentional requires that we make time for reflection, con-nection, thought, and invention. It requires sitting with that "why" we talked about earlier in the book. Finding your why or your mission in life is how you discover your talents, your gifts, and your abilities. But it all requires a devoted focus. In the workplace and in our pro-fessional goals and aspirations, we need to be both brave and bold. We need to be willing to break the rules and change the norm. We must be intentional about teaching and learning core emotional intel-ligence skills, such as: how to be present in a room; how to choose good mentors and sponsors; how to structure time management; how to engage people who think differently than you do, look differently, and live differently; how to show empathy; how to say thank you when people lift you as they themselves climb.

In short, good leaders, good workers, and good managers need to redefine the behavioral norms around what it means to focus and to strategically multitask so that it will produce the most value, not just for their business, but for their human capital as well. This is something that all of us need to have a conversation about. If we can change policies around public safety and health, enforce seat-belt rules in vehicles and no-smoking rules in airplanes and restaurants, we can also start to reform our culture of distraction and begin to change the habits and attitudes that devalue the very human need for focused attention.

> *"You can't do big things if you're distracted by small things."*
> —Anonymous

## Don't Get Distracted in Your Relationships

Human relationships require work. They require nurturing, attention, pruning, growth, devotion, loyalty, and most of all attentive love, or in other words: focus.

Most relationships fail because they die from two things: poor communication and drifting apart over time as people change and grow. I am no expert on relationships, but I have been in several long-term romantic relationships, and I have friendships that date back to grade school. I have a family. I have had struggles in my relationships, like all of you. The reality is that whether it's romantic love, agape love, filial love, or passionate love, all relationships require our attention. And they must be regularly tended to just like a garden or nothing will grow and blossom.

In our multitasking world, we think we can treat our relationships like our devices. We text instead of talk. We ghost people when we no longer have the desire or interest to be with them. We hide. We cower. We duck. And we feel justified. And what has happened over the course of the past decades, in which distraction has become king, is that people have suffered. Depression. Suicide. Mental-health issues. Emotional challenges. Divorce. A huge surge in people in the US taking antidepressants. And on and on.

We have allowed our inability to stop, look, and listen to truly impact even our most sacred of spaces: our relationships with other human beings. I want to give you a few tips on how not to allow distractions to destroy your relationships. At the end of the day, love is all we take with us. And love is worth the fight. People are worth the fight. And we better start figuring that out, or we are lost as a civilization. Relationships need ample positive exchanges. You must fill up one another's cup. You must have a mutuality of reciprocity, gestures of affection, kindness, compliments, and you must listen deeply with empathy and helpful cooperation.

I needed to have a conversation recently with someone I had not spoken to in a very long time. We did not have a good parting. But we reconnected and we both wanted to talk. I asked for permission before we even called one another to use a communication tool I learned as a young attorney. It has served me well in both my personal and professional relationships. It works best on the telephone, but it can work well in person if you have the discipline to follow the rules of courageous conversation. It goes like this: Each person gets a total of up to ten minutes to talk as the other person listens quietly. They must mute themselves. Or, if in person, they must sit quietly and not interrupt. Under no circumstance are you allowed to speak as the other person is speaking. The point is to HEAR and not to RESPOND; to take notes and to have to state back what you heard. Then you switch roles. Once you have both been heard, you can dialogue openly about what each of you has shared and wants.

I was glad that we did this, because our thirty-minute talk turned into a two-hour talk. And it was a healing, much-needed conversation. I blocked out the time and so did she. We were intentional to pick a good day, one when we would be alone in our homes, and when we would be uninterrupted for that block of time. My point is this: being intentional about your relationships and the people you love, value, and care for is essential in a busy world full of distractions. We made the time. We both acted in good faith toward one another. And I can tell you that it unleashed a wellspring of good feelings that refreshed us both. When goodwill is extended, negative moments from our past don't drain the well dry. But you must put in the work. If you want good relationships, you must invest in them. Put down the devices and make yourself emotionally available and accessible.

> *"Don't be on your deathbed someday, having squandered your one chance at life, full of regret because you pursued little distractions instead of big dreams."*
> —Derek Sivers

## The Price We Pay for Distraction

Distraction is not just a word we throw around. Distraction can have deadly consequences. According to a *Forbes* magazine article entitled, "Why Distraction Is So Dangerous and What We Can Do About It," in 2011, 1.3 million auto accidents in the US involved cell phones, about 23 percent of all crashes. Also in 2011, 3,331 people were killed in crashes involving a distracted driver, compared to 3,267 in 2010. The author, David DiSalvo, gives amazing statistics on just how dangerous distraction is. Citing data that is sobering and upsetting all at once, he writes, "For drivers 15-19 years old involved in fatal crashes, 21 percent of the distracted drivers were distracted by the use of cell phones. Text messaging while driving makes the chance of an accident 23 times more likely. Sending or receiving a text takes a driver's eyes off the road for an average of 4.6 seconds; at 55 mph, that's the equivalent of driving the length of an entire football field, blind." That was almost ten years ago. What about now?

Let's fast forward to 2021. According to NCS Data Systems, using a cell phone while driving accounts for over 1.6 million auto accidents in the US, an increase of roughly 300,000 annually. Despite better technologies in our cars' accident-warning systems, we can't stop the dangers of distraction. We can only be diligent about mitigating the things that distract us and ultimately make us unsafe.

What kinds of distractions are there? **Personal ones:** for example, marital problems, or caring for a sick family member. **Financial ones:** for example, overspending and running up your credit cards, with no money to pay bills when they come due. **Emotional ones:** for example, people who know how to pull on your emotional heartstrings, manipulate you, and pull you out of your peace and into their life storms.

Distractions have a scientific impact on our bodies and brain functions, too. According to a 2018 *Medium* article entitled, "Seriously Distracted: A Report on Our Interrupted Life," by Oksana Tunikova, she shares some data points that once again drive home the impact of distraction on our lives. For example, she noted that, "A typical office worker cannot focus on a task at hand for more than eleven continuous minutes. The average student can't focus on a given task for more than two minutes without getting distracted. If you are a typical Internet user, your online screen focus lasts a mere forty seconds on average. The worst part? No matter what task you are distracted from or what form the interruption takes, once distracted, your brain needs an average of twenty-five minutes to get back to the original task." She goes on to say that our brains are actually hard-wired for distraction. In other words, attracted to distraction. She says, "In fact, we all have an internal urge to be distracted. To the human brain, any distraction means novelty, and everything new is associated with an increase in dopamine levels (the neurochemical associated with pleasure and reward). This means we are predisposed to fall for distractions, biologically."

The takeaway is that we need to be more aware of how we choose to manage our time and how we deal with distractions in our daily lives. Here are a few things that I have incorporated into my daily routine that have made a huge impact on my focus, time management, and self-care.

1. I have specific times a day to check emails: first thing in the morning, again at noon, and later before the day ends.

2. I have specific times a day when I check my phone for texts or calls. People who need to find me, can.

3. I have specific days for specific tasks. I do not allow distractions, or people who distract me, to get access to me on a daily basis. I have a good assistant who protects my peace and my time.

4. I do not text and drive or answer my phone while driving unless it is hands-free and I am on a long drive where I am on open roads and can talk and drive safely. I do not talk on the phone on highways or in traffic.

5. I have a daily task and to-do list. I follow it and check items off. I put everything on a list and give it a date by which I need it done.

These are just five tips that help me to not become distracted. The key is for you to identify your blind spots and know what you need to do. Know what you need to keep or what you need to get rid of. Distractions keep us from the life we want. You must do the work of intentionality and focus if you want to keep distractions from derailing your life.

"When we clutter our lives with imagined obligations, unnecessary activities, and distractions that only kill time, we dilute the power of our lives."

—Anne Katherine

# LESSON 15

## Your Faith Is Your Fuel:
## Fill Up Daily

*"The reason birds can fly, and we can't is simply because they have perfect faith, for to have faith is to have wings."*

—J.M. Barrie, *The Little White Bird*

## Your Compass for Living

*"Now faith is the substance of things hoped for,*
*the evidence of things not seen."*

**(Hebrews 11:1)**

F aith is something that every human being has had to confront at one time or another. Our faith is what sustains us. Our faith is what anchors us. Our faith is what allows us to get through the most unthinkable and challenging things that life throws our way. One's faith is something deeply personal, deeply sacred, and deeply held. It is the essence of who we are. I should be clear that faith and religion are not the same. Religion is a set of practices that come together around a set of values, traditions, texts, canons, and beliefs. When I think of religion, I think rigidity. I think rules. I think closed and not open.

Faith, however, is something much deeper. It is a guide. It is a compass for living, for how to be resilient in life. It is what tells you to keep going when everyone and everything around you tells you to stop. It is that whisper that sustains you in your most challenging life storms. It is hope that overrides appearances and propels you to go places you've never gone before, to try things you've never tried, to love again even if you've been hurt.

Find your faith because it's not the only thing in life—it's everything.

Faith derives from Latin *fides,* meaning confidence or trust in a person, thing, or concept. And of all the faith walks we make, the greatest is the walk to have faith in ourselves. And that is the walk that I want to discuss with you in this life lesson. Having faith in yourself is really another way of saying that you know your value, that you know you have worth, that you know you have gifts, and that you want to share those gifts with the world. And that no matter who or what may come against you in life, ultimately you will succeed because you believe in yourself. For me personally, it also means that there is a force greater than me, who has faith in me, too, and that force has a direct impact on my day-to-day living in the realm of things unseen.

One of the first things that they teach you in Alcoholics Anonymous or Al-Anon (which is where I spent many years, trying to heal from my childhood trauma) is that first you must admit that you are powerless over your addiction, and, second, you must submit to a higher power, a power greater than yourself that can restore you to a good, healed, whole place. That power is another way of saying faith. When we have faith in something, we are committed to it. When we have faith in ourselves, then possibilities in life are endless. But faith requires something of us. It requires humility, submission, and surrender. That is the part that most people miss. In other words, faith is empowering, and, at the same time, it requires you to surrender to the power that pushes you, drives you, and helps you to soar. My goal in this lesson is to drive home just one simple but invaluable point: your faith is necessary to get through life. You cannot live without faith. Again, faith is not to be confused with religion, or dogma, or attending church services. Faith is something far more fluid, far more meaningful, and far more impactful. It's important to understand and know what faith is, and then put your faith to work to radically change your life for the better.

To grasp the true nuance of faith is to explore something far beyond what you may think of as faith. But there's a catch. The Bible says, "Faith without works is dead." Translation: If you say you have faith, but you aren't applying that faith in your life, you are wasting your time, because faith is not for the faint of heart. Faith requires you to not just believe in something, but, far more importantly, to actually do something.

Let me start with a premise. Everything in your life starts with a belief system and that belief system comes from your family and your community. We operate our lives from our beliefs. Beliefs run the show. One of our most basic beliefs is in self. It is an immutable fact that every successful human being who has ever lived believed in himself or herself when everyone else around them may not have. They not only believed in their own abilities and ideas, but they also believed that they could be the first, that they could blaze the trail, that they could go where no one else had gone before. The Wright Brothers. Henry Ford. John D. Rockefeller. Andrew Carnegie. Thomas Edison. John Glenn. John F. Kennedy. Martin Luther King. Mahatma Gandhi. Rosa Parks. Shirley Chisholm. Abraham Lincoln. America's founding fathers. All these men and women believed in themselves. They had faith that helped them overcome their fears, that helped them do the extraordinary things that most regular people never dream of.

**Everything in your life starts with a belief system and that belief system comes from your family and your community. We operate our lives from our beliefs. Beliefs run the show.**

So, what makes them different? Faith. The unyielding belief in your own success. Marching to the beat of your own drum, with a spiritual connection to that higher power, to God, to whatever you call that force that gives you the bravery to run with the wolves and ascend the mountain. Without belief in yourself, you will inevitably hit a career wall, or become stagnant in your relationships, or, worse, be unable to reach your goals in life.

Here are three faith builders practiced by successful people that you must incorporate into your life if you want to follow the same path:

1. Successful people do not engage in self-doubt.

2. Successful people are optimists.

3. Successful people do not care what others think.

You must be able to consistently adhere to the belief that you can, and will, succeed. A determined belief that you can be successful in life requires an unyielding confidence that, regardless of where you are in life, or what has happened to you in your past, anything is still possible. Those who struggle with their faith and self-worth are very unlikely to be successful. Faith provides the emotional fuel we need to keep going. And I, for one, see my faith as the fuel that has saved me time and time again. When I think of all I have been through, there are times when it seems impossible that I did not end up in a very different place in my life. I look at people I know who had every advantage I did not. They came from loving families. They came from wealth and privilege, which gave them access and connections. And yet they somehow gave in to those darker impulses of life that I was able to avoid. Let me be clear: I am no saint. I have made some poor choices. I have been in some bad relationships. I have done some dumb stuff. But I never, no matter what, lost faith in myself. And thank God for that, or I would not be here.

My faith was put to its greatest test when I lost pretty much everything I had in the span of just one year: my relationship with a man I really liked

> **Faith provides the emotional fuel we need to keep going. And I, for one, see my faith as the fuel that has saved me time and time again.**

and loved, my home, my health, my financial stability. It all vanished due to an illness and huge medical bills, and my own lack of physical and emotional self-care. This is where the rubber meets the road. It can happen to any of us, and it can happen at any time. Being a single woman, you are very vulnerable to the storms of life because you have no support to back you up if the bottom falls out from underneath you. And when it does, what you often find is that your support system is some great friends if you are lucky, some family if you still have them, but most of the time it is just you. You and God. You and **your faith.**

Loss, death, financial collapse, divorce, a sick child, a sick parent—all these can devastate you. They can turn your life upside down quickly. And if you do not have a strong faith, a strong belief in your ability to get through it all, the truth is you won't.

All of us face storms in life. But the people who rise like the phoenix from the ashes are those who dig deeper. They lean into the pain. They lean into the lessons. And they learn, they grow, and then they teach others how to do the same. That is why I wrote this book. I do not want all the hell I have been through to go to waste. There are many times the only encouragement I had in my life as a small child; as a young woman struggling through college and graduate school; as a young career woman in a profession in which I was often the only person who looked like me, was my faith. I had to believe in me when everyone and everything around me said this cannot be done.

**Here's the bottom line.** Successful people have one huge thing in common: they understand the power of choice. At any given moment, they may have one foot on the side of possibility and greatness, and the other in fear and doubt—just like the rest of us often do. What sets them apart, however, is that they listen to the voice inside, the voice that is fueled by faith in themselves that never allows them to quit. Or give in. Or give up. All the resources in the world can be at your fingertips—money, friends, support, innovative ideas, and a solid game plan—but the best preparation and expert guidance is all for naught if you're not able to hold on to the belief that genuine success is attainable and sustainable. You must see it, you must believe it, and you must make it happen. So, let's look at those three faith builders I mentioned, and I want you to really take them in. Of all the life lessons in this book, this one is on you, more than any other. Because your faith is deeply personal. It's you and your faith against the world.

> **You must be able to consistently adhere to the belief that you can, and will, succeed. A determined belief that you can be successful in life requires an unyielding confidence that, regardless of where you are in your life, or what has happened to you in your past, anything is still possible.**

## Successful People Do Not Engage in Self-Doubt

Faith is indeed fuel for success. Successful people use their faith not only to keep moving forward in life but also to expel doubt. That's really what faith is about after all. It's getting rid of fear, doubt, worry, and regret. Of course, all those emotions are normal. We all suffer from self-doubt at some point. But people who have a dependable faith are good at talking themselves out of their doubts. Or, at the very least, they do not take their self-doubt too seriously. Instead of overanalyzing all that could go wrong, they concentrate on their strengths. They replace doubt with daring. They take the risk. They use their strengths to serve as a strong foundation from which to leap into the big wide world to show off their skills.

Self-belief accounts for a large part of your success in life. I have seen many people without the great gifts of charm, intelligence, or natural talent achieve some pretty great things due to their faith and self-belief. I have also seen super-gifted and talented people waste their potential completely due to their lack of faith. Believing in yourself is the springboard for how high you can go. Without self-belief, self-love, and faith in yourself, your talents will likely never see the light of day. You will find yourself limited and stuck. You will struggle to be the best you can be. But if you work hard to surround yourself with positive people, positive thoughts, and a positive outlook, it will make all the difference in the world.

## Successful People Are Optimists

Despite all I have been through, I am still an optimist. My friends joke about that all the time. They marvel at how I have kept going through so much grief, trauma, and loss. The secret is once again: my faith. Despite moments of despair, moments when I didn't know how to keep living, I always found a way forward. I learned how to truly lean into prayer. I created vision boards. I built altars of positivity all around me when all I felt was dread. I forced myself to look for the next thing. To create the next thing. To be the next best thing in my life. I had to learn to be the one that I needed. I had to find something to look forward to, even when all seemed lost.

Successful people all have the ability to do this. And a huge part of being successful is being resilient. Being resilient is 100 percent about having faith in God, or whatever higher force you believe in; having faith in yourself; having faith in your future. It is the ability to see the good in situations even when no one else can. Even in the face of glaringly negative facts, you summon the courage to get back up. Your faith is your fight. Your faith is your purpose. Your faith is your voice in the world. That is why I write inspirational books. That is why I give inspirational speeches. That is why I am sharing with you all I know about making the choice between being negative when things go wrong, versus choosing to find the silver lining.

Nothing in life would ever be accomplished, invented, established, blazed, mended, built, or achieved if we all focused on what could go wrong, versus focusing on what is possible. Faith is all about optimism and the art of the possible. Successful, resilient people look for the good in situations and then go about creating and building the structures and strategies that will help them to succeed. Optimism doesn't mean you don't have worries, fears, or challenges. It simply means that you have learned how to be mentally strong and mentally tough so that you can face and overcome life's difficulties.

## Successful People Do Not Care What Others Think

I have already given you a life lesson about dealing with haters. In Lesson 7, we talked about how no matter what you do in life, no matter how kind, good, or accomplished you are, you will always have haters.

Every successful person I know cares a lot about their own opinions. Follow me here. I am not talking about someone who is arrogant or self-important. I am talking about someone who hearkens to their own voice when other voices are arrayed against them. I am that person. I have been that person my whole life. I will be that person until I die. It gets back to the life lesson on trusting your instinct, trusting your gut. Yes, we all need advice, coaching, and people who correct us. But successful, resilient, and brave people listen to their own voice above the naysayers. They hear that voice that says, "Forget about what they said. You got this. Go."

Your faith is what helps you weed through the fear. Your faith is what helps you cut through the noise of the mob. It all comes down to knowing what you are capable of when others may not. You must have strong belief systems, a set of core values that line up with your faith. Values like humility. Honesty. Integrity. Faith alone will not get you there, but faith is that fuel you will need to travel the highway to a successful life.

I know some of you are probably saying, "But, Sophia, I don't think I can do this faith thing you're talking about because I don't believe in God or a higher power. I believe that life is made up of good luck and bad luck." Well, here's what I say: you are free to believe that. But life will be better if you can believe in something bigger than yourself. Because in so doing, you learn to draw from that source and believe more in you. At the end of the day, the difference between, say, my belief system as compared to someone else's is that I know my value. I like myself. I believe in myself. I have learned not to let my detractors and haters get me down or hold me down. I like what I stand for. They don't have to. If you want to win at life, you must walk in your truth. You must be authentic. You must have strong values and live a life that is true to what is important to you. It's easy to be wishy-washy when you don't have clear values. Successful people don't just say, "That's the way it is." They don't just let life happen to them; they go out and make things happen. They constantly look for ways to improve the "way it is." They are leaders, not followers, and they aren't afraid to go against the grain. The more people tell them something can't be done, the more determined they become to prove it can be done.

*"Fear finds an excuse while faith finds a way."*

**—Seth Adam Smith**

# SECTION IV
## Relationships Are Not Transactional—They Are Reciprocal

*We were made for relationship. We are not meant to do this thing called life alone. We all need the tools to help us win at our relationships and bless others in the process. But our most important relationship is the one we have with ourselves.*

# LESSON 16
## Don't Cancel and Publicly Shame People

*"Humanity is fallible and every single one of us is capable of sin but if it were not for the hopes of one day being redeemed none of us will seek to understand our flaws and make the effort to rectify the damage our actions have made."*

—Aysha Taryam

## *How You Extend Grace to Others*

You can't say anything anymore. That's the truth of where we are in our public discourse, and even in our private lives. We are suffering from the death of dialogue and a lack of grace in our twenty-first century communication. We are mean. We are unkind. And we are always ready to ruthlessly destroy other people who do not agree with us, or who may not see life the way we see it, or who experience life differently in day-to-day living. None of us experiences life the same way as others. None of us sees the world the same way as others. We are complex, layered. It is for that reason that I want to talk about this very concerning emergence of what we now know as "cancel culture."

We've all heard the term. *The Cambridge Dictionary* defines cancel culture as "a way of behaving in a society or group, especially on social media, in which it is common to completely reject and stop supporting someone because they have said or done something that offends you." Some people say the term is overused or that it is an overtly political term used by aggrieved people who do not want to be held accountable. Or that it has become a meaningless term. I disagree. We are living in a world deeply caught up in cancel culture frenzy.

Everywhere you look—from Hollywood to the NFL, from college campuses to corporations, from churches to organizations—you see news of yet another "cancelled" person being cast out, fired, blackballed, removed, and shamed. Once respected people whose views and opinions may differ from the norm—comedians, sports heroes, and university professors—are being made to prostrate themselves with a virtual scarlet letter hung around their necks due to some perceived, made up, or even real slight against some group. In this life lesson, I want to avoid the politics of this issue and dig deeper into why we want to cancel others, and to encourage you not to do it. It is a battle that nobody wins. And one in which everyone will lose sooner or later.

I opened this book talking about the way the dynamics of the American family have shifted because of the impact of the Millennials, Gen Yers, and Gen Zers. These age groups do not engage in relationships the way those of us over forty do. We learned our values from our parents and grandparents. They learn theirs from social media and the Internet. We learned faith and values from our churches, our community, our Little League coaches, our teachers. We learned the importance of having basic good manners (I will address this in the next section of the book). We respected our elders even when they were grumpy, mean, or unkind. We got up when our grandparents entered the room. We sent Christmas cards, birthday cards, and thank-you notes. We were taught about duty and understood the importance of family. Our current generations feel empowered to say that people and situations that require grace and forgiveness are "toxic." They refuse to engage in dialogue because it "triggers" them or "traumatizes" them. I have seen this firsthand in my family and on the college campus where I teach in Virginia. We kept family secrets even when it was not healthy or helpful for us to do so. We forgave our parents their trespasses and took them in if they needed love and comfort in their old age. We revered our grandmothers and grandfathers. We helped feed hungry neighbors. We looked out for other kids growing up. We would never have allowed blatant bullying to go unaddressed. We didn't have cell phones; instead, we learned the art of conversation. The art of friendship and of courtship. We learned about empathy because our personal connections fostered it. Our culture and our times demanded no less. Publicly shaming someone was unheard of. It was considered impolite, cruel, and unforgivable.

There has been a breakdown of the social order in this PC culture. In my opinion, this new generation embraces "group think." They have been raised that way. They don't do forgiveness. They don't do redemption or grace. They don't do dialogue face-to-face. They do not like that—they do not want to be "triggered" or "unsafe." They block, delete, unfriend, cut, put you on blast, take embarrassing videos, secretly record you, call people out, protest, petition (they really love the online change.org petitions), and harass you if you do not do what they want, when they want. That said, I honestly don't believe it is their fault. They learned it from the adults in the community and high office, from the US President Donald Trump and other politicians to attendees at school-board meetings. They have learned that life is a zero-sum game. Like *Game of Thrones*, there are Dragons and Dragon Slayers. There is only black or white. There is no gray. There is the only way they see the world, and the way they experience the world. And if you don't agree with them, you must be removed or discarded. Technology may have liberated us in many ways, but it is dealing a devastating blow to human dialogue, human dignity, and basic human respect.

One of my favorite quotes by evolutionary biology professor Heather E. Heying, who was "canceled" into resigning from Evergreen State College, is: "Please engage me: First, as a human. Second, as an individual. Last if you must, go tribal."

A new phenomenon has emerged where young adults are now cancelling their parents, siblings, friends, and colleagues. They hold grudges. They do not suffer slights. They expect forgiveness to come swiftly but do not offer it themselves. They do not like to be held accountable. They judge harshly and then condemn people if those people make mistakes or missteps. Folks, I must tell you, this is really a problem.

Do you know what it means to get cancelled? It means you can lose your career, your income, your good name, your identity.

The question is: who gets to decide who should be held accountable? Who gets to decide what we are allowed to say, or who can speak and who must stay silent. In the eyes of the law, there are things we can do and things we cannot do. And ignorance of those laws is no excuse. For example, you can't tell the judge that, even though you admit you were doing 85 miles per hour in a 40-mile-per-hour zone, he should let you off with no fine because you didn't know the speed limit. That won't fly.

Likewise, there are laws against hate speech, intimidation, and harassment of people in the workplace and in public spaces. You cannot, for instance, use racial slurs toward your colleagues of color, claiming this is your free-speech right and therefore your employer cannot discipline you or fire you. Yes, you do have that free speech, but you will also have to deal with the consequences of your words. We should all be in favor of standards of lawfulness, respect, and decency. Those standards, ethics, and laws keep a free society free, safe, and open to all her citizens. But cancel culture is quickly becoming a part of our normal, everyday life. Let's start with the powerful words of author Abhijit Naskar, in "Sonnet 52," from his book *Giants in Jeans: 100 Sonnets of United Earth*:

> *Humanhood isn't him, her or them,*
> *Humanhood requires realization beyond sex.*
> *Pronouns may be a step in the right direction,*

*But they are not passport for arrogance and disrespect.*
*The purpose is to erase hate from society,*
*And we ain't gonna do that by passing judgment.*
*If we want there to be equity and acceptance,*
*We must learn to trample first our own arrogance.*
*Rebelling for the sake of rebelling achieves nothing,*
*Arrogance only produces just another bitter creature.*
*In trying to fight against prejudice and oppression,*
*Be cautious that you don't end up as the new oppressor.*
*Revolution is the foundation of civilization's evolution,*
*But it must be rooted in gentleness, not cancellation.*

Naskar's powerfully elegant poem describes the reason why we should never cancel one another's humanity. Cancel culture is real. It is a form of public shaming that aims to destroy people. It calls people out and not in. It seeks to shame the person who has broken some PC rule, or new ever-evolving cultural norm, or dared to ask a question. I know. I have been there. And it is horrible. I touched on this a bit in Lesson 1 but after further reflection, I realized that I needed to address this in a much bigger and more thorough way.

> *"Cancel Culture grows because we accept (and gluttonously consume) social violence. We no longer seek truth or both sides of a story. Whichever side is loudest, wins . . . gardless of its relationship to the truth."*
>
> **—Steve Maraboli**

## My Cancel Culture Experience

In the fall of 2021, I was publicly shamed, berated, and humiliated repeatedly by a group of angry faculty and students at Christopher Newport University in Virginia where I was serving as a scholar-in-residence. Their collective behavior can only be described as mob-like—hell-bent on seeking revenge without knowing all the facts. It was a situation that quickly spun out of control and was the worst experience of my entire professional career. I have never been so traumatized in all my life, and as you've gathered from reading this far into the book, you know that is saying a lot.

People who could have talked to me, engaged me, heard my heart, and, I believe, grown to respect and like me, instead made it their mission to not just call me out for a tweeted question they did not like (I had asked respectfully, in good faith, about the effect on children of a cartoon's character "coming out" as bisexual), but to attempt to destroy my reputation and career. I suffered severe damage online, in media reports, and sensationalized headlines. As you know, once something appears on the Internet it can never be taken off. My speaking engagements were cancelled, my corporate engagements were cancelled, I lost needed income to take care of my life and that of family members dependent upon me. I was made out to be a bigoted monster, a racist, a homophobe. My life's work and my life itself prove how ridiculous and false such allegations are, but facts do not matter once the mob of anger and correctness comes for you.

Some people believe that canceling others leads to a more just society. In reality, however, it leads to an angrier and more divided society. How boring would the world be if all of us agreed all the time, thought the same way, spoke the same language, loved the same way, laughed the same way? It's like the 1990s movie *Pleasantville* (young people, look it up on streaming and watch it). I grew up in a community much like that movie. There were definitive rules, norms, and conduct. But it was almost all uniform. We were isolated in our own neat little world. When I left my childhood home of South Jersey and went to college in Southern California, I discovered a whole new world. I met a diverse group of people and experienced different cultures I had never encountered before. The point is this: when we stifle our diversity, we stifle our richness, our collective individuality.

The new mantra from those who like to tell the rest of us how to think, live, and speak is that cancel culture is not real, that in reality it is just a new "consequence culture" meant to "deplatform" the social capital of those who cause offense or harm. What an arrogant, holier than thou, tragic way to live. Who empowered these people to tell us whether we need to suffer consequences or not?

> *"Do not confuse the crippling hauntedness of judgment with the transformational power of awareness."*
> —Abhijit Naskar

The next time you feel the urge to cancel people, to try them in the court of public opinion, instead pause and reflect on the four points that I'm going to share with you. Take the time to take them in. Remember, our goal should be to call people IN, not cancel them OUT. Let karma have her way, and you go on your way, and remember that the judgment and condemnation you render to others will be returned to you in the same manner.

Here are my four fundamental truths about why you should never cancel people and what you should do instead:

1. Vengeance is God's purview, not ours.

2. Judging others is not your business.

3. We should offer grace in abundance.

4. Extend forgiveness liberally.

## Vengeance Is God's Purview, Not Ours

This point harks back to Lesson 15, about using your faith as fuel for good in your life. Faith allows us to move beyond our wounds and to envision a better way forward, whereas vengeance mires us in regret and anger. Vengeance is as old as humanity itself, fueled by dangerous emotions, and it becomes an action that we often cannot take back once executed. This is why you find it embedded in texts throughout history: *Lex Talionis*—the law of retaliation, the law of retribution, the Old Testament—all of it has to do with punishment, banishment, and consequences for socially unacceptable behavior. We are more evolved now than the time in which those concepts of justice and punishment were written. Or are we? My good friend, author Steve Maraboli, speaking about the online carnage of cancel culture or retribution, says it like this: "It's an online coliseum now. We feel evolved, but we're still throwing those we disagree with to the lions. Entertained with the social bloodshed we see." I couldn't agree more.

We need to leave vengeance or retribution to someone smarter, higher up, and more objective than us. We have rightly enacted laws to make clear that people know the rules of the game. But this new culture of canceling people on a whim is dangerous. We should not have the ability to ruin other people because we're offended. Do not operate out of vengeance. Operate in a spirit of letting karma have her way. Let the law decide the proper punishment. Vengeance and seeking it mars the human soul. Let it go. It's not a good way to live.

## Judging Others Is Not Your Business

As children like to say, "You're not the boss of me." And that is the bottom line. We do not have the right to judge and sentence people. That is what courts are for. That is what due process of grievance is for. We would all do well to focus on our own foibles and failings. When we get into the business of judging people without proper context, facts, motives, and understanding how they experience the world, we make mistakes. We end up passing judgment on good people because we didn't do the hard work of having courageous conversations. Stop judging people. Mind your own business. And if something bothers you, reach out, ask questions respectfully, and try to come from a place of engagement and understanding.

## We Should Offer Grace in Abundance

All of us fall short. As I have aged, I understand the importance of extending grace. What is grace, you ask? It is kindness, courtesy, and mercy. And it starts from a place of humility, a virtue that we are sorely missing in our modern-day ethos. My advice to you is to always extend grace because you will need grace extended to you. Grace opens the door to growth, conversation, healing, and hope. It opens the door to change. It's easy to be a critic. It's easy to judge. It's easy to want revenge when people hurt us or make mistakes. But remember that as we sow, we will reap. If you are quick to condemn and to rage against other people, that is going to come back at you. It will. I promise. Consider how you feel when you are angry: likely unsettled and awful. But when you operate from a place of grace, you feel good and positive. You will never ever regret acting with grace, and you can feel good about allowing people to have second chances instead of being forever labeled by their mistakes and shortcomings.

## You Will Need Forgiveness, So Extend It Liberally

In the final analysis, people cancel others for several reasons: they want to squash free thought, free behavior, or behavior that does not conform with their view of the world; they are hiding from something; they want to protect their turf; they want to control people. None of those is a good way to live. A better way to live is by the Golden Rule: *Do unto others as you would have them do unto you.* That rule has great, positive reverberations not only in your own life, but in the lives of your children and grandchildren. I have an entire life lesson to come on radical forgiveness, because I have now lived long enough to know that I need forgiveness every day in some form or fashion. I have learned to look at why people do what they do or say what they say. I have learned that grace is a huge precursor to being able to offer forgiveness.

I will end this life lesson by imploring all of us to take a step back from our rage. We have become an angry, vengeful lot of human beings. We need a self-check. We need a social grace movement. Because if we are going to solve the great issues of our time—racism, climate change, domestic violence, sex trafficking, poverty, and injustice—it will require us to talk to one another and not at one another. It will require us to listen to points of view we may not like; to hear other people's hearts; to engage in a great public debate about who we are and who we want to become. Cancelling each other is not the way to get there. Please, do not choose it!

*"It isn't hate to speak the truth."*

—JK Rowling

# LESSON 17

## Go Where the Love Is:
## Stop Being the Go-To for People
## You Can't Go To

*"Some people won't love you no matter what you do,
and some people won't stop loving you no matter
what you do. Go where the love is."*

—Unknown

## *Your Self-Worth and Value*

I f you follow me on social media, you will notice a familiar post: "Go Where the Love Is." I post it often. I do so because there are so many sad, dejected, broken, rejected people walking all around us every day. People who accept the unacceptable. People who endure unkindness and disrespect at the hands of people who are supposed to love them, take care of them, and be kind to them. They accept it because they don't believe they deserve better. I was like that for a long time. Thank God I found my voice and my self-respect. I no longer live that way and you don't need to either.

My goal in this lesson is to help you to find the strength and the self-love you need to connect yourself to people, places, and things that make you feel loved, that honor your whole being—people who embrace you, people who really like you. I want to give you the tools that will help you develop self-value and self-worth, so that you will never tolerate or abide anyone or anything that offers you less. As the old saying goes, "Be around those who feed your soul, not eat it." Life is too short. Know your front row. Stop burdening your soul with people who suck the life force out of you.

COVID should have taught us about the importance of love, family, and connections, but writ large many seem to nevertheless persist in their addiction to those things in life that don't last—things like our possessions, our jobs, our success, or our smartphones—when we should be focused on the precious glory of life and living, of relationship and fellowship. We will never get there unless we become intentional—focused on having deeper, richer, lasting relationships. My hope is that I can help you to better disconnect yourself from anyone or anything that no longer blesses you, loves you, encourages you, celebrates you, supports you, or who makes you a better, wiser human being. This life lesson is your reminder that life is too short for the bullshit. Live your life around people who radiate light, kindness, loyalty, respect, and love.

There are good people out there. You find them and attract them by respecting yourself and by being one of them—respectful to others! Here's a quick test to help you gauge whether or not someone is in your corner. You are the one who always initiates calls and texts. You leave messages but get no response. They don't check on you or look out for you. Do you really believe they are thinking about you and that they care for you? No and no. Stop chasing, folks, hoping that if you are just nicer and more accommodating, they will change. They will not. People do not respect people they can walk over.

Let me tell you what I know to be true. Trying to love or be nice to folks who show you repeatedly how little you mean to them is an exercise in futility. The best thing any of us can do in the face of such callousness is to NOT accept it. Reject it and move to higher ground. Connect yourself to people who feel like warm sunlight, who radiate light and love. There are many of those people all around you. You must first know how to be one of them, and, second, how to spot them.

You are better off letting go of people who don't want to be in your life. Go where the love is. Protect your circle. Protect your network. You simply cannot and should not introduce everyone you meet into your safe place, your sanctum sanctorum. You cannot let Judas eat at your table. He will betray you, steal from you, turn you over to your enemies. Some people cannot appreciate your goodness and support. They don't think you're worthy of the love and adoration you have earned. Too many times I have opened doors, granted access, lifted, and helped those who were simply unappreciative and unworthy.

I think most people probably start out with good intentions. They begin by admiring you, singing your praises, and they are genuinely thrilled to be connected to you. But then because of envy and jealousy, or just plain old insecurities, they end up hating you. They let their insecurities or mistrust seep in, and they begin to ask why her and why not me? Or they co-opt your relationships, sometimes even poisoning them with their issues. If you are doing all the work to keep the friendship alive, is it really a friendship if you are the only one giving and never receiving? Please be careful to whom you expose your inner circle. Guard it. Protect it. Nurture it. Once ruined or tainted, you cannot go back. Use wisdom and discernment when letting new people into your life, your network, your business, and your friendships.

In this life lesson we will address three important ways to break away from the wrong people in your life and move toward attracting the right ones:

**Choose people who choose you.**

1. Take your power back.

2. Dig deeper.

3. Be what you want to attract.

## Take Your Power Back

If you want more love, more peace, if you want better for your life, it all starts with you. And it begins with you taking your power back.

How? By taking care of yourself. As the title of this book says, by being the one you need, and by connecting your life to good, emotionally healthy, and emotionally available people.

The year 2020 changed all our lives forever. It was a tough and challenging year for every human being on this earth. All of humanity had to deal with the COVID virus. Our families, neighbors, friends, loved ones, strangers, we all faced our mortality. The massive loss of life globally topped millions, and there will be millions more. Food banks were overwhelmed. Businesses closed, never to return. Incomes were cut in half or gone. Savings were drained. Millions of women had to drop out of the workforce. We all felt it. We all needed to take care of our souls, our bodies, our minds. And the way we did that was to connect for birthdays, for baby showers, for fellowship, even during a deadly pandemic. We Zoomed. We called. We checked on our neighbors. We helped stock food banks. We wore masks. We sat outside on lawn chairs and got together at a safe social distance— sharing a glass of wine together, breaking bread together, or sharing a cup of coffee together. Most of all, I pray that we learned how much we need one another.

But, as we move incrementally back toward a normal existence, I see us regressing. Back to busy. Back to exhausted. Back to stress. Back to putting our families and our relationships last. To take your power back from the twin addictions of *distraction* and *busyness,* you need to set healthy boundaries. You need to keep bad energy away from you. You need to keep bad people away from you and draw good people closer. You need to make time to pray, to sit, to reflect, to nourish your soul, to read, to rest, to re-energize your mind, to re-imagine your life, to reset your focus. Take your power back. The past is gone. It cannot be changed. It can only be learned from. Stop being a victim and start being a VICTOR! It's all in what you choose. It's all in how you take care of and love yourself.

I was in a training session recently related to workplace emotional trauma. And I realized how many of us are walking around in trauma without realizing it. We have had all hell break loose on us and yet we keep getting back up. We keep pressing. But we are playing life wounded, not at our best, not fully healed. We never catch our breath. We are trying to breathe in so many things happening around us—the pandemic, how to balance our needs with those who need us, new workplace rules, Zoom meetings, online classes, masks on our faces 24/7—things that we are not hardwired as human beings to absorb. Trauma rewires your brain, your physiology, and your responses to relationships and life itself. If you have been through, or are going through, some type of trauma, please get some help. Please take care of you. Please take a minute to just BREATHE. Stop allowing people to dump on you. You are a person. You need love. You need care. You need touch. You need encouragement. You need kindness. You need some self-care.

So far, I have shared with you sixteen life lessons I have learned, and a number of sub lessons. But this seventeenth lesson is vitally important. Because if you do not honor you, others never will. This is your daily reminder to GO WHERE THE LOVE IS. Stop chasing after people who do not want to be caught. Stop begging people. Stop trying to change people. Stop trying to get what you need from people who will never give it to you. Instead, move on. Find greener pastures. There are people who will love you, care for you, lift you, be there for you. Find those people. And be that person for others, too. Go where the love is! Stop holding on to people who keep letting go of you. Pay attention to the loyal people. The ones you can trust. The people you don't have to impress. The ones who always have your back and who love you with no strings attached.

One of the greatest lessons we can learn is to be clear about what we want, what we need, and what we can no longer tolerate. Start speaking up. Stop suppressing. There is not a single person on this earth who is entitled to disrespect you, dishonor you, hit you, lie to you, lie about you, curse you, yell at you, demean you, cheat on you, hurt you. Stop making excuses for people because you love them. NOBODY has the right to treat you like crap. Period.

## Dig Deeper

If you want to know why you accept less in your life, why you put up with people's unkindness and lack of respect, you are going to have to dig deeper. Meaning, you are going to have to ask yourself some hard and uncomfortable questions. Here are a few I had

**Stop holding on to people who keep letting go of you. Pay attention to the loyal people.**

**The ones you can trust. The people you don't have to impress. The ones who always have your back and who love you with no strings attached.**

to ask myself and then get help for with a mental-health professional:

1. Do I value myself?

2. Do I like myself?

3. Was I taught how to honor my voice, my boundaries, and my needs as a child?

The answer to those questions will help you determine where you are with the all-important process of knowing your value. Because that is really what this life lesson is about. Learning to stop being the "go to" for people you can't go to is all about understanding and standing firmly in your own worth. If you answer one or more of those questions in the negative, you have work to do. Remember, we attract who and what we are. And if you do not feel good about yourself, others will not feel good about you either.

We must know who we are and what we want. We must be intentional every day of our lives (which, granted, is not easy). Once we know who we are, what we are worth, what we value, and what gifts we have to give the world, we are unstoppable. My point is this: you will never be more than the work you put in. Life is a sowing and reaping process. When you are willing to go deeper and deal with your trauma, your losses, your regrets, or your shame, what you unlock is a life of wonderful vulnerability and possibility. But you will never ever find out who you truly are unless you do the work.

So, how do you dig deeper? Here are a few tips that I have used in my ladies' prayer group, and they have really helped me along my way:

1. **Find your life mission.** We talked about this earlier in the book. It is imperative in order to find and embrace your full value and worth.

2. **Stop comparing yourself to others.** Susie's life is not yours. And yours is not hers. You have to focus on you and your journey, not on what everyone else has or is doing. Doing that will eat you alive, make you feel less than, and cause you to settle for less in your relationships.

3. **Build up your physical strength.** It is a biological fact that our physical wellness and strength have a direct impact on our emotional health and wellness. If you can build your body, stay healthy, and be intentional about being physically strong, I guarantee you will feel better emotionally and feel better about your life. They go hand in hand.

4. **Create a support group of people who are with you.** I did this and it changed my life. I gathered with some friends who

were all dealing with similar issues, and we all wanted to shift, to pivot, and to change our lives in our forties and fifties. We started reading books to help us, we talked, we shared, we encouraged one another, and along the way created strategies to do the work we needed to change our lives.

## Be What You Want to Attract

The law of attraction, which is explored in many ancient texts, was popularized in our day by author

**Nobody has the right to treat you like crap.**

Rhonda Byrne in *The Secret* and it says this in short: *Basically, the law of attraction tells us whatever we will believe, we will manifest. If we believe we are deserving of great love, then we will manifest it. If we believe we are going to be poor, we're going to stay poor. If we believe we don't deserve something, it's not going to come to us.* Another way of saying what Ms. Byrne puts forward is, in a word: energy. As I have said before, we are walking human magnets.

Positive people connect with other positive people. Successful people hang out with other successful people. Kind people like other kind people. Quiet people do not like noisy ones. We are creatures of habit. And we are creatures of our tribe. We like to be around people with similar energy. It makes us feel in control and comfortable.

The problem with this, of course, is that if you are negative, or depressed, or feel defeated in life, you will not improve your situation by being connected to other depressed, defeated people. Get the point? That gets us back to digging deeper. When we dig deeper, we get to the things that are holding us back from the life we want. If you want to feel loved, you must give love to healthy, whole, loveable, good people. If you want to feel safe, you must be around trustworthy, honest, good people who will protect your emotions, your secrets, and your privacy. I have learned, much to my delight, that there was a whole world full of wonderful people all around me who were exactly like me. People who gave of themselves. People who would listen. People who would care. People who would be there for me, love me, pray for me, stand in the gap for me, but I could not see those people for the longest time because I was too busy saving people, fixing people, giving to people who had zero capacity, desire, or ability to give back to me. I was connected to a bunch of social vampires and family vultures who had become very adept and comfortable feasting on my goodness.

Admitting that you are being taken advantage of is hard. But you must. I kept wondering, "God, why is this happening to me over and over again?" And once I started to let go of people who were takers not givers, set healthy boundaries, and work on me, I started attracting good, caring, authentic, and amazing people into my life. It was effortless. They literally showed up across the board. It was, and is, humbling, to say the least. People can joke about the law of attraction, but it is real, and it has been forever. It is as old as time. You attract who and what you are.

Here are a few tips you can use to start attracting better people into your life:

1. **Follow your heart.** Take the path that resonates for you, not others' expectations for you.

2. **Tune in to your soul.** It's that small voice leading the way. Follow it.

3. **See the big picture.** Don't get stuck in the rearview mirror of your life. Look at what is beyond the vast windshield in front of you. Focus on having something to look forward to.

**4. Develop self-control.** Self-control helps us to avoid making impulsive and dangerous life decisions. It makes us settle down. It makes us think through what we want and need, with a clear mind and a clear focus.

**5. Follow your intuition.** Your intuition is everything. Trust it. When your gut says "no," or "wrong way," or "bad person," trust it. Then follow its lead.

"Love isn't something natural. Rather it requires discipline, concentration, patience, faith, and the overcoming of narcissism. It isn't a feeling, it is a practice."

—Eric Fromm, *The Art of Loving*

# SECTION V

## Fill Your Cup First: Be Intentional About Your Choices, Your Living, Your Life

*Successful people are intentional. They live a life that integrates common sense with respect for others, with grace, and collaboration. They are not afraid to compete with anyone, anywhere, but they do so with a firm code that allows them to climb while still lifting others along the way.*

# LESSON 18

## Practice Radical Forgiveness, It Can Heal Everything

*"It is essential that we adopt a way of living not based on fear, control, and abuse of power but on true forgiveness, unconditional love, and peace."*

—Colin C. Tipping

## *Your Ability to Forgive*

O f all the life lessons we have considered so far, this is the one I am still actively working on and working through. It is also by far the hardest. I would love to meet the person who has forgiveness all figured out. This life lesson is more of a life tool than a tried-and-true roadmap to "forgiveness success." Contrary to twenty-first century popular belief, forgiveness is not a meme with words saying, "I forgive you, but I don't have to have you in my life anymore." It's far deeper than that, folks. It's far more complicated. Forgiveness is a process, a long and difficult one at best.

You need to learn this life lesson early and practice it often. Forgiveness is the superglue of life. It is the only way we make it through intact, filled with love, at peace. Because at the end of the day, we will all leave this life, and we don't want to exit carrying the burden of things unforgiven. And the process of learning to forgive is indeed just that—a process. It is not something that happens instantaneously. The deeper the cut, the offense, or the wound, the deeper the walk you must make toward forgiving—first yourself and then those who have hurt you.

I suppose, on balance, I have made a good life out of a rough start. But I often wonder what might have been if I had had a different beginning. A different set of life experiences. More love, less trauma. More courageous conversations. Honest and earnest forgiveness, coupled with genuine repentance and a promise to change. I think that's the part that everyone misses; forgiveness is as much for the forgiver as it is for the offender. But the person who receives the forgiveness must also do the work to fully reconcile the harms caused. Forgiveness is another way of extending grace and giving a second chance. Forgiveness is a gateway to becoming better and doing better, to learning and growing. But that works only if both parties want it to. The fact of the matter is none of us walking this earth has the power to make someone who has hurt us ask for our forgiveness, or apologize, or help us in our healing. Only we can do that. So, in a sense, forgiveness is actually for the one who extends it, not the one who receives it.

I have found that the people who caused me pain rarely helped in my healing. It was only through doing the work on myself, and learning the lessons that pain taught me, that helped me to heal. Forgiveness is the most important thing that will help you heal yourself, and you must start with forgiving your family. Then you must forgive yourself. And only after you have mastered those two very tall orders, can you grasp how to truly forgive others. Why do we need to learn the art of forgiveness? Simply put, it will be a big factor in how you play the hand you are dealt and how you continuously move forward stronger and wiser in your life.

Here's the thing: we all make mistakes. And we all need forgiveness. And as Billy Joel says in one of my favorite songs, "Sorry seems to be the hardest word." I don't know why we can't just say, "Hey, I got it wrong." Or "I love you; can you please forgive me?" "Sorry" is one of the greatest healing words in the human language. Yet, in this time of unfriending, cutting off, and ghosting (you can tell I really hate that, right?) we have become accustomed to hurting people and just moving on. Likewise, we accept being hurt by people as the price of doing life in the twenty-first century. Neither of those choices is correct. And, as I have said throughout these lessons, life is 100 percent about the choices we make. So, if you can learn early in your life to forgive other people quickly, whether they ask or not, and if you can learn to continually show yourself some grace and forgiveness daily, you will do well in this life.

Forgiveness means different things to different people, of course, but the short answer is that it means to let go of something that has hurt you or caused you to feel shame. It may even mean giving up thoughts of revenge. It's important to understand, though, that even if you extend forgiveness, the hurt or offense you feel might always be with you. But forgiveness lessens the grip on you and helps to free you from the control of the person or trauma that harmed you. Holding on to anger and resentment can be a very painful, and a potentially harmful, process. As Stephen Hayes, one of the founders of Acceptance and Commitment Therapy (which is a therapy used by federal agencies like the Veterans Administration to help returning soldiers deal with PTSD and anger issues) says, "Unforgiveness is like being on a giant hook. Next to you on the hook is the person who has hurt you. The hook is extremely painful. Wherever you go, so does the hook and so does the offender. The only way you can get off the hook is if you allow the offender off first. The cost of not allowing the offender off the hook is, perhaps, a lifetime of unhappiness."

For the purposes of this life lesson, I want to focus on five tools that you will need to help you successfully navigate the terrain of unforgiveness in your life and instead take your power back by focusing on forgiveness. 1.) Why do we forgive? 2.) When do we forgive? 3.) How do we forgive? 4.) When do we restore people who have hurt us, and 5.) When do we release those who have hurt us, left us, passed away from us, and leave them to their own journey as they are no longer a part of ours?

## Why Do We Forgive?

Simply put, we forgive so that we can move forward in our relationships with others who have hurt us, or life experiences that greatly

impacted us. That is one part of forgiveness, for sure. However, there are
other forms of forgiveness as well—
and these are every bit as important

**Forgiveness is an
intention.**

to our emotional well-being and our ability to move forward as the
former. We may be struggling to forgive ourselves. Or we may find
ourselves needing to ask someone else for forgiveness. We may need
to accept a request for forgiveness. We may even find ourselves needing to find forgiveness related to existential concerns—for example,
the need to forgive the world—the domino effect of the circumstances
that came together to create the spread of COVID-19—for a pandemic that caused so much widespread suffering. We may need to
forgive God for not preventing the death of a child or loved one after
we prayed to Him for healing. The point is, the need for forgiveness
is always with us. And always around us. It's in our DNA. Part of the
reason I write, that I share my life story and the things I have learned,
is because I am trying to forgive others, or perhaps even myself. Writing is how I heal. It allows me to open a deep part of myself to others
that I find difficult to do in day-to-day life or conversation. We need
more of that. We need people to discover themselves, or, in my case,
rediscover themselves. We need to embrace the mistakes we've made
and dare to walk through them with an eagerness to learn and be
better. That is why we should practice radical forgiveness. By radical,
I hearken to the guidance of radical forgiveness guru Colin Tipping.

What I love about what Tipping says is that forgiveness is a lens
through which we can see for ourselves a life where *life happens for
us, and not just to us.* That is powerful. So, to answer the question I
opened with—why do we forgive? —we forgive so that we can change
our perspective. So that we can lean into what hurt us, what we lost,

and press forward to something better. The big takeaway here is to see forgiveness as a way forward. It frees you. It releases you to fly. It reconciles your pain. And it allows you to keep living, to keep loving, and to keep giving of yourself.

For those of us who follow Him, God *requires* us to forgive. It is an essential core tenet of the Christian faith—indeed, of all faiths. It's how we keep our relationship with God in a whole state, as we seek His forgiveness for our own trespasses and sins. We must likewise forgive others' trespasses and sins against us. In one of my favorite quotes from Scripture, Matthew 18, 21-22, Peter (my favorite apostle) asks Jesus, "How many times shall I forgive a brother or sister who sins against me? Up to seven times?" And Jesus replies, "I do not say to you seven times but seventy times seven!" What's Jesus's point? His point is not to just forgive those who hurt you four hundred ninety times and then stop, but that when we are in relationship, in fellowship, in love, and in faith with people, we must keep extending the long and loving arm of forgiveness.

## When Do We Forgive?

This part is a bit tricky. As I have aged, I have learned to try to let go of things quickly. Not allow them to fester. Not allow them to sit too long in my craw, in my heart, in my soul. Because there is less road in front of me than behind me, I need to say what I need to say. I need to resolve conflicts quickly, or I need to decide not to resolve them and move on. But what I cannot do at this stage of my life is not forgive. I simply do not have the capacity to hold on to pain, regret, or unkindness. So, when you are considering the right time to forgive someone, or not forgive them, here are a few things I have learned that helped me from my younger years up to my present-day life. First, if you are suffering over something that happened to you, and you are unable to release it through the normal human grieving process, or with the help of a therapist, that is when you must practice and walk out forgiveness. Dr. Deepak Chopra says, "When we hold onto a resentment, grievance, shame, guilt, or pain from the past, our entire body and mind suffers."

Forgiveness is an intention. We must feel the need to forgive for it to have value to us. For example, if your neighbor's tree branch fell on your car windshield in the storm and broke the glass, you don't need to forgive him. It was not his fault. What you want is for him to make it right and fix your windshield with his homeowner's insurance policy. However, if you were in a long-term marriage that you thought was good, and your spouse comes in one day to tell you that he or she is leaving you for someone else and wants a divorce, then you will need to forgive them for many things. You will need to forgive them at some point for breaking their wedding vows, for breaking your heart, for breaking your family. And all that comes with such a sudden and unexpected blow.

> *"Radical Forgiveness is something infinitely greater, more all-encompassing and more revolutionary than conventional forgiveness. Through it, we see for ourselves that life doesn't happen to us—it happens for us. This perspective changes everything."*
>
> —Colin Tipping

## How Do We Forgive?

How we forgive is complex because everyone has a uniquely individual response. Each of us is different, so the way we process, the way we react, and the way we respond to the things in life that hurt us, or upended our lives, is different. There is no tried and true, 100 percent guaranteed method to fix all the hurt with a single apology. It simply does not work that way for any of us. As I said at the outset, forgiveness is a process, a complex, layered journey into self and others.

Just as in Al-Anon, where you have twelve steps to help guide you to healing, author and psychologist Robert Enright says there are eight keys to forgiveness:

1. Know what forgiveness is and why it matters.

2. Become "forgivingly fit."

3. Address your inner pain.

4. Develop a forgiving mind through empathy.

5. Find meaning in your suffering.

6. When forgiveness is hard, call upon other strengths.

7. Forgive yourself.

8. Develop a forgiving heart.

These eight keys are steps designed to help you through the process. I remember reading Enright's article "Eight Keys to Forgiveness," in the October 15, 2015, edition of *Greater Good Magazine*, in which he walked through each of the steps listed. I am not going to do that here because, honestly, they are self-explanatory. However, I highly recommend that you read his books because they all support what I am saying to you in this lesson, and that is this: Forgiveness is not a meme on Instagram or Twitter. It is not something to be taken lightly. It is not a game you play with yourself or with others. Forgiveness is all about self-care, self-respect, and a commitment to others that they can find grace in your relationship when it is needed and, more importantly, forgiveness when it is hard. We all want and need second chances, even third ones. But remember, forgiveness starts with you.

## When Do We Restore People Who Hurt Us?

You cannot talk about genuine forgiveness without restoration. Because forgiveness is truly about restoration. As I said at the beginning of this lesson, many people in our day and age see forgiveness as cutting people loose and then moving on. The problem with this way of thinking is that, if you do this too many times in your life, you will have no friends, you will have no family, and you will have no meaningful relationships.

The fact is all relationships face trouble at one time or another. All humans fall short. We tell white lies sometimes. We fail sometimes. We hide from others and ourselves. We get depressed. We get angry. We get fearful. We lose faith. We break faith. We mess up. And then we do it all over again. All of this makes us human. And forgiveness is what keeps our marriages and families intact. It keeps our teams at work connected. It keeps us connected to our friends. It keeps our dreams alive. It keeps our hopes alive. It keeps our faith alive. Forgiveness, as I said, is the superglue of life because it truly can mend and put things back together again that we never imagined could be restored.

Restoration does not mean we necessarily take people back the way they once were in our lives. It does not have to mean that we see them all the time. *Restore* means to bring back, or to put something in its former position, to repair, to make new or to renovate. It's that last definition—to renovate—that I like. Because when we forgive, we do more than restore the one who fell short. We create and build something new where there used to be something else. We repair the cracks and breaks. There is nothing more amazing than having what was taken from you restored. And there is nothing more restorative than second chances to make things right in our lives and in our relationships.

## When Do We Release Those Who Have Hurt Us?

The hardest part of forgiveness is making the decision not to extend it any further. Or to *cut what you can't untie,* as my nana would say. Life is all about choices, and one of the hardest is knowing when we need to walk away from someone or something we love or value. Part of forgiveness is most certainly forgetting, which is one of the hardest things to do. We can forgive an offense, or even a deep emotional wound. But it is hard to forget it if we continue to feel the effects or if we continue to dwell on it. Sometimes, we simply cannot repair things or restore people who have hurt us. It's just too much water under the bridge. And that is okay. If you are someone who suffered immense emotional, physical, or sexual trauma from a family member or close acquaintance, your best way forward for you is to forgive them. That does not mean you have to see them or ever speak to them again. You must do what is best for you, and only you know what that is.

However, before you walk, I want to encourage you to talk, if it is safe for you emotionally to do so. Make sure that you do the work on you to be able to make healthy decisions around forgiveness. Deciding to forgive someone does not mean that you are excusing their behavior or condoning it. It means that you are making a conscious choice not to hold on to the hurt, pain, disappointment, or resentment any longer. For example, deciding to get a divorce, or deciding to end a relationship with a friend, or choosing to never see a sibling again is a really big deal. So, make sure that when you end it, you're doing so for all the right reasons. And make sure that you aren't holding on to the past and in the future missing out on someone who has grown, and who has done the work to change from their past mistakes. We are all a work in progress. All of us. We all need grace. We all need forgiveness and most of all we need the loving grace that comes with forgiveness.

*"When you forgive, you love.*
*And when you love, God's light shines upon you."*

—Jon Krakauer, *Into the Wild*

# LESSON 19

## Mind Your Manners, They Matter

*"Respect for ourselves guides our morals;
respect for others guides our manners."*

—Laurence Sterne

## *Your Manners*

Pe
ople might think that putting a life lesson on manners in a book about self-care is strange. It isn't. A huge part of self-care is how we treat others. Remember, we are all energy—like magnets we attract who and what we are. So, if I am kind, I attract kindness. If I am friendly, I will attract friends. If I am respectful, respect and so on. Yet, I think we can all agree that good manners are not high on the list of things people practice these days. In fact, it seems as if rude is the new cool. I have been watching basic manners decline for years now, and it has had a very serious impact on families, on relationships, in the workplace, on college campuses, in politics, and in our day-to-day lives. I'm not alone in this opinion. The Rasmussen polling group started tracking Americans and our attitudes toward manners in 2011 and found that 76 percent of respondents at that time thought that Americans were becoming ruder and less civilized. Fast forward to our present time, 2022, and that number has remained stable at 75 percent. Things have gotten so bad, that I'm sometimes left wondering if people know what manners are anymore. We have become uncivil people who have the lost the great art of human courtesy and treating people well. My goal in this life lesson is to reintroduce some of us who may have forgotten, to the life-changing power of good manners. For those of you in younger generations, my hope is to give you a leg up on your peers professionally, personally, and relationally by introducing you to what manners are, what they are not, and how when used with great emotional intelligence they can open doors for you that you never imagined possible. Manners are defined quite simply as the proper or polite way to

behave in public, in society, and in the treatment of elders and others in positions of respect and authority. Manners means refraining from inappropriate behavior. Manners also means "etiquette"—for instance, men standing when a woman comes to be seated at the table. Or using the right forks and spoons. Opening the door for an older person or extending your arm for them to hold. Good manners mean saying "please" and "thank you." But manners are so much more than that.

Manners let other people know that you appreciate them and respect them. Manners allow us to display courtesy, kindness, grace, and gratitude. Manners also help us to build bridges with other cultures and people unknown to us. A handshake, for example, is a polite universal greeting in Western cultures, as is a slight bow in Eastern cultures. Breaking bread together or having tea are ways we connect with others across race, class, gender, and culture.

> *"Politeness [is] a sign of dignity, not subservience."*
>
> —Theodore Roosevelt

For the purposes of this life lesson, I want to add manners as another tool for your EIQ toolkit. Having good manners is not only a means for advancing your social standing. When used as a matter of course, a way of life, manners can create opportunities, build lifelong relationships, and propel you to great positions. Good and conscientious manners signal to people that you care, that you are thoughtful. And most of all that you are approachable as a human being first, not as a boss, not as a leader, but as a person with a heart and good will. Manners matter a lot, and the sooner you can learn them, the better off you will be. Manners never go out of style. They are a currency every bit as valuable as gold or silver, dollars or francs. And they increase in value, in human capital value, just the same.

Manners may have gone out of style in twenty-first century culture, but they should never go out of style in your life. I have valued and practiced good manners all my life. I learned them at the knee of my paternal grandmother when I was a little girl. Manners were very important to her and to my mother. We sent cards on every birthday and holiday, we wrote thank-you notes for every gift we received, we practiced proper telephone etiquette, our table manners were impeccable, and we were well versed in small-talk pleasantries.

If you want evidence that manners matter, according to LinkedIn, there is a lot of scientific proof that manners are very important for your career advancement. A study of over five hundred employers conducted by Career Builders found that an overwhelming 95 percent of executives and managers surveyed said that good manners matter when it comes to advancing a person's career or promoting them to senior ranks. And, further, a 2020 study conducted by the *American Journal for Public Health* tracked a large group of children for twenty years, evaluating them on many things including their social skills. At the end of the study period, they found that those children who ranked highest had the best social skills and were the

> *"Manners are a sensitive awareness of the feelings of others. If you have that awareness, you have good manners, no matter what fork you use."*
>
> **—Emily Post**

most successful, and those who did not have good social skills were the ones who were more likely to have substance-abuse issues, be unemployed, or have very low-paying jobs. Social skills, of course, being good manners.

I want to break down five life skills that fall under the manners umbrella. They will serve you well if you can learn them and live by them each day.

- The grace of gratitude
- The power of thank you
- The spirit of kindness
- The humanity of empathy
- The blessing of humility

Each of these are subcategories of good manners, social graces, or social etiquette. Here's the most important thing to take away from this life lesson: at the end of the day, we are all social creatures, interconnected whether we like it or not. We depend on each other, and we all saw just how much during the darkest days of the COVID-19 pandemic. This is exactly why we need to have a sense of not just personal well-being, but compassion for one another. Manners is another way of saying compassion. And we can all use a little more compassion in our lives. Practicing good manners, having compassion, and being mindful of others is a powerful trifecta of how to live a meaningful life. When all is said and done, isn't that what all of us really want?

## The Grace of Gratitude

One of the greatest manners we can extend to others is grace. Extending grace is a very important tool in the emotional intelligence toolkit. What is grace, you ask? The word grace and the word grateful are first cousins. When we extend grace to someone, we are giving them a gift for something they haven't earned; we favor them. In my life I have been blessed by being favored many times. I have been given opportunities that I am not sure I earned, simply because I showed up as a considerate, thoughtful person. Case in point, when I worked on Capitol Hill in the late 1990s as a young, congressional committee counsel, I was invited to go on C-SPAN, which televised gavel-to-gavel coverage of congressional sessions and committee hearings. I worked on the House Government Reform and Oversight Committee investigations into alleged illegal foreign money being put into the 1996 presidential campaign. Supreme Court Justice Clarence Thomas happened to be watching the broadcast and afterward invited me to meet with him. The funny thing is, I did not want to meet him. As a first-year, first-semester law student, I had watched in shock, as did the rest of the nation, Justice Thomas' confirmation hearings in the fall of 1991. Anita Hill's riveting, detailed testimony alleging sexual harassment when she was in his employ was deeply disturbing. I believed Anita Hill. I still do.

After seeing this, I had reservations, which I shared with my mother. She said, "Sophia, I know how you feel. But I raised you to be respectful and wise. When a sitting United States Supreme Court Justice invites you to meet with him at the Court, you go. You show grace. You listen. You take his secretary some flowers. And you hear him out." She was right, of course. I had to push my emotions down and not pass judgment on him for something that had nothing to do with me. I just needed to show up. And I did.

When I arrived at the hallowed halls of the Supreme Court a few weeks later, I stood in awe. It is a special experience for a lawyer to be in a place that is the pinnacle of our judicial system, and it took me back to my childhood dream, when I wanted to be the first Black female Supreme Court Justice. The feeling was surreal. I sat with Justice Thomas in his chambers, and he could not have been more gracious and kind. We had a great conversation about the photos on his wall of Frederick Douglass and Malcolm X (imagine that), and about what it was like to be a Black conservative. Our visit lasted about an hour. He told me that he had asked to see me because of how I handled myself on television. He said I was respectful, prepared, and graceful with an opponent from the other side who was aggressive and interrupted me at every turn. Those words meant so much to me.

Almost a decade after I met Justice Thomas, and had been admitted to the bar in Washington, DC, I was extended an invitation by my alma mater, American University, Washington College of Law, to be sworn into the bar of the United States Supreme Court. I accepted, but did so past the deadline to show up and be sworn in. Well, as fate would have it, a simple act of kindness helped me with this. Justice Thomas's mom had passed away a year before, and I had sent him a condolence card—handwritten. He was touched by it. And when I called his assistant to see if he could move the swearing-in ceremony, he immediately responded that he was able to accommodate my request. It was one of the proudest moments of my mom's life to see me admitted to the bar of the nation's highest court. All the justices were present, and Justice Thomas came to say hello to me afterward. And it was all made possible because I exercised good manners and thoughtfulness. It works every time because people never forget when you show that you care about them or what has happened to them in their life. Think about how you feel when someone does the same for you versus someone who is rude or indifferent to you. It's a win-win for all.

What gratitude allows us to do is remember our own shortcomings, and it forces us to reckon our own humanity with others. It allows us to look at that person with compassion, sympathy, and concern for their sufferings and misfortunes. And, in so doing, we grow richer, wiser, and more resilient ourselves. The grace of gratitude is that it gives us more. It opens pathways

> *"Life is short but there is always time enough for courtesy."*
> —Ralph Waldo Emerson

and byways that take us deeper beneath the surface. Being courteous to a very important person in my life when I was a young woman opened countless doors for me later in life. Take it from me, I know the power of both gratitude and grace. And I want you to know it, too.

## The Power of Thank You

You've noticed by now that I have used the word *power* a few times in this lesson. I want to use it again now. Power is a word that means more than just strength. Power is an energy. It is a feeling. It is, to me at least, the ability to use the force of will within for external impact. This means that when you thank someone you empower them to feel good, to feel appreciated, and to feel valued. Everybody loves to get a handwritten thank-you note in the mail. Everyone loves to get thank-you flowers, or a thank-you memento or gift. We all love to feel appreciated. We love to make gestures of love. And we love for our gestures to be received and appreciated with love.

Saying thank you is another one of those EIQ tools that should be used every day of your life. When you pick up your Starbucks at the drive-through window, you say thank you. When you pay for your gas with the clerk at the 7-11 store, you say thank you. When your assistant hands you some important papers, you say thank you. When your spouse brings you a warm cup of coffee, you say thank you. Thank you is a universal love language. It acknowledges the other person's existence. It shows the team at the job how much you value them. It lets your kids know how much you appreciate the lawn being cut or their chores being done. Thank you empowers others to feel good. And, in so doing, they pass it on and on and on.

When you activate a "thank you," it's like pushing a button of good will. It takes little time to execute, as all manners do. But when you put positive gratefulness, grace, and appreciation into the universe, it unleashes more of the same and the residual good feelings last and last. So, do yourself a favor and say "thank you" every day, all day, for the smallest of things and the biggest of things. It will serve you well. Invest in some nice notecards, get some old-fashioned things called postage stamps, and an ink pen. When an occasion merits it, write a personal note. Say thank you. Say I love you. Say I appreciate what you did for me or what you mean to me. Say it. Because it matters. And it will never be forgotten.

## The Spirit of Kindness

When we act with kindness toward others, we encourage the spirit of kindness. You've likely heard about random acts of kindness and the chain of goodness that results from them. Well, having good manners creates a groundswell of kindness. When you open the door for the elderly woman at the grocery store, grab a cart for her, and extend your hand, you have no idea the human warmth and respect that you create for her in that moment. And it ripples. When others see you do an act of such respect and honor, they want to emulate it. I know. Just this past Thanksgiving, I was driving in the car with my family. We had just come from grocery shopping for the holiday and, as we waited for the traffic light to change, I noticed a woman holding a sign asking for food. She was young. She said she had kids, and that she would work for food or money. The light turned green, and the traffic was about to move. I put on my brake, put on my flashers, and got out of my car. I literally stopped traffic.

I motioned for the young woman to come to my car. My family was perplexed and the cars behind me were beeping their horns. That is, until they saw what I was going to do. I opened my trunk and started handing the woman bags of food. Dead silence on a busy, major thoroughfare in Northern Virginia. People waited patiently until I could get that woman some groceries. She started to cry. I started to cry as I ran away, waving and hopping back into my car. I wanted to do more. But I had no cash that day, and I had no work for her to do, so I improvised. I gave her what I had to give at that moment, and I drove off knowing that literally dozens of cars filled with people saw that act of simple kindness and humanity. And for me that is where the gold lay. I know that people who saw what I did were inspired to do something similar: donate to a foodbank, support a family's meal, donate clothes, or something even greater. My point is this: one small, unplanned act of humanity causes ripples of other similar acts, often unknown to us and unseen by us. But the good news is that they happen. And that is the biggest blessing of all.

> When we live a life of displaying good manners, we help others to want to do the same. When we show compassion, kindness, grace, and goodness, others follow.

## The Humanity of Empathy: Knowing Others' Feelings Matter, Too

When we live a life of displaying good manners, we help others to want to do the same. When we show compassion, kindness, grace, and goodness, others follow. When we consider other people's feelings, we do three things:

1. We see them beyond their faults, their failings, or their needs and see their humanity;

2. We put them front and center in our thought process and decision-making; and

3. We engage the all-important human emotion of empathy.

According to The Conversation, a nonprofit organization working for the public good through fact- and research-based journalism, there are three ways of looking at empathy. First, there is *affective empathy*. This is the ability to share the emotions of others. People who score high on affective empathy are those who, for example, show a strong visceral reaction when watching a scary movie. They feel scared or feel pain strongly within themselves when seeing others scared or in pain. Then there is something called *cognitive empathy*, which is the ability to understand the emotions of others. A good example is the psychologist who understands the emotions of the client in a rational way but does not necessarily share the emotions of the client in a visceral sense. Finally, there's *emotional regulation*. This refers to the ability to regulate one's emotions. For example, surgeons need to control their emotions when operating on a patient.[3]

Empathy is critical to your success in life as a parent, as a leader, as a pastor, as a teacher, as a human being. When we use good manners in our everyday lives, we are thinking of the courtesy we can express to others first. It becomes a reflex. It becomes a habit, and that is exactly what we all want and need more of in our present-day world.

## The Blessing of Humility

Of all the virtues that matter in life, I think that humility is the least talked about and the one, perhaps, that we need most. What is humility? The short answer is it means to be humble, to not be a glory seeker, to not be afraid to admit when you are wrong, to consider others' needs above your own, or, as the great C. S. Lewis once said, "Humility is not thinking less of yourself, it's thinking of yourself less." A more clinical definition of humility is a modest or low view

[3] https://theconversation.com/us/topics/charities-4583

of one's own importance. The common thread in all these definitions, however, is that humility allows us, once again, to get out of our own way and to see a better way forward that may, at times, seem like we're eating humble pie or crow. But what we are really doing is blessing others by walking in humility. We most certainly could use some of that in our modern world.

The rub is that our culture places so much value on external accomplishments: money, status, false appearances, carefully curated images of our lives on Instagram, and self-aggrandizement—all things that are intangible and fleeting at best. Yet seldom do we see acts of humility. Why is it so challenging for us to express humility? Is it because we often misinterpret its demonstration to be a sign of human weakness when it's actually a sign of tremendous inner strength? I don't have the answers, but I do know that the times in my life when I had to humble myself, I was always lifted higher. Humility is simply that tool that allows us to walk the pathway of life with some good sense, some kindness, some grace, some gratitude, and some good manners; showing respect, affection, and goodness to other human beings. That is humility in a nutshell. And that is why manners matter so very much.

> *"Good manners will open doors that the best education cannot."*
>
> —Justice Clarence Thomas

# LESSON 20

## Just Say No—It's a Complete Sentence!

*"There are often many things we feel we should do that, in fact, we don't really have to do. Getting to the point where we can tell the difference is a major milestone in the simplification process."*

—Elaine St. James

## *Your Self-Care Boundaries*

When I was a preteen growing up in the early 1980s, then-First Lady Nancy Reagan started an anti-drug abuse campaign known as "Just Say No." It was what you should say if someone offered you illegal drugs. We heard that slogan everywhere. People made fun of the campaign as being too simplistic to deal with the drug problem in America. But it was actually very effective, and pretty much every school district in America adopted the slogan and drilled it into their students. *Just say no.* I have often wondered why it was at once so effective and so ridiculed. My guess is that the campaign was so straight to the point that it defied logic. There was no beating around the bush, no subterfuge. Just a direct answer to a big problem: Just say no.

In short, what Mrs. Reagan was saying to young people and adults alike was: make a choice. Choose to say no. Don't take the bait of drugs. They will ruin your life, ruin your community, and wreck your future. What it taught me at a young age was that sometimes we don't need things to be over-complicated to work. Sometimes, the best path is the easy road. The simple, right-there-in-front-of-your-eyes road that works best, and that yields the best results. Saying no should be easy, but it's hard for most of us to do, particularly those of us who are women. We are just not hardwired to take care of our needs and our work first. That needs to change. Whether married, single, single moms, aunts, grandmothers, or best friends, women are the heartbeat of our homes and our communities. If we are always running on empty and totally drained, who is going to be there to keep the world spinning and running on time?

Men, on the other hand, are better at setting boundaries and saying no because they have been socialized to set the rules, the norms, and to decide who gets access and who does not. Men are cared for by the women in their lives: mothers, sisters, wives, girlfriends. This allows them to say no more frequently and to be free of guilt. I have often heard the older married women I know joke, "I need a wife." Their point is that they needed help and the ability to manage things in their lives. While the women were dutiful wives, tending to the children and sometimes having their own careers, their husbands, although often the primary breadwinners and heads of the household, did not reciprocate by offering that same support or help regardless of childcare duties and work outside the home. I think that has changed some with men of Gen X, Y, and Z, but men are most often guilty of perhaps giving too little rather than giving too much.

The answer rests with you. It's time to take your power back. And it all starts with a simple two-letter word: NO! What a novel concept in a world where we have no clue how to say no. Our modern ethos and work ethic is to be on call 24/7, and then we wonder why we're exhausted all the time, complaining that we don't have enough time to do what we want and need to do. Well, just say no! My goal in this life lesson is to help you learn to say no! This is not a lesson that requires a lot of explanation or deep thought. The way to successfully incorporate this into your life is to start by making a habit of saying no to the wrong things so that you are freed up to say yes to the right things.

The earlier that you can learn to say no—and set healthy self-care—the

> *"Real freedom is saying 'No' without giving a reason."*
>
> —**Amit Kalantri,**
> **Wealth of Words**

better off you will be. I have failed this life lesson too many times to take it for granted any longer.

The long and short of saying no is that it allows you to be empowered and focused, not caught up in the distractions of life (see Lesson 14). Saying no is a way to weed out what matters and what does not. It ultimately gives you the power of choice, allowing you to focus on those things that must get done as well as those you want to get done. Remember, all of life is a choice.

One of the reasons people do not say no enough is because they allow themselves to be guilted into saying yes. They feel obligated to say yes, even when doing so inconveniences or harms them. I read a great book years ago by Carmen Renee Berry entitled *When Helping You Is Hurting Me: Escaping the Messiah Trap*. She makes several key points:

1. **Watch out for what she calls the "Messiah Trap," or God complex.** One of the hallmark character traits of this person is that they live by the motto "If I don't do it, nobody will." Many of us constantly try to rescue and save people from themselves. We literally think we are their savior. We never say no. We always say yes, even when we know that people are crossing our boundaries while we ignore our own wellness needs. We simply cannot help ourselves. Be clear not to confuse "empathy" or "kindness" with the trap. They are radically different. One is healthy and natural. The other is dangerous and very unhealthy.

2. **Understand how your childhood trauma often forces you to become caught in the Messiah Trap.** As I have reinforced throughout this book, our childhood is the epicenter of our lives. It is what shapes and molds us into the adults we

become—for better or for worse. If you get used to being the go-to as a child, or the responsible one, or the rock of the family, you will continue that syndrome to your detriment. When we miss the important balance of happiness, carefreeness, safety, and love in our lives as children, we tend not to have healthy boundaries as adults. If we want to fix that, we must do the work.

3. **Escape the unhealthy life cycle of the Messiah Trap by starting with a few simple steps:**

  • Understand that you are caught in the trap.

  • Learn the word "no."

  • Work on your own unresolved pain.

If you are constantly taking care of everyone but you, your issue is much bigger than just being "too nice." I had to learn this. And it is a tough lesson to learn. I got burned many times, as I've have shared with you, in my relationships with family, in dating, and with friends because I let my boundaries become flexible—and boundaries must be immovable. As a people pleaser and empath, I used to get overly involved in other people's affairs or needs and failed to limit the access that people had to me resulting in them asking more and more of me. And I often gave until it broke me—mind, body, and soul.

The most important thing about saying no is that you can feel empowered by it while still maintaining loving, reciprocal, and healthy relationships. Saying no helps you to establish healthy boundaries and enables others to have clarity about what they

> *"When others are not okay with your NO's, they should not be allowed around for the YES's either."*
>
> —Christine E. Szymanski

can expect from you and what they should not. This is a goal every human being should have with everyone in their life: to take care of self while balancing the needs and wants of others you love and are in relationship with.

## Whom to Say No To, the Reason to Say It, and How to Say It

We have established that saying no is important. But the question is whom to say no to, why should I say it, and how do I say it in such a way as to be firm, but also to not hurt the people I care about. Those are all very good and very real points. I will do my best to answer them all briefly, but thoroughly, based on my life experience, which is always the best teacher.

Let's start with the important question of **whom** you have to learn to say no to. The short answer is that you should say no to anyone who is asking more of you than what they give to you. Someone who expects more of you than you are able or willing to give. Most of all, you say no because it's what you really want to do. This is not complicated stuff. But it takes courage to break bad habits and dysfunctional life patterns, and deal with self-esteem issues. It seems so easy to follow Mrs. Reagan's advice to just say no. But it really isn't—at first. It takes time. It takes being intentional, and it takes work. I want you to know, however, that you can do it. It starts with understanding what I have said repeatedly in this book: you must be the one you need. You must put yourself first. You must honor your voice and your heart. You must take care of yourself, because, if you do not, no one else will. Trust me on this. You are first. They are second. It's okay.

The **why** you say no is situational. If your boss asks you to do to something for the company, trusting that only you can see it through, can you really say no? It depends. But most of the time you will do as he asks. If he keeps coming to you, however, when he has others he can ask, who are more senior and who make more money, you need to speak up and say no. By doing so, you translate your value. And you make sure that others know your value, too. It's all about finding your voice, your courage, and your strength.

Most importantly, though, the why we need to say no is to address the internal struggle we experience when setting boundaries between ourselves and others. As author William Ury says in his book *The Power of a Positive No: Save the Deal, Save the Relationship, and Still Say No,* the reason we struggle with saying no often stems from an internal struggle (I referenced this earlier with the Messiah Trap) between tending to your own needs and a simultaneous desire to cater to, or foster, a relationship. Ury says we often find ourselves doing one of three things in response to a request that we really do not want to answer in the affirmative:

1. **We accommodate.** We say yes when we really want to say no. This brings us a temporary, false sense of peace, which is later replaced with apprehension and deep resentment. We defer to the relationship (parent, spouse, sibling, boss, friend, or colleague) with no regard for our own power and, ironically, end up undermining the relationship in the long run. We do so because, once again, we violated our own human needs and boundaries. And inevitably resentment builds.

2. **We attack.** We often do this with those we love the most, the ones we take for granted. We say no aggressively, stepping strongly into our power, but with no regard or attention to the connection with the other person.

**3. We avoid.** We don't prioritize our personal power or the relationship. In other words, everybody loses. We dishonor ourselves and amp up our own discomfort by leaving something unresolved and disrespecting the other person by not providing them with an answer.

> *"Saying NO is an art, master it."*
> —CA Vikram Verma

Last, but not least, is the **how** we say no. How we do anything matters. When it gets right down to it, it's more important even than what we do. You say no with three things in mind:

- Whom am I saying no to, and what do they mean to me?

- What is the benefit of saying no or the burden of saying yes?

- How do I say no to this request while preserving my own well-being and not damaging my relationship with the person who is asking?

I have come up with some creative ways to say no, particularly to those people in my life who have taken advantage of my goodness, loyalty, and love too many times to count. The first thing I had to recognize and act on was to stop being a people pleaser. Only then could I realize that saying no was okay, and very important to my self-care. Here are some very tangible ways you can say no, while still preserving your relationships:

**1. Do not stall or beat around the bush or avoid.** When you want to say no—say it. Say it and mean it. But do it with respect. Use what I call a buffer: "I would love to help you, but I'm not able to at this time. Charge it to my crazy, busy life and not my heart." This removes the sting by implying that you would help them if you could.

2. **Put the question back on them.** If they say, "I need your help with X," you can say, "Well, I can do that for you in two weeks or a month; when did you need it done by?" It makes them consider the timeline. If the situation is urgent, you've made it clear that they will have to ask someone else. But you must remain firm. Do not back down or be manipulated.

3. **Know your relationship.** By knowing whom you are dealing with, and what the status of your relationship is, you will not fear saying no.

Sometimes, we have a hard time saying no because we haven't taken the time to evaluate our relationships and our role in those relationships. When you truly understand your role, you won't feel as worried about the consequences of saying no. By roles, of course, I simply mean if you are a mother, be unafraid to ask for what you need, and say no to your children when it is required. If you are a husband and you work twelve hours a day, but you are missing your kids' games and recitals, you need to say no to working as much. Put your kids first for once. You'll realize that your relationships are more solid than you think and that they can withstand your saying no.

The bottom line is that saying no is important. It protects you. And it protects others in relationship with you. It sets important boundaries of mutual respect, time management, and self-care. It keeps you from building up hidden resentments and fears. Saying no to children can be hard, but it is necessary. As an aunt of two nieces who, as little girls, had me wrapped around their little fingers, I never said no. But as they have become grown women, I have learned to do just that. Teaching your children the value of the word no is good for them, too. None of us should hear "yes" all the time. Because if we do, it makes us entitled, spoiled, and we become rotten. It ruins us if we do. No is a showstopper. It makes us stop in our tracks and pay attention. It also forces us to be self-sufficient and to find other ways to get things done for ourselves. Learn the life-changing power of no. It is the most powerful two-letter word ever invented.

> *"Love yourself enough to set boundaries.*
> *Your time and energy are precious. You get to choose*
> *how you use it.  You teach people how to treat you by*
> *choosing what you will and won't accept."*
>
> —Anna Taylor

# LESSON 21

## Exits Matter in Life— Exit Gracefully

*"Look on every exit as being an entrance somewhere else."*

—Tom Stoppard

## The Way You Leave Things

How we leave things matters. I once exited a relationship with someone I loved very much in a really bad way. The relationship was toxic to us both and neither of us had the courage to end it. When I blew that bridge up, I blew it up. And it was 100 percent intentional. Sometimes, simply burning a bridge doesn't go far enough; we must blow it up leaving no doubt. Some bridges should never be crossed again. And yet, when we leave, we leave parts of ourselves in that place and with that person. And no matter how far we travel, or how long we stay apart, we are still there in that place we thought we left behind. There are also things in us that can heal only by going back there, to that place we swore we would never again go to find the answers we seek or to rediscover that part of ourselves we lost long ago.

I did that recently. I had an opportunity, through a serendipitous chain of events, that put me in a place to have a conversation with this person—one that was almost two decades overdue. I knew that one day I would reach out, but what I did not know is that this person had attempted to reach out to me years earlier, sending correspondence through a mutual friend that I never received. But I finally found the courage to track this person down. And I was amazed at how a flood of stirring emotions, stored away in the recesses of our brains, can be triggered and flood to the forefront again.

My point is that both of us walked away deeply hurt and we lived separate lives for a long time. We have had very different journeys. Yet, even after all that time, there needed to be a clearing of the past. A reckoning, of sorts. An honest discussion about what happened, and why. We both said unkind, cruel—downright ugly—things to each other. That is what happens when you don't exit when you should, and then the situation festers and explodes, causing needless hurt, destruction and ill will. If you have to exit, make it worthy of your character. Make it worthy of your heart and do your best, even under the most challenging of circumstances, to walk away in a way that, when you look back in time, holds up to the mirror of your heart at the time.

Here's the thing, timely, thoughtful exits are opportunities for better beginnings. Exits make it possible for you to go in a new direction. In my case, we both needed the closure we hadn't received when things broke apart so abruptly. There was this huge hole, a void, that even time couldn't quite fill. But having a chance to talk made it more palatable, even if it still stung. The truth is human beings are far better at entrances than exits. Entrances, after all, are easy—there is hope and optimism for what is ahead. Breaking up, falling apart, walking away is much harder.

It's funny the things that stay with us long after they are no longer a part of our day-to-day reality. Time passes and we think we've put it all away. But when we exit the wrong way, particularly with people we care about, there is never any peace. There is no escaping an exit gone wrong. I know. I lived with that pain and regret for years. And I feel grateful and blessed that fate gave me a second chance to handle myself like a woman of grace and not a child acting out of unbridled grief and sadness. Yes, exits matter. A lot.

When all is said and done in life, only two things matter: how we began our lives, and how we end them. That is what people remember most—the end of the story. When you look at an obituary or memorial service program it starts with the day we are born and ends with the day we die. I have met many amazing men and women in my life. Literally, I have been in the presence of paupers and of kings; of presidents and of celebrities, and of sports icons. And we each owe a death. We all exit this life. The people who do it right are the ones we remember fondly when they are gone, the people who had the greatest impact on our own lives. They are the ones who taught us how to live and how to love, the ones who modeled kindness and care.

> *"The most telling part about a person's character is how gracefully they exit from your life."*
>
> —Nitya Prakash

Our deaths say everything about how we lived—who shows up at the end, and who speaks well of us when we pass on to the next state of consciousness—our legacy we leave behind us. Death is an exit. It is a transition. The living we do in between is the part we take with us.

I have **three points** to make about the importance of how we leave life situations and people. And then this lesson and all of them are yours.

**First: talk before you walk.** Unless it is physically or emotionally unsafe to do so, everyone is owed a conversation: a chance to get it, a chance to know how you feel. Don't wait twenty years, like I did. And don't let things escalate to the point where the love you once felt turns to dark emotions like resentment, anger, and even hate. Talk.

**Second: look for the glaring exit signs.** For example, when a relationship brings you more pain than joy. When you are always arguing with someone, or unhappy in your job, or just not feeling that friendship anymore—you need to pay attention.

**Third: leave people better than you found them, even if you must walk away.** Don't let your emotions get the best of you by not talking and working through what you need to with another person. You will regret the time you let slip by. This happens to people all the time, but it doesn't have to. You can learn to use your EIQ tools to work through conflict. And, if for some reason you cannot work through it, you can exit through the front door versus sneaking out the back door. We live and we learn. And we grow up. I learned. I grew up. At least I hope I so. Each of us must find our own way, for sure.

## Talk Before You Walk

This one is simple. Almost all exits in life happen because people don't talk. They have one-sided conversa-

> *"If you can't elevate, enhance, or encourage—Exit."*
>
> **—Charmaine J. Forde**

tions with themselves, building things up in their mind—but they fail to have the difficult conversations with the people they love, that they care about, or that they work with. They might treasure these people more than life itself, but instead of working it out, getting things out in the open, they run. They walk away in anger, or in fear, or, worse, in shame. Down the road, this only leads to regret. Let me tell you what I know for sure—that is not the way forward. There is a better way and here are a few tips you can use that I know work well.

## Don't Wait Until Things Get So Bad That You Can't Talk

If you fell in love with this person once, maybe when you were both young and idealistic, you must take a minute to step back, reflect, and remember what brought you together. Focus on the good in that person—even if what you see right now is not so good. We are like the iceberg that sank Titanic: part what you see on the surface, and part what's submerged. We all have the façade we show to the world—the smooth veneer, the controlled—and then there is that other much larger part lurking underneath, the part we rarely reveal and show to others. That is the part that you must reckon with when your feelings get hurt and you're feeling like you need to run, versus staying and doing the hard work of relationship. You must find the courage to have a conversation.

## You Must Know Your Partner's Emotional EIQ

You must be able to read their emotions, their wants and their needs. And then you must talk about it with them and listen. Truly listen to hear, and not to formulate your response. You must be able to take emotional and relational feedback. And man up. Or woman up. That is how you do the work of avoiding a bad exit. I believe most marriages, friendships, and business relationships could be saved and thrive if people just learned how to say what they need and ask others for the same.

## Do Not Try to Force People to Change

That will fail every time. Change is something that must come from within. Even if the person does change, sooner or later we will find something else we want them to change. The point is, you must take people as they are, where they are, or simply don't take them at all, otherwise you will never be satisfied. The goal is not to make people fit your expectations or to become a shadow of you. That isn't a relationship. That is an exit waiting to happen. Talk. Listen. Do the work. If after that it all falls apart, let it go. But give it your best shot so that years down the road you are not regretting what could have been or should have been.

## Look for the Glaring Exit Signs

If after you have a given a relationship, a job, or a passion your all, and it still isn't working right, you need to pay attention to the "exit signs" that are all around you:

> *"Sadly enough, the most painful goodbyes are the ones that are left unsaid and never explained."*
>
> **—Jonathan Harnisch**

- You argue all the time.
- You hate going home.
- You avoid their calls or texts.
- You find you don't share anything in common anymore—visions, dreams, passions, exercise, financial goals.
- You find it impossible to be civil to one another.
- You feel drained and used, burdened in the relationship.
- You yell at one another often.
- You are no longer interested in being intimate with them.
- You begin to look elsewhere for love, companionship, and sex.

These are just a few of the exit signs. Any office, school, or theater posts big red exit signs for a reason. They want you to clearly know where to go and how to get out safely. It's the same in your life. The signs are there, but we ignore them, pretend not to see them, or just overlook them. We do so because we know that exits hurt. Nobody likes goodbyes, even good goodbyes. But saying goodbye is a natural and normal part of living. You get to keep very few people forever. Very few. Over 50 percent of marriages end in divorce. That's a lot of people who don't make it through a vow they took to love someone for life.

The point is that you must live in awareness. Don't stick your head in the sand and deny what you know to be your reality. Either be brave enough to change yourself, or talk to your partner, spouse, kids,

> *"Exit is a letter away from Exist. A part, just a space away from Apart."*
>
> —**Noor Iskandar**

siblings, business partners. Or walk away with the clarity of knowing that you know where you want to go after you leave. You have a plan. You have a life strategy. You have something to fill the inevitable void of emptiness that always comes when we exit from someone's life or leave a familiar place where we feel safe. We have been trained to believe that break-ups or goodbyes are bad. They do not have to be. Exits can be positive, good, life changing, and life affirming if we have the courage to see the signs and make a conscious choice either to face it so we can fix it or admit that it cannot be fixed and find a good way out and forward.

## Leave People Better than You Found Them Even If You Have to Walk Away

Exits can be learning experiences if we allow them to be. That is why almost all the Fortune 500 companies, tech industries and global foundations, even the federal government, ask their employees who decide to leave and take new jobs to do an "exit interview." The purpose of doing this is to get valuable information: to learn where the company can improve; to make sure employees leave feeling good about their service; and, to encourage the employee to stay if the things that were not satisfactory can be made better or improved upon. By asking the right questions of someone who is leaving you, your company, your life, you can gain invaluable information to help you grow and do better the next time.

Even if you must exit, do so in a way that leaves the people you once loved and cared for better off. The way you do that is to grow as a person, to do the important work on yourself first. My most rewarding relationships are amazingly reciprocal. They flow. We genuinely like each other. We are there for one another without having to ask. We have shared life experiences that are powerful, real, authentic. But they did not get that way overnight. They grew because we did the work. If you do, you will find that, over time, the wrong people get weeded out. The people who needed to exit, leave. The people you do not want around you anymore you can let go. And it works if you make a commitment to do people no international harm. And when you do cause harm, own it. Apologize and do the work of apology by changing the things in you that need changing.

When all is said and done, however, I think the most important thing to remember about this life lesson is that you don't have to leave a job, a family member, a friendship, a lover, or marriage on bad terms. All exits and goodbyes are hard. But if we can grow up a little, and act like rational, thoughtful human beings, we can have "exit interviews" in between our life milestones, too. It's all about how you see the exit. As for me, at this stage of my life, I have come to see every exit in my life, every closed door, every bad learned lesson as an entrance to another place, to another joy, to another opportunity, and to another positive human connection. I hope you will come to see it that way, too, because exits really do matter, a lot.

"Life is similar to a bus ride. The journey begins when we board the bus. We meet people along our way of which some are strangers, some friends, and some strangers yet to be friends. There are stops at intervals and people board in. At times some of these people make their presence felt, leave an impact through their grace and beauty on us fellow passengers while on other occasions they remain indifferent. But then it is important for some people to make an exit, to get down and walk the paths they were destined to because if people always made an entrance and never left either for the better or worse, then we would feel suffocated and confused like those people in the bus, the purpose of the journey would lose its essence and the journey altogether would neither be worthwhile nor smooth."

—Chirag Tulsiani

# AFTERWORD

Now we come back to the beginning: How do you become the one you need?

It starts with a question we rarely ask ourselves: **What do I want?** and taking the time to find an answer. It's hearing your own voice and listening to your life rhythm or pace. It is asking yourself often: **What do I need? How do I feel?**

In asking those three questions, you are practicing the most profound, practical, and powerful form of daily self-care. You are checking in on you. You are listening to your heart's desires. You are making sure that your cup is full and not empty. You are nourishing your soul by connecting with your heart and with what you are lacking so that you can tend to what you need. Trust me, nothing is more freeing or powerful. Nothing.

I know it seems counterintuitive to put yourself first, but you must do it every day. It is the key to unlocking more in your life. Through the twenty-one life lessons I have shared with you, I hope that I have provided you with a guide of emotional intelligence tools and practical strategies to practice deep and meaningful self-care, not the surface stuff we tell ourselves will quench our deepest needs: a day at the spa, a walk in the park, or meditation in the morning. Those things are great, but they are how we rest and take respite. They will not fix your childhood traumas or get you the life that you truly want to live. By guarding your emotional health, you empower yourself to take the risks that lead you to success and happiness. By trusting your intuition and stopping to honor and fulfill your most neglected needs, you enable yourself to both give and receive love more deeply.

As I reflect on this work, I wanted to do more than just dispense advice. Instead, what I have tried to do with these life lessons is to give you a window into my life—*human to human*—a window that allows you to see what happens when we do not face our life traumas or our past, a window into the stumbles we all make in life and the recoveries that are still possible if we will just practice good self-care. A window that may have given you glimpses into yourself, and in so doing inspired you to make better life choices and to break free of the often-painful bonds of toxic family ties, broken relationships, shattered dreams, or disappointments—whatever it is that holds you captive, stuck in place, or feeling like you just can't catch your breath. My challenge for you is to live. Go out and find the life you want, not the life they told you that you had to live, but instead a life of curious wonder and wandering.

> **Self-care is what happens when we stop lying to ourselves, when we stop trying to be a hero to everyone else and instead save ourselves. Self-care is a radical act of bravery.**

Self-care is what happens when we stop lying to ourselves, when we stop trying to be a hero to everyone else and instead save ourselves. Self-care is a radical act of bravery. It truly is. It means you do not give up on your-self, and you never allow others to treat you in ways that dishonor, demean, or negate your worth. So much damage is done to our souls when we are subject to emotional, physical, or relational trauma. As I said at the beginning of this book—this is a book about you, for you, and it's about being what you need for your peace of mind. It all starts there.

The most successful, well-balanced, and fulfilled people I know all like themselves. In fact, they practice self-love because they know that, in doing so, they are better lovers to their spouses or partners, better parents to their kids, better leaders, better siblings, and better children. They do not dwell in the past. They do not dwell in distrac-tions. They are very aware of their own energy and of that of their friends. They practice radical forgiveness. They do not stay stuck in the prison of regret, guilt, or shame. They move. They pivot. They shift as needed, and they walk out good manners and social graces daily. They are the ultimate risk takers.

They are resilient, bouncing back time and time again from the worst life has to offer. However, as Dr. Bruce Perry says in *What Hap-pened to You*, resilience is a two-way street. Be careful to not use your resilience as a shield or allow others to do the same. The truth is—and God knows I have experienced it in my own lifetime—that when we are hurt, or have experienced serious trauma in our lives, most people tend to move away from us or look away from us. They do not want to experience the discomfort of grief, pain, or loss. They do not want to be in the orbit of our sorrow. They see us as resilient super-beings who never need help and who are only there to help others. And when we need their care, they do not step up. They run, scatter, or simply go on with their own lives. Don't allow yourself to get boxed in as a super-fixer, super-hero. You are neither of those things. You are human. Act like it. Let people see your vulnerability. Let people help you. Let people love you. Pull the walls down. Share your secrets with a trusted friend and confidante. No one can carry it all alone.

**Remember: you are just like every other mortal walking this earth.** You need what we all need: love, kindness, support, and empathy. Successful people also know what to keep and what to get rid of. They are very intentional about both their thoughts and their words. They don't sweat the small stuff, and they use their haters as fuel for success. They do no harm, and they most certainly take no shit. They do not allow anger to hold or control them. They know well the art of surrender and of faith. They trust their instincts and intuition. They do not cancel people; they have courageous conversations instead. And they have built a wise tribe, or "Front Row" as I like to call it, of good people to walk through life with. And most of all, they excel at managing life's expectations as well as their own.

When all is said and done, my friends, life is an amazing, fabulous, crazy, wild, romantic, awesome, challenging, brilliant, heartbreaking, and at times pain-in-the-ass trek that we all make every day from the time we're born until the time that we leave this life for the next. I may be a wise sage now, yet the optimistic, happy, hopeful teenage girl still resides inside my spirit. I have been your guide and the best piece of advice I can offer is that whatever road you take in this life, you will need to meet yourself first along the way.

*God bless you. You can do this! Now, go take care of you! First!*